"If you're wondering why evangelical worship is often so thin—and what can be done about it—you could hardly do better than to read this book. Professor Davis offers a cogent and deep analysis combined with arresting reflections on the nature of worship. I'll be reading it again, to be sure."

Mark Galli, senior managing editor, *Christianity Today*

"John Jefferson Davis is one of the most thoughtful persons I know. In his new book, *Worship and the Reality of God,* he reminds us that a follower of Jesus inhabits an alternate reality. With passion and verve, he invites readers to a deeper sense of what it means to worship God. He casts a grand vision that is 'Reformed in its soteriology; trinitarian in its understanding of theology; doxological in seeing worship as the highest priority of the church; charismatic in its affirmation of the gifts and presence of the Spirit in the life of the congregation; and liturgical in its ancient-modern form of worship.' I dare say this vision will find resonance with all kinds of Christians, from emerging Christians to traditionalists; from the new monastics to the megachurches. Not everyone will agree with Davis at every point, but I promise you, he will make you think."

Frank A. James, provost and professor of historical theology, Gordon-Conwell Theological Seminary

"Professor Davis recaptures what has been lost in most contemporary worship: a theologically rich understanding of the presence of God in our midst during congregational worship and of how we should rightly respond to this incomparable Reality. This is a book to reawaken the heart and mind to true worship, and as such, it is desperately needed."

Douglas Groothuis, Ph.D., professor of philosophy, Denver Seminary

Worship and the Reality of God

AN EVANGELICAL THEOLOGY
OF REAL PRESENCE

JOHN JEFFERSON DAVIS

IVP Academic

An imprint of InterVarsity Press
Downers Grove, Illinois

InterVarsity Press
P.O. Box 1400, Downers Grove, IL 60515-1426
World Wide Web: www.ivpress.com
E-mail: email@ivpress.com

InterVarsity Press® is the book-publishing division of InterVarsity Christian Fellowship/USA®, a movement of students and faculty active on campus at hundreds of universities, colleges and schools of nursing in the United States of America, and a member movement of the International Fellowship of Evangelical Students. For information about local and regional activities, write Public Relations Dept., InterVarsity Christian Fellowship/USA, 6400 Schroeder Rd., P.O. Box 7895, Madison, WI 53707-7895, or visit the IVCF website at <www.intervarsity.org>.

All Scripture quotations, unless otherwise indicated, are taken from the Holy Bible, New International Version®. NIV®. *Copyright ©1973, 1978, 1984 by International Bible Society. Used by permission of Zondervan Publishing House. All rights reserved.*

Design: Cindy Kiple
Images: Harnett/Hanzon/Getty Images

ISBN 978-0-8308-3884-4

Printed in the United States of America ∞

Library of Congress Cataloging-in-Publication Data

Davis, John Jefferson.
  Worship and the reality of God: an evangelical theology of real presence / John Jefferson Davis.
    p. cm.
  Includes bibliographical references and index.
  ISBN 978-0-8308-3884-4 (pbk.: alk. paper)
  1. Public worship. 2. Presence of God. I. Title.
  BV15.D36 2010
  264—dc22

2010019873

| P | 20 | 19 | 18 | 17 | 16 | 15 | 14 | 13 | 12 | 11 | 10 | 9 | 8 | 7 | 6 | 5 | 4 |
| Y | 26 | 25 | 24 | 23 | 22 | 21 | 20 | 19 | 18 | 17 | 16 | 15 | 14 |

Contents

1 INTRODUCTION 7
   Why God Has Been Lost and Where We Can Look to Find Him

2 GOD, THE CHURCH AND THE SELF 37
   Searching for Reality in Evangelical Worship

3 REALITY IN WORSHIP 77
   The Real Presence of God on Sunday Morning

4 THE EUCHARIST 113
   Meeting the Risen Christ at the Table

5 FROM ONTOLOGY TO DOXOLOGY 171
   From Theory to Practice in Worship Renewal

APPENDIX 207
   Theology and Practice of Worship: Selected Readings

SELECT BIBLIOGRAPHY 215

ACKNOWLEDGMENTS 225

NAME AND SUBJECT INDEX 226

SCRIPTURE INDEX 229

Introduction

WHY GOD HAS BEEN LOST AND
WHERE WE CAN LOOK TO FIND HIM

Scene One: My wife, Robin, and I pulled into the parking lot of the shopping center in a Denver suburb, parked the car and went inside the seeker-style community church for the Saturday night worship service. We were a few minutes early, and as we waited for the 5:30 service to begin, we noticed the message on the TV monitors in the lobby: "If you find that the volume of music is too loud, ear plugs are available at the information desks in the lobby." We went inside the partially darkened auditorium for the service, sat down and watched the countdown video on the screen tick off the seconds remaining to the start of the service. As the digital clock on the screen reached "zero," the praise band entered the stage and began with an ear-deafening musical set. People were standing, but many were not singing the praise choruses, their voices being drowned out by the massive electronic amplification. My wife went outside and brought back two sets of ear plugs, and with their help we made it through the "worship" portion of the service, which was followed by an excellent topical message on marriage. People filed out of the auditorium at the end of the service, and ushers held cardboard popcorn buckets at the doors for those who wished to leave an offering.

Scene Two: We were a few minutes late that Sunday morning for a contemporary worship service at a well-known evangelical mega-church in the Denver area, so we decided to make our way up to the second floor balcony to look for a seat. As I looked around, I noticed more coffee cups than Bibles in the hands of those who were present. I settled back in the comfortable theater-style seat, and my eyes were immediately drawn to one of the large TV monitors suspended from the ceiling to the left and the right, projecting the larger-than-life images of the praise band musicians who were live on the stage. I found myself thinking, *Here I am in "church," and I find my attention focused on the television screens, not on the real human beings down front.* After the service we went downstairs and spent a few minutes looking around the church's gift shop, where many who had attended the service were doing some last-minute Christmas shopping before heading home. As we left the church, I had something of an epiphany, realizing that even the church furnishings—in this case, the theater-style seating—were sending a subliminal message, one that my culture sends continuously: "Sit back, relax, and enjoy the show." When, indeed, does the church's attempt to be culturally relevant cross the line and become entertainment, or, so to speak, "worshedutainment"? Those questions continue to haunt me.

Those services were only two of the thirty-five different church services that my wife and I attended that fall in the greater Denver area. When we are at home, we are not church hoppers, but since I am a seminary professor, training future pastors and teachers, when I am away for a research sabbatical, as was the case that fall, we try to visit as many churches as possible to see how theological education is being played out at the retail outlets. These thirty-five worship services ran the entire gamut from very traditional to very contemporary, from the very quiet to the very loud, from the very large to the very small. In terms of denominational traditions, these churches included Quaker, Pentecostal, charismatic, Presbyterian, Lutheran, Nazarene, Congregational, Episcopal, Anglican, Roman Catholic, Greek Orthodox, Russian Orthodox, Antiochian Orthodox, Coptic Orthodox, independent and nondenominational, several varieties of "emerging" churches, and several seeker churches, including Willow Creek Community Church in South Barrington, Illinois.

As my wife Robin and I struggled to process the tremendous diversity and variety in worship styles that we had experienced, we realized that at the heart of it all was a strange and paradoxical situation. In most of the evangelical churches with contemporary worship styles, the expository or topical preaching was often excellent, and the praise bands were generally performing at very professional levels, but we still were left with disturbing questions:

• Where is God in all this?

• What are we really doing here?

• Is there a vivid consciousness of the presence of the living, holy God among his people at these services?

As I pondered those questions, I somewhat reluctantly concluded that in most of these services a vivid awareness of God's presence as the central reality in worship was indeed missing. Along with this I had a sinking feeling as I asked myself a further question: If indeed a consciousness of the presence of a holy and living *God* as the dominant reality on Sunday morning has been lost in many evangelical churches,[1] whose fault is that? Who is to blame? The culture? Hollywood? Megachurch pastors? TV evangelists? Such blame-shifting answers were too easy; in the pit of my stomach I sensed something of a spiritual wake-up call as I realized that *evangelical seminary professors like myself*—and especially the theologians—needed to look in the mirror and assume a heavy share of responsibility for the current realities (or unrealities) in American evangelical worship. I began to see that the strengths and the weaknesses of the contemporary evangelical churches and their worship services tended to reflect the strengths and weaknesses of the curricula of the evangelical seminaries where these pastors had been

---

[1] I acknowledge the danger of making generalizations about the realities of worship in "American evangelical churches." The concerns raised in this book are most visibly focused in evangelical megachurches that have adopted seeker-driven styles of worship, but I believe that the problem of the loss of the awareness of the presence of the Holy God and the risen Christ as the central reality of worship is present to some degree in most evangelical churches today, whether charismatic or noncharismatic.

trained. Where seminaries such as Gordon-Conwell and Denver Seminary are strong and place great emphasis—Bible, sound doctrine, expository preaching—the graduates tended to do well; my wife and I do not recall any obvious instances of faulty doctrine from the pulpit, and the preaching was generally good. In areas such as *worship*, which tends to receive less attention in the curriculum, the problems were more evident.

As I continued to reflect on what I had seen in those thirty-five church visits, I realized that the greatest strengths of the evangelical tradition—preaching and evangelism—had unwittingly contributed to its greatest weakness: lack of depth in the theology and practice of worship. A variety of historical and theological factors, to be explored in this book, have unintentionally conspired to deflect our attention on Sunday morning from the invisible, holy, living God who is present in the midst of his people, to the human preacher, the musicians on the stage, and to the expectations and responses of the "audience."

My level of concern continued to grow as I realized that worship is not a peripheral but a central concern in the life of the church. In fact, I have come to believe that the church's highest priority and purpose on Sunday morning is not just preaching the Bible or evangelizing the lost but worshiping the living God. Missions and evangelism are important, but worship is more important still. Powerful missionary outreach and lasting spiritual formation in fact arise in the context of deep encounter with the living God in his temple (Is 6). In the new creation of eternity, when the Great Commission will have been fulfilled, and the body of Christ will have been discipled to full maturity, the saints of God will still forever be singing the praises of their great redeemer God and enjoying joyous communion with him forever. I have also come to believe that worship is the highest and most fulfilling act of which a human being is capable; it is that experience in which we in fact become most truly human, for communion with the living God is the eternal purpose (Eph 1:4-6) for which human beings were created. The human being's highest purpose and greatest joy is to "glorify God and to enjoy him forever"; as human beings we were created for a doxological purpose: "for the praise of his glory" (Eph 1:6, 12). If this is indeed the case biblically—and I am convinced that it is—then the evangelical churches need "to get it right" on worship, and to recover the centrality of God's presence as the heart of every Sunday's gathering. If God has been shoved away from the center of the stage on Sunday morning, then God is not happy about that; "Houston, we have a problem."

I make no claim to originality in pointing to this God-vacuum in evangelical worship; thoughtful observers have been calling attention to various symptoms of the problem for years.[2] Not long before his death, James Montgomery Boice pointed to the "thinning" of evangelical worship and the disappearance of many of the traditional elements of worship:[3]

> In recent years, I have noticed the decreasing presence, and in some cases the total absence, of service elements that have been associated with God's worship. . . .
>
> *Prayer.* It is almost inconceivable to me that something called worship can be held without significant prayer, but that is precisely what is happening. There is usually a short prayer at the beginning of the service, though even that is fading away. It is being replaced with chummy greetings to make people feel welcome and at ease. . . . Longer prayers— pastoral prayers—are vanishing. . . . There is no rehearsal of God's attributes or confession of sin against the shining, glorious background of God's holiness. . . .
>
> *The reading of the Word.* The reading of any substantial portion of the Bible is also vanishing. In the Puritan age ministers regularly read one chapter of the Old Testament and one of the New. . . . But our Scripture readings are getting shorter and shorter, sometimes only two or three verses, if the Bible is even read at all. . . . So what is going on in our churches if we neither pray nor read the Bible?
>
> *The exposition of the Word.* We have very little serious teaching of the Bible today, not to mention careful expositions. . . . Preachers speak to

---

[2]Notably, for previous generations of English-speaking evangelicals, A. W. Tozer, *The Knowledge of the Holy: The Attributes of God; Their Meaning in the Christian Life* (Harrisburg, Penn.: Christian Publications, 1961), and J. I. Packer, *Knowing God* (Downers Grove, Ill.: InterVarsity Press, 1973); and more recently, my colleague David Wells, *God in the Wasteland: The Reality of Truth in a World of Fading Dreams* (Grand Rapids: Eerdmans, 1994).

[3]Cited in Philip Ryken, Derek Thomas and J. Ligon Duncan, *Give Praise to God: A Vision for Reforming Worship* (Phillipsburg, N.J.: Presbyterian & Reformed, 2003), pp. 18-20.

felt needs, not real needs, and this generally means telling people only what they most want to hear. . . .

Confession of sin. Who confesses sin today . . . as God's humble, re-pentant people bow before God? . . . That used to be a necessary ele-ment in any genuine service. But it is not happening today because there is so little awareness of God. . . .

Hymns. One of the saddest features of contemporary worship is that the great hymns of the church are on the way out. They are not gone en-tirely, but they are going. . . . The old hymns expressed the theology of the church in profound and perceptive ways and with winsome, memorable language. . . . Today's songs reflect our shallow or nonexistent theology and do almost nothing to elevate one's thoughts about God.

All these disappearing elements are symptoms of the growing God-vacuum in modern American evangelical worship. At this point some readers may be tempted to put down this book, concluding that this is just another cranky diatribe against contemporary worship styles, by an older generation that does not like drums and is out of touch with to-day's culture. I ask such a reader to suspend such judgments for a while, for the fundamental concern of this book is not styles of music or a call to return to traditional styles of worship. Rather, the fundamental issue is the recovery of the centrality and reality of God in the worship and life of the evangelical church generally: *Jesus Christ is risen from the dead; Jesus is still alive today, and is present here with us in the power of the Spirit to enjoy communion with his people.*

It is the recovery—each and every Sunday morning—of the con-sciousness of this fundamental fact, without which the New Testament church would not have been born, and without which there would have been no new, continuing religion called Christianity. This is the reality for which I am contending. The reality of the resurrection of Jesus Christ was the sine qua non of the birth of the church,[4] and the recog-nition of the continuing real presence of the risen Christ in the church here and now is the heart and soul of the recovery of the truth and

---

[4]This emphasis on the resurrection of Jesus Christ as the core reality of the existence of Chris-tianity and the continuing existence of the church has been made recently in the magisterial treatment of N. T. Wright, *The Resurrection of the Son of God* (Minneapolis: Fortress, 2003).

power of biblical worship today. It is my conviction that such a recovery of New Testament worship is both desirable and possible; I am convinced that there are no good biblical or theological reasons why it cannot be so today as it was in the first-century church. We do, however, need a Copernican mind shift to see it happen. There are no quick fixes available to solve the problem of the poverty of evangelical Protestant worship.

As I see it, there are at least six areas of deficiency in the American evangelical subculture's theology and practices of worship: (1) a deficient understanding of the importance and priority of worship, (2) a deficient understanding of the nature of worship, (3) a deficient understanding of the participants in worship, (4) a deficient understanding of the elements of worship, (5) a deficient understanding of the "ontologies" (understandings of reality) of modernity and postmodernity and how they undermine true worship, and (6) a deficient understanding of the need to learn new behaviors and new "doxological skills" for the enjoyment of true worship. Chapters two, three and four will address all six of these deficiencies and propose remedies. In order to move toward renewal in worship and a "Copernican revolution"[5] in how evangelicals understand and perceive the act of worship, it will be necessary to build a more adequate understanding of the nature of the church itself (ecclesiology) as well as a more adequate theology of worship (doxology). But even more fundamentally, we need a new framework for perceiving reality itself—an "ontological framework" so to speak—within which worship takes place. Now we turn to an outline of that task.

---

[5]Karl Barth's massive theological project in his *Church Dogmatics* can be seen as one long tremendous protest against the man-centered orientation of liberal Protestant theology from Schleiermacher down to the present: "man, namely his piety . . . had become its object of study and its theme. Around this it revolved and seemed to revolve without release . . . here man was made great at the cost of God—the divine God who is something other than man, who sovereignly confronts him, who immovably and unchangeably stands over against him as the Lord, Creator, and Redeemer" (Barth, *The Humanity of God* [Louisville: Westminster John Knox, 1968], pp. 39-40). I wish to thank my colleague Peter Anders for drawing my attention to this reference. This "turn to the human subject" can also be seen in a parallel trajectory in the evangelical tradition that reaches from Charles Finney to Bill Hybels. As did Barth, this book calls for a new Copernican revolution—a return to "God as primary Subject" in the worship and life of evangelical churches.

YOUR "GOD" IS NOT REAL ENOUGH:
THE NEED FOR A BETTER ONTOLOGY

Tinkering with the music or with the technology or even the elements
of the contemporary worship service will not fix it; the problem is at a
deeper level. Getting to grips with the problem will require a better
theology of worship to inform the practices of worship. But the fundamental point here is that the problem is even deeper than theology: The
problem lies at the level of *ontology*—that is, at the level of a fundamental background theory of the real that is operating in the hearts and the
minds of the people, the preacher and the praise band, even before they
walk through the door of the church or onto the stage. My claim is that
alien, nonbiblical ontologies are at work to wash out the churchgoers'
consciousness of God even before the "worship" service begins. A new
way of perceiving reality more Christianly is needed, together with new
cognitive skills that need to be intentionally formed ("doxological intelligence") to enable authentic worship. Unless we recognize these alien
ontologies and counter them with a biblical background theory of the
real, we may miss God on Sunday morning, and real worship in "Spirit
and in truth" will probably not take place.

There are at least four reasons why such an ontological project for
the renewal of evangelical worship seems particularly timely at our
present cultural moment: the growing religious pluralism in America,
the impact of economic globalization, the digital media revolution and
the explosive growth of the church in the Global South. Long gone are
the days when the religious landscape of the United States could be
described in terms of "Protestant, Catholic, Jew." America is now one
of the most religiously diverse nations in the world, with more Buddhists than Episcopalians, more Muslims than Presbyterians, and with
representatives of virtually every religious group on the planet found
somewhere within our national boundaries.[6] The question is now no
longer simply, do you believe in God? but, which "God" or deity, if any,
do you believe in, and if any "God," why that one? Americans have
never before had the choice of so many alternative religious "realities"

---

[6]See Diana L. Eck, *A New Religious America: How a "Christian Country" Has Become the World's
Most Religiously Diverse Nation* (New York: HarperCollins, 2001).

available in today's super shopping mall of religion. We need to explain and sometimes defend our personal choices of a religious (or atheistic) worldview; ontologies can no longer be taken for granted without further justification.

The globalization of the world economy, increasing international airline travel and the waves of immigrants from southeast Asia, the Middle East and Latin America have exposed Americans to new levels of diversity in cultures, lifestyles, religions and belief systems. More and more Americans are living and working beside others whose perceptions of God, family, sexuality and even reality itself may differ radically from their own.

Perhaps even more dramatically, the explosion of electronic and digital media in the last generation—cable TV, movies, DVDs, talk radio, satellite radio, 24/7 news, the Internet, Google, email, cell phones, Blackberries, text messaging, iPods, MP3 digital music files, video games (Xbox 360), high-definition TV, home entertainment centers, *American Idol, Survivor,* online simulation gaming (World of Warcraft), virtual worlds (Second Life), touch-screen smart phones, hand-held electronic devices—the list seems endless—appears to be altering the nature of human consciousness itself.[7] Never before in human history has it been possible for the human mind to be so overstimulated, so distracted and so overloaded with a never-ending, Niagara Falls–like cascade of information, images, entertainment, texts, sounds, fantasies, pornography and commercial advertisements. Here is a state of mind in the new world of postmodern virtuality that may span the globe in its breadth with the click of a mouse, but its depth be as shallow as the play of electrons on the computer screen. This is a digital world of "continuous partial attention," as Thomas Friedman has described our current

---

[7]Nicholas Carr ("Is Google Making Us Stupid? What the Internet Is Doing to Our Brains," *Atlantic*, July/August 2008, 56-63) surveys current research on how the Internet and search engines such as Google are beginning to affect cognition, noting, for example, the increasingly common "skimming mode" of visiting Internet sites and sources: "It is clear that users are not reading online in the traditional sense; indeed there are signs that new forms of 'reading' are emerging as users 'power browse' horizontally through titles, contents pages and abstracts going for quick wins. It almost seems that they go online to avoid reading in the traditional sense" (p. 58). He cites researchers at University College London and their five-year study of online research habits.

16

state of consciousness: constantly interrupted, rarely giving anyone or anything our undivided attention for significant lengths of time.

Popular films such as *The Truman Show* (1998) and *The Matrix* (1999) play with the modern world's blurring of the lines between the real and the simulated. The plot summary of *The Truman Show* in Wikipedia tells us the film "chronicles the life of a man who does not know that he is living in a constructed reality soap opera, televised 24/7 to billions across the globe—the film is set in a hypothetical world, called Seahaven, where an entire town is dedicated to a continually running television show. All the participants are actors, except for Truman Burbank [played by Jim Carrey], who is unaware that he lives in a constructed reality for the entertainment of those outside. Central characters simulate friendship to Truman, and in the case of his 'wife,' bury their real feelings of disgust with the whole concept of the show."[8]

The new digital media tends to blur the lines between reality and fantasy in other ways. Joni Gleason of Haverhill, Massachusetts, says she is spending about $100 a year sending virtual gifts to her pet-loving friends. As a member of Dogster.com, Gleason can send, by email, fellow dog owners virtual candles and virtual angel wings when their pets get sick or die. "They may not be something that you can hold in your hand," said Gleason, "but the sentiment that comes with giving or receiving is the same sentiment. . . . To us, they're real."[9]

When I went to the mall recently to shop for a new cordless mouse for my laptop (the store happened to be Best Buy, a large outlet for consumer electronics, computers and appliances), I noticed a teenage girl in the video game section absorbed in playing an Xbox module, the bestselling Guitar Hero. I stopped to watch for a few minutes, musing on how in this one store the quintessential artifacts of modernity (refrigerators, stoves, vacuum cleaners) and postmodernity (computers, video games, cell phones, HDTVs) were all conveniently available for

---

[8]"The Truman Show," *Wikipedia* <http://en.wikipedia.org/wiki/The_Truman_Show> (accessed July 24, 2008).
[9]Meredith Goldstein, "It's the Icon that Counts: Virtual Gifts Make Real Impact," *Boston Globe*, July 12, 2008, pp. A1, 14.

purchase under one roof. The teenager had a guitar-controller in her hands, controlling the music and gyrations of the scantily clad female rock musician on the stage, receiving the adulation of the fans in the virtual concert hall. As long as the simulation lasted, at least, she *was* a rock star; this was better and more compelling than ordinary real life at home or at school. If not, why would billions of dollars be spent on these digitally simulated experiences each year? Guitar Hero makes it possible for the player to become a god or goddess for the hundreds of virtual fans expressing praise and adoration to the Rock Idol on the stage. Here are alternative universes for sale at the mall or online. The production, distribution and sale of simulated experiences—"entertainment"—is an enormous economic and social reality; in fact, entertainment is a mainstay of the economy. In a recent year, *American Idol* drew 40 million viewers each week, and Las Vegas was drawing 2.5 million visitors each month to its simulated experiences. Movie theaters sell over 565 million tickets per year.[10]

It can be said that the One who has captured your imagination has captured your soul. So we can ask, Christian, what reality are you living in? Where is your heart's true "ontological home"? The philosophical and theological reflection on the significance for the church of these "alternative ontologies" has only just begun; the present book is an attempt in that direction. It is not just American adolescents whose imaginations have been captured and colonized by alien ontologies; this is a huge challenge to the church at large. The evangelical church in its worship assemblies needs a fresh manifestation of an *ultimate reality* that can recapture its imagination with a Presence that is more compelling than anything that Spielberg or Pixar Studios can manufacture.[11]

---

[10]These figures are from Grant McCracken, *Transformations: Identity Construction in Contemporary Culture* (Bloomington: University of Indiana Press, 2008), p. xi.

[11]In a famous sermon, "The Expulsive Power of a New Affection," Thomas Chalmers (1780-1847) of Glasgow argued that the worldly man was unlikely to give up his attachment to the world simply by hearing criticisms of the world; but if, "during the time of his contemplation, some happy island of the blest floated by, and there . . . burst upon his senses the light of its surpassing glories . . . then without violence done to the constitution . . . may he die unto the present world, and live to the lovelier world that stands in the distance from it" (on the Thomas Chalmers Sermons & Writings website <www.newble.co.uk/chalmers/comm9.html>). Chal-

Much of North American church life and programming seems to operate on merely human energy and planning. The reality of God and the supernatural power of the New Testament is not that evident. In the Global South, however, much of this growth is taking place in charismatic and Pentecostal churches. According to Lamin Sanneh, this charismatic version of the faith has in fact been the driving engine of Christian growth in the Global South and "is largely responsible for the dramatic shift in the religion's center of gravity."[12] Some scholars have estimated that by 2025, Pentecostal and charismatic Christians around the globe may number nearly 800 million. "Now exploding in Brazil, Mexico, Russia, and China, Pentecostal Christianity may become the most widespread form of the religion," notes Sanneh, "with as yet unquantifiable effects on the mainline churches and global politics."[13]

One outcome of this growth is likely to be a challenge from the avowedly supernaturalistic worldview of Christians in the Global South—a worldview in which biblical signs and wonders are considered normal Christianity—to the worldviews and ontologies of North American churches that, from the Southern churches' perspective, seem to be stuck in the naturalistic assumptions of Enlightenment naturalism and materialism. The idea that the age of miracles ceased with the apostles or when the biblical canon was closed seems strange to majority-world Christians, who seem to be saying to their northern brothers and sisters in the faith, do you *really* believe the Bible? What universe are you really living in?

Yet another reason for evangelicals in America to become more reflective about their basic assumptions about what is real is that by doing so, it will be easier to push to a deeper level the current discussions of moral relativism and "truth decay." In recent years there has been much hand-wringing by religious leaders and academics concerning the rela-

---

mers today might say that powerful Christian worship—the presence and manifestation of the risen Christ in the Spirit among his people—can be the "new affection"/reality that has the power to drive worldliness from the church.

[12]Lamin Sanneh, *Disciples of All Nations: Pillars of World Christianity* (New York: Oxford University Press, 2008), p. 275.

[13]Ibid.

tivism that seems so endemic in our postmodern settings. Even if this is a soft and selective rather than a hard and consistent relativism—after all, how many real Holocaust deniers or justifiers of Hitler's genocide or of child abuse are there out there?—there is nevertheless a real problem here. The explosion in the number of alternative realities and lifestyles for sale in the digital universe has produced a situation in which, as the number of possible choices increases, the brand loyalty to any particular choice seems to diminish. This can be just as true for one's choices in religion, gender constructions, or a particular brand of granola or designer jeans. "Too many choices, too many brands, too many 'realities' are out there competing for my attention."

As North American evangelical Christians we are not, of course, fundamentally concerned with the effects of the choice explosion for our consumer purchases of yogurt or designer clothing. Rather, we are concerned about its impact on our Christian beliefs; here is where the chickens of relativism are coming home to roost. For example, pollsters working for the Barna Research Group expected to find an increase in Americans' belief in absolute truths after the 9/11 attacks on the World Trade Center, but this was not the case. Defining adherence to absolute truth as assent to the statement "there are moral truths or principles . . . that do not change according to the circumstances," the pollsters found that before the attacks about 38 percent of Americans said they believed in such absolutes, but about a year later, only 22 percent answered affirmatively to the same question—the opposite of what had been expected. Among "born again" individuals, only 32 percent said they believed in absolute moral truths, as defined in the sense stated above.[14] In a comprehensive "U.S. Religious Landscape Survey" of 35,000 Americans conducted by the Pew Forum on Religion and Public Life, the researchers found that most Americans agree with the statement that "many religions—not just their own—can lead to eternal life." More than half the members of evangelical Protestant churches (57%) said they agreed with this statement; only among small bodies such as the Jehovah's Witnesses (80%) was there a supermajority for the

---

[14]"How America's Faith Has Changed Since 9-11," *The Barna Update*, November 26, 2001 (Ventura, California) <www.barna.org>.

opinion that their religion was the one true faith leading to eternal life.[15] The implications of such surveys seem clear enough, and are disturbing: however much the absolute truth of the Bible and the Christian faith may be preached from the pulpit, these absolutes are in fact being washed out by the pluralistic social realities in which American Christians live, by the real ontological frameworks that dominate their lives outside the walls of the church.

Another symptom of the erosion of Christian belief by the powerful influence of these alien ontologies is the alarming disconnect between evangelical profession and evangelical behavior in America. National statistical surveys have shown that conservative Protestants are more likely to end their marriages in divorce than the general population, and that the South, the heartland of the Southern Baptist Convention, has a higher divorce rate than the rest of the nation.[16] Russell Moore, a faculty member at Southern Baptist Theological Seminary in Louisville, has noted that "the shift in Southern Baptist attitudes toward marital permanence does not seem to have come through any kind of theological reflection or conversation at all. Instead, the Southern Baptist approach to divorce seems to have meandered just a bit behind the mainstream of American cultural patterns of acceptance of 'one wife at a time' as a sad, but normal part of life."[17]

What Russell has called the "mainstream of American cultural patterns" is the powerful ontological riptides of modernity and postmodernity that have carried the (nominal) evangelical beliefs out to sea like so much flotsam and jetsam. Evangelicals at times are tempted to dismiss the "nominal" commitments of some Roman Catholic and Orthodox churchgoers whose adherence to their religion is viewed as being more cultural than a matter of deep conviction; but the ugly truth is that under the conditions of modernity and postmodernity, we are all

---

[15]"Religion in America: Non-Dogmatic, Diverse, and Politically Relevant," *U.S. Religious Landscape Survey*, Pew Forum on Religion and Public Life (Washington, D.C., 2008), p. 3 <http://religions.pewforum.org/>.

[16]Russell D. Moore, "Southern Baptist Sexual Revolutionaries: Cultural Accommodation, Spiritual Conflict, and the Baptist Vision of the Family," *Southwestern Journal of Theology* 49, no. 1 (Fall 2006): 3-29 at p. 8.

[17]Ibid., p. 9.

"nominal" Christians now, to a lesser or greater extent, and our convictions may not have as much traction as we would like to believe. It is to those competing frameworks of daily reality that we now turn, with a view to bringing them to the full light of consciousness, in order to protect our Christian confessions from their corrosive effects.

HOW THEN SHALL WE BE REAL? THREE COMPETING ONTOLOGIES

This section briefly sketches three ontologies that are competing for shelf space in the Christian mind today, and then chapters two and three will develop them more fully. This ontological schematic can function like a worldview template or a global positioning device to serve as a mental map as we navigate around the increasingly diverse versions of reality that Christians encounter in different cultural settings today. These three ontologies will be called (1) *scientific materialism* (the ontology of modernity); (2) *digital virtualism* (the ontology of postmodernity); and (3) *trinitarian supernaturalism* (the ontology of eternity). In the first, there is one ultimate reality (matter-energy); in the second, there are many "realities" ("pick one; construct your own"); in the third, there is one ultimate reality (the triune God), and many lesser (natural and simulated) realities.

In the ontology of scientific materialism, the ontological center is the natural world of energy and matter and natural selection, the world that can be studied, measured and controlled by the scientific method and by the technology based on it. The natural world is the truly real, and the basis of much economic life. This is the ontology of the atheistic and materialistic side of the eighteenth-century Enlightenment, exemplified in different ways in the work of thinkers such as Karl Marx, Charles Darwin and Sigmund Freud. This is the world of a Carl Sagan, who could say, "The (material) universe is all there ever has been or ever will be," or of Chairman Mao, who said, "All power comes out of the end of a gun." In this model, human beings may have religious beliefs, but these beliefs about gods, spirits, demons, angels, miracles and a life beyond the grave have no basis in reality; they are simply human constructions that reflect psychological needs, wish fulfillment and a now-outmoded prescientific view of reality. An ontology of scientific materialism (or naturalism) provided a basis for an economy of industrial capitalism and a lifestyle that could revolve around consumerism and the acquisition of the material goods produced so abundantly by the Industrial Revolution.

This ontology of scientific materialism became the established worldview in the elite universities in the latter part of the nineteenth century, it is now presupposed in secularized American law, and it provides the working assumption for much of the world of American business and military operations. God is not in the picture. In this universe the virtual realities of human culture do exist, but are ultimately reducible to the material objects known by the laws of physics, chemistry and biology. For a quintessential image of this ontology, imagine the fiery images of sweating workers pouring molten iron in one of Andrew Carnegie's Pittsburgh steel mills in the nineteenth century; this was the world of iron and steel and railroads and factories that built America's industrial economy.

In the second ontological framework, digital virtualism, the virtual or the *simulated* is at the center. Here the iconic institution is not the factory, but the television studio, or movie theater, or Pixar's computer animation laboratory, or Disney World, or Las Vegas, or Bill Gates's Microsoft campus in Redmond, Washington. The natural world of flowers and mountains and trees certainly exists, but one could go for days at a time not noticing the natural world, since both one's job and one's leisure-time entertainment revolve around the center of socially constructed images, services and experiences that are the basis of the digital and information age economies. Religion has a place in this model, but no one version of religion is better than another, being simply an individual choice. Any such choice is purely optional and lies at the margins, not at the center, because the ontology of postmodern virtuality, like that of scientific naturalism, places the autonomous self at the center of its universe of meanings.

In practice, these first two ontological frameworks—scientific naturalism and postmodern virtualism—can combine to form what can be called an "ontology of everyday experience" that characterizes much of our contemporary lives (apart from church, for churchgoers), from

Monday morning to the weekend, so to speak. This can be epitomized by three seemingly mundane but formative human activities: driving a car on a freeway, going to a mall to shop, and watching television or surfing the Internet. These three activities now seem so commonplace that we can engage in them with little thought or self-reflection, but in fact, most human beings in the history of planet Earth have not engaged in these activities; they are artifacts of the modern and postmodern periods.[18] Driving my car (perhaps to the mall to shop) encloses me in a bubble of steel and glass (an artifact of the Industrial Revolution and modernity), separates me from my neighbors and neighborhood, and reinforces my belief that I am an autonomous, individual self who is in control, able to go where and when I choose. Arriving at the shopping mall, I enter a socially constructed environment where I can purchase the products of industrial capitalism and the entertainment industry, and in so doing enhance my sense of personal value and place in the social order. When I go to the mall and enter the movie theater or surf the Internet at home, I may be consuming not material goods, but experiences and simulations. As I surf the net or watch the ads for the coming attractions in the theater, I am drawn into the commercial nexus that connects driving in my car, a trip to the shopping mall and the world of entertainment. All three worlds of everyday life are interlocking and mutually reinforcing. When I walk through the doors of the church, I need to change my mindset and consciously remind myself: This is not like driving my car; I am not in control; I will go where God wants to take me; this is not a trip to the mall; this is not about "consumption," this is not about "entertainment," but about the praise and presence of God—the God who is more lastingly real than the car in which I drove to get here.

The third ontological framework, that of trinitarian theism, places the triune God, Father, Son and Holy Spirit, at the center of the universe as the ultimately and eternally real. The triune God is the cen-

---

[18]It is certainly true that premodern humans shopped at village fairs and markets and exchanged goods and services in the agoras; but nevertheless, there does seem to be something new about a vast emporium like the Mall of America that is totally enclosed and that places the visitor in a thoroughly constructed, man-made environment dedicated to consumer spending.

tral reality around which the secondary and tertiary realities of nature and virtual simulations revolve. In this world, *persons in holy, loving, committed relationship* are the weightiest and heaviest realities toward which all other beings should be pulled by the inexorable reality-field of God at the center. In this ontology, the world of the supernatural— God, heaven, hell, angels, demons, miracles, the saints and martyrs and prophets and apostles of the invisible church above—is as real as the natural and is more real than the socially constructed world of the virtual. In fact, as will be argued more explicitly in chapters two and three to follow, the triune God, as the eternal, uncreated great *I AM*, is more eternally and powerfully real than Mount Everest; in the world of biblical, trinitarian theism, "the mountains melt like wax" (Ps 97:5) in the presence of the burning ontic intensity of the almighty Creator God. This trinitarian ontology, in which the unseen things of the Spirit are as real, and in fact, more powerfully and enduringly real, than temporal, material objects like sticks and stones,[19] implies a spirit-empowered epistemology of the Word, Spirit and faith that opens the eyes of the believer to the unseen realities of heaven. Thus, worship in "Spirit and in truth" implies and requires a new vision of the real, and new cognitive habits and practices that give access to heavenly realities in worship.

---

[19]In the ontological model presented here and in chapters two and three, reality is seen as a gradient in which some entities have more ontic weight than others, the triune God being at the very top of the scale (or more properly, *off* the scale, being the uncreated source and ground of all reality). Reality markers on this scale, or criteria of the real, include *coherence, durability, causal efficacy* and *accessibility*. Logical coherence is a necessary and minimal condition of the real; a "square circle" or "a color patch that looks simultaneously blue and yellow" are examples of incoherent verbal formulae; they have no ontic weight or reality. Entities that have great durability over time (God; Mount Everest) are more enduringly real than things that are dreamlike or ephemeral (e.g., my confused, barely-remembered dream last night); entities that have great *causal efficacy* or impact on their surroundings are assigned greater ontic weight. In this respect a literary artifact such as Shakespeare's *Macbeth*, or the search algorithms that underlie a Google search, are more efficaciously real than the laughter on a late night comedy show or a speck of dust on my kitchen window. Real entities are *accessible* in that they are the objects of possible human experiences, whether spiritual, material or virtual, and accessible not only to me but also to other human observers, given the proper circumstances: Realities are objective to the extent that they can, at least vicariously, be shared by others. The ontological framework being proposed here is not to be confused with a form of Platonism or Neo-Platonism, for in this biblically based ontology, matter is not illusory, and neither the body nor matter are intrinsically evil, but rather are expressions of the good creation of God.

Ideally, the Christian would live consistently—24/7—in the realities of the world of trinitarian, biblical theism; in practice, this generally does not happen. We are inconsistent human beings and are pulled in many different directions, living compartmentalized lives, or even with our fractional selves inhabiting several worlds at once.

Driving on a long cross-country trip on the interstate, far from a major urban center, I may scan the FM dial for a good station and find myself in a place where two different stations, two different signals, are coming in at once. This can be a picture of my Christian life, where I would like to think that the signal of trinitarian theism is the one (and only one) to which I am tuned, but in fact, the signals of modernity and postmodernity are fighting to be heard on my spiritual receiver. Alas, even in our "Bible-believing" churches, heaven is only dimly seen, and hell and the day of judgment are rarely mentioned. Or to suggest another image, picture a teenager at the back of the church on Sunday morning, supposedly listening to the sermon, but daydreaming about the car he would like to own and also surreptitiously listening to his favorite tunes on an iPod: the world of trinitarian theism is being drowned out by the images and sounds of the natural and the virtual.

As a practical reality diagnostic, we can ask ourselves the following question: What do I really consider worthy of my focused, continuous and undivided attention? My strenuous effort? That's what's "real" for me. In the case of our teenager at the back of the church, the compelling reality this morning is not the world of Jeremiah or Jesus, but the world of Pearl Jam or . . . ? Are we really all that different? Christians today have to fight to take back biblical reality and to train themselves to see reality in a thoroughly different way, through a different ontological grid. A true ontology needs to be embodied and practiced as well as understood, or else our God-consciousness will be swept away by the culture around us.

NEXT EVANGELICALISM: WHERE DO WE GO FROM HERE?

Before concluding this chapter, I want to offer some observations on the current and possible future trajectories of the evangelical movement in America. These are only my own personal speculations on what shape the "next evangelicalism" may take, but since every book, including this one, is written from somewhere, I owe it to the reader to indicate where I am coming from ecclesiologically, so to speak. Everyone's understanding of worship will reflect their own views of the current state of the segment of the church with which they identify, and I am certainly no exception.

As we are now standing in the second decade of the twenty-first century, there seem to be a growing number of reasons that prognostications concerning possible "next evangelicalisms" are in order. The founding fathers of the modern postwar American evangelical movement—Harold John Ockenga, Billy Graham, Carl F. H. Henry—have either already passed from the scene or will soon be doing so, and it is far from evident that any unified cadre of younger leaders is emerging to take their place. The vision of these earlier leaders for the broad renewal of mainline Protestantism in America has been at best only partially and fragmentarily fulfilled. They have, however, left behind them a host of schools, mission organizations, publishing houses, campus ministries and many other parachurch institutions, together with a passion for worldwide evangelization, biblical preaching, and theological orthodoxy that constitutes a comprehensive and enduring legacy.[20] As we have previously noted, the dramatic growth of the church in the Global South has changed the demographics of the world Christian movement, and North American evangelicals, as they look to the future and their place in it, will need to get used to the idea of being partners, not the unquestioned leaders, in the global evangelical movement. It is no longer a time of mission from "the West to the rest"; the emerging reality now is Christian mission "from everywhere to everywhere."[21] Looking around the American evangelical subculture[22]

---

[20]An appreciative yet critical and scholarly assessment of this legacy has been written by my colleague Garth M. Rosell, *The Surprising Work of God: Harold John Ockenga, Billy Graham, and the Rebirth of Evangelicalism* (Grand Rapids: Baker Academic, 2008). Rosell notes that there are some 100,000 parachurch organizations—many of them evangelical in their staffing and mission—in North America alone (p. 221).

[21]I wish to thank my colleague and missiologist Moonjang Lee for this reminder.

[22]These remarks focus on the *white* American evangelical subculture and in that respect are parochial; the evangelical African American, Hispanic and Korean churches would have their own distinctive issues and perspectives in such matters.

today, at least six groupings call for brief comment, each having certain strengths and weaknesses: the evangelical left, charismatics and Pentecostals, popular apocalypticism, Willow Creekers, emergents and Reformed orthodoxy.

The evangelical left, associated with prominent spokesmen such as Jim Wallis and Tony Campolo, have seen themselves as responding to the call for evangelical social engagement that was issued by Ockenga, Henry and other founding fathers of the evangelical movement. They have acknowledged the disappointing response of many white evangelicals to the challenge of the civil rights movement in the 1960s, have attempted to frame a political agenda that is not simply a reflection of "the Republican Party at prayer," and have challenged the evangelical movement to commit itself to responsible environmental stewardship and care for the earth. Whether revisionist moves by Campolo and others on the biblical understanding of homosexuality represent the beginning of a liberalizing theological trajectory remains to be seen, and is a matter for some concern.

Popular apocalypticism, on the other hand, represented by the wildly popular series of *Left Behind* books, derives from the dispensational wing of the American evangelical church originating in the nineteenth-century world of John Nelson Darby, prophecy conferences and the Scofield Reference Bible.[23] True to its dispensational heritage, this wing of the evangelical movement has preserved its commitment to doctrinal orthodoxy, biblical preaching, and missions and evangelism. Its preoccupation with biblical prophecy has, unfortunately, generally left behind the Old Testament prophets' passion for social justice, and has also been tied to a rather uncritical and one-sided support for the state of Israel in Middle Eastern politics, to the detriment of any just claims of the Palestinian people.

Charismatics and Pentecostals, associated with prominent figures

---

[23]For an excellent historical treatment of the rise of dispensationalism and its impact on American foreign policy, see Timothy P. Webber, *On the Road to Armageddon: How Evangelicals Became Israel's Best Friend* (Grand Rapids: Baker Academic, 2004). The problematic nature of the *Left Behind* phenomenon has been studied by my colleague Gordon Isaac in his recently published *Left Behind or Left Befuddled: The Subtle Dangers of Popularizing the End Times* (Collegeville, Minn.: Liturgical Press, 2008).

such as Pat Robertson, Benny Hinn, Peter Wagner and many TV evangelists, have challenged the American evangelical movement to come to grips with the reality of the presence and power of the Holy Spirit in the life of the church. The emphasis on faith healing,[24] speaking in tongues and on signs and wonders has been controversial and at times divisive. The Pentecostal and charismatic movements at their best represent a healthy and needed witness to the supernatural dimensions of New Testament Christianity. But at their worst, they can degenerate into a health and wealth gospel that minimizes repentance and the centrality of the cross. They can focus on dramatic spiritual experiences rather than depth of biblical teaching and growth in personal holiness. Some wings of the American charismatic and prophetic movement need to be reminded that the Holy Spirit is a Spirit of *holiness*, and that signs and wonders and prophecies in and of themselves do not produce spiritual maturity. Recent interests in angelic visitations, dream interpretation, third-heaven visitations and the like open the door to aberrant practices that can be spiritually and theologically dangerous indeed.[25]

Since the 1980s the Willow Creek version of seeker-friendly or seeker-driven evangelical Christianity has had a high national profile and has projected its evangelistic and contemporary philosophies of worship around the globe. The Willow Creek movement appears to be losing altitude and may have passed its peak, however, for a variety of demographic, cultural and theological reasons. A church growth methodology targeted at baby boomers will inevitably need to rethink its strategies as this generation ages and as younger generations of Americans increasingly are showing greater interest in more liturgical and ancient-modern approaches to worship. Willow Creek's own major internal study of 2007, *Reveal: The Brutal Truth about Spiritual Growth*,

---

[24]The ministry of healing was a strong concern for A. J. Gordon, one of the founders of the Gordon-Conwell Theological Seminary: A. J. Gordon, *The Ministry of Healing* (Boston: Howard Gannett, 1882).

[25]See, for example, from the current "prophetic" movement, Patricia King, *Spiritual Revolution: Experience the Supernatural in Your Life Through Angelic Visitations, Prophetic Dreams, and Miracles* (Shippensburg, Penn.: Destiny Image, 2006). King's website is www.extreme prophetic.com.

was a wake-up call to the church staff, when the findings showed that substantial numbers of its most highly committed members and regular attenders reported feelings of spiritual stagnation and dissatisfaction.[26] The leaders concluded that church programming alone could not bring the most committed to the higher level of spiritual growth, that biblical teaching needed to be strengthened, and that Sunday mornings should have more of a focus on worship for believers, rather than being almost exclusively devoted to the evangelizing of the unchurched. It seems that the Willow Creek leadership is moving toward a recognition, however partial and belated, that making the unchurched the primary focus of Sunday morning is a flawed and unbiblical strategy. This element of the evangelical and revival tradition, reaching from Charles Finney to Bill Hybels, which displaced the centrality of worship in the life of the church with evangelism, may now have passed its peak and deserves to be laid to rest.

In the last decade the emerging church movement associated with Brian McLaren, Rob Bell and others has attracted the attention of many American evangelicals, not the least among them a younger generation that has become dissatisfied with seeker versions of contemporary worship and that is looking for a greater sense of mystery and transcendence. The emerging movement, in its renewed interest in liturgy, tradition, ancient-modern worship and the weekly Eucharist affirms many of the renewal elements that are advocated in this book.[27] However, there are significant concerns being voiced in other quarters of the evangelical movement—and I share these concerns—that the emerging church takes postmodern culture too seriously and is showing signs of theological softness at the core which, if continued, could land the project in the camp of Protestant liberalism in a generation or

---

[26]Greg Hawkins and Cally Parkinson, *Reveal: Where Are You?* (Barrington, Ill.: Willow Creek Association, 2007).

[27]Recent studies of the "emerging church" include Eddie Gibbs and Ryan Bolger, *Emerging Churches: Creating Christian Community in Postmodern Cultures* (Grand Rapids: Baker Academic, 2005) [cautiously favorable]; D. A. Carson, *Becoming Conversant with the Emerging Church* (Grand Rapids: Zondervan, 2005) [more critical]; and Dan Kimball, *The Emerging Church: Vintage Christianity for New Generations* (Grand Rapids: Zondervan, 2003) [favorable].

two.[28] A too-generous orthodoxy may be in danger of giving orthodoxy away altogether.

Since the inception of the modern American evangelical movement, Reformed orthodoxy has given intellectual and theological leadership to the movement, and it is likely to continue to do so in some significant measure in the future. This is a wing of the broader evangelical tradition that has its roots in the Old Princeton of Hodge, Warfield and Machen, and is continued today in denominations such as the Orthodox Presbyterian Church, the Presbyterian Church in America, and in theological seminaries such as Westminster, Covenant and Reformed. Reformed orthodoxy brings to any discussion of the renewal of worship in American evangelicalism a strong commitment to historic biblical doctrine, a firm sense of the sovereignty and glory of God, and a staunch commitment to the centrality, primacy and sufficiency of Scripture in the faith and life of the church. Any renewal of worship in the evangelical churches of America will need to incorporate these strengths of the Reformed tradition.[29]

Some branches of this Reformed tradition have, unfortunately, from my point of view, saddled themselves with cessationist views that can handcuff the Holy Spirit in the life of the church and blind it to where the Spirit may be working dramatically in the world today.[30] Are there intrinsic theological reasons why Reformed theology must affirm the sovereignty of God at the expense of the freedom and power and presence of the Spirit? Does the manifestation of a tongue or prophecy necessarily mean that Scripture is demoted to secondary epistemic and theological status?

Some of the New Calvinists associated with John Piper and Bethlehem Baptist Church in Minneapolis and his associates have com-

---

[28]My colleague David Wells, for example, has pointed to a "looser and less definitive" understanding of the authority and function of Scripture in the emergent movement: Wells, *The Courage to Be Protestant: Truth-Lovers, Marketers, and Emergents in the Postmodern World* (Grand Rapids: Eerdmans, 2008), p. 16.

[29]The work by Ryken, Thomas and Duncan, *Give Praise to God*, is a notable contribution in this regard.

[30]If in the "land of charismania" it is the Holy Spirit with a wrecking ball, in the "land of Hodge and Warfield" it seems to be the Holy Spirit in handcuffs: are these the only choices for the churches?

bined a conservative Reformed theology with greater openness to the work of the Holy Spirit today.[31] Wayne Grudem's *Systematic Theology*[32] could be cited as a current example of an evangelical theologian with a high view of the primacy, sufficiency and inerrancy of Scripture, a Reformed soteriology, *and* a strong emphasis on the gifts and presence of the Holy Spirit. Perhaps it is time for the cessationist tradition to revisit some of these questions in the light of current realities. This would open the door to an understanding of worship that would equally affirm the centrality and sovereignty of God and the presence and power of the Spirit in the Sunday gatherings of the church.

A grouping not mentioned above but worth briefly noting could be denominated as "former evangelicals," who have left the evangelical movement and migrated to Rome or Constantinople. The reasons for their spiritual migrations are complex and various, but their stories are relevant to this present effort at the renewal of worship, for they—like significant numbers of younger (and older) evangelicals—have longed for a deeper and richer experience of worship than they found in their nonliturgical evangelical churches. This trickle has not become a flood, and there are likely very many more globally who migrate in the opposite direction. And yet the stories of these seekers should cause the evangelical home guard to ask if all is indeed well in the evangelical sanctuaries on Sunday mornings—lest others in the future conclude with those who already emigrated that "the glory has departed" and head for richer, greener pastures.

What, then, for the next evangelicalism? It is always easier, it seems, to see the limitations of present offerings than to build a more attractive alternative for the future, and yet something needs to be said. The next evangelicalism, the outlines of which I can only dimly imagine, would have some similarities with the emerging churches, but with a more robust commitment to doctrinal orthodoxy and biblical authority. This

---

[31]Collin Hansen, *Young, Restless, Reformed: A Journalist's Journey with the New Calvinists* (Wheaton, Ill.: Crossway, 2008). I wish to thank my colleague Scott Hafemann for pointing me to this reference.
[32]Wayne Grudem, *Systematic Theology: An Introduction to Biblical Doctrine* (Grand Rapids: Zondervan, 1994).

next evangelicalism would be Reformed in its soteriology, trinitarian in its understanding of theology, doxological in seeing worship as the highest priority of the church, charismatic in its affirmation of the gifts and presence of the Spirit in the life of the congregation, and liturgical in its ancient-modern form of worship. This next evangelicalism would see itself as a post-Christendom project, and even perhaps as post-American, in that it would have more of a concern for partnering with its brothers and sisters in the faith in the global church than in identifying itself too closely with America and its global economic and military hegemony.

This would be a church marked by the attributes *deep, thick, different:* that is, a deep church that is marked by the depth of its encounter with God in worship and the spiritual disciplines, rather than a church oriented toward numerical growth; a thick church characterized by thick relationships and commitments rather than thin personal relationships of consumerist and postmodern culture; and a different church of "resident aliens" (Hauerwas) that is unashamedly distinct from the culture in its ontology, theology, worship and moral behavior. Such a resistance church, while not renouncing calls for cultural transformation and political involvement, would be based on the premise that the church must first be transformed itself by God before it can deeply impact the culture. And while not renouncing its historic interests in foreign mission, it would emphasize the church's service to its own local neighborhoods and communities: thinking globally, acting locally. Such a next evangelicalism would even encourage a new monastic[33] lifestyle and the ethical ideals of poverty, chastity and obedience: poverty and simplicity in the face of consumerism and materialism; sexual purity and fidelity as the Christian standard in the midst of a sexually saturated culture; and obedience as a new Christian way of being human, and as an alternative to the autonomous self of modernity and postmodernity. Such a church could have a very simple mission statement and list of priorities: (1) to worship God well, (2) to love one another, (3) to engage in mission to the world.

---

[33]On the "New Monastic" movement, see Jonathan Wilson-Hartgrove, *New Monasticism: What It Has to Say to Today's Church* (Grand Rapids: Brazos, 2008).

A PREVIEW OF THINGS TO COME

As its central concern this book argues that American evangelical churches need to recover a sense of the holiness and majesty of God, and of the real, personal presence of the risen Christ in the midst of his people in the power of the Spirit as the central realities of biblical worship. Such a renewal of worship will require a deeper theology of worship, which in turn rests on a better ontology of God, of the church and of the self. We need a new ontological framework to see God, the church and the Christian—and Christian doctrine as a whole—in their proper light.

These claims will be presented as follows in the ensuing chapters. Chapter two, "God, the Church and the Self: Searching for Reality in Evangelical Worship," argues that the renewal of evangelical worship calls for a fresh way of looking at the major participants in worship: God, the church and the Christian (or the self). The chapter also shows how the competing ontologies of modernity (scientific naturalism) and postmodernity (the digital universe, simulations, virtual realities) tend to wash out our Christian beliefs even before we enter the church, and how we need to be consciously aware of these influences, and intentionally adopt a new mindset (trinitarian theism) in order to experience worship in a more fulfilling way. The chapter comments on the loss of the sense of the holiness and majesty of God in the contemporary church, and argues for an understanding of the heaviness of God, in the sense that the eternal, self-existent great *I AM* of the Bible, who is the source of all existence and all reality, is the most intensely real being in the universe, in the face of which the "mountains melt like wax" (Ps 97:5). This point is meant to counteract the effects of modernity and postmodernity that make God seem lightweight in the modern Christian's typical experience. It is also stressed that God is a God who is joyful, beautiful, relational and available—a God who is to be praised and enjoyed, now and forever.

The chapter presents a vision of the church in the New Testament that is a unique theanthropic (God-human) reality, that is, an utterly unique, sui generis reality, unparalleled anywhere else in the universe, consisting of a communion of communities: the Holy Trinity, Father,

Son and Holy Spirit, eternally united by the Holy Spirit to the body of Christ, the believing church. This is a high view of the church, since Jesus Christ, the head of the body, is high in authority, power and glory, exalted at the right hand of the Father, sharing his glory with the church in the communion of the Holy Spirit. The church as the body of Christ is seen as an end in itself, the reason for which God bothered to create the universe—and not just as a voluntary collection of individuals, existing instrumentally for the pursuit of other tasks.

This theanthropic view of the church implies a new view of the Christian self, for the Christian, in Christ, is indeed a new creature (2 Cor 5:17). The Christian who participates in worship can and should see himself or herself as a trinitarian-ecclesial self, not a consumerist or therapeutic self of modernity or postmodernity, or a sovereign and independent self disconnected from the body and the triune God. In this new way of seeing the Christian self, worship is not an incidental activity, or only one among many others during the week, but rather, worship is the highest act of the human being—for in worship we fulfill the purpose for which we were created and for which we exist: "to glorify God, and to enjoy him forever."

The central focus of chapter three, "Reality in Worship: The Real Presence of God on Sunday Morning," is the real, personal presence of the risen Christ in the assembly in the power of the Spirit as the central and fundamental fact of true worship—not the singing of praise songs, not preaching and listening to sermons, however valuable these can be. It argues that the real presence of God as the fundamental fact of worship makes the assembly a special place and a special time because the real God is really there—investing the space with God's own holiness and glory, in the unseen yet very real presence of the angels and archangels and saints and martyrs. The time of worship is no longer just ordinary, worldly time because the powers of the age to come can be experienced in the presence of the Spirit in the church and in the exercise of spiritual gifts.

This chapter also shows how the competing ontologies of modernity and postmodernity have combined to erase from the Christian imagination a vivid sense of God's real presence and make God seem more distant and unreal, replacing it with a focus on the human preacher, the musicians on the stage and the audience. It argues that the Reformation's reaction against the Roman Catholic understanding of real presence as transubstantiation had the unintended effect of producing a sense of the "real absence" of God in Protestant worship services. The chapter concludes with a discussion of an online simulation game (World of Warcraft) as an analogy and metaphor of Christian worship, where the believers, by faith, step into an interactive parallel universe that transcends everyday life, interacting in kingdom space and kingdom time with the risen Christ, present in the world of kingdom life through his "avatar," the Spirit present in the church.

Chapter four, "The Eucharist: Meeting the Risen Christ at the Table," argues for a restoration of frequent Communion in the evangelical churches, based on a new ontology and theology of the Lord's Supper. It is argued that the central reality in a New Testament understanding of the Lord's Supper is that *the risen Christ, alive and present in the Spirit, continues to meet his people in joyful fellowship at the table.* Jesus Christ is really present in the celebration of the Lord's Supper, not on the table, circumscribed by the elements, but at the table, as the true minister and celebrant, continuing to enjoy fellowship with his disciples as he did during his earthly ministry. This presence is real, dynamic and personal, mediated by the Holy Spirit, the personal "avatar" of the risen Christ in the midst of the church. The chapter traces the historical development of the doctrine of transubstantiation in the Roman Catholic Church, focusing the worshiper's attention on the material elements themselves, rather than on a more personal understanding of the presence of Christ, and how Protestant Zwinglian (bare memorial) reactions to transubstantiation tended to produce a sense of the real absence of Christ at the table. The chapter argues that frequent Communion, understood in this "real spiritual presence" way, has many spiritual benefits, including the strengthening of the church's distinctive Christian identity and contributing to the Christian's spiritual formation and discipleship.

Chapter five, "From Ontology to Doxology: From Theory to Practice in Worship Renewal," suggests ways for the pastor and church leadership to implement this new understanding of worship. It offers guidelines for the teaching of the new ontological framework and recommends the adoption of an ancient-modern blended form of worship. Suggestions are also given on the topics of contemporary music, the visual arts, use of digital technology, and the encouragement of the discovery and use of spiritual gifts. The chapter concludes with specific suggestions concerning the practice of frequent Communion.

2

God, the Church and the Self

SEARCHING FOR REALITY
IN EVANGELICAL WORSHIP

Over a generation ago A. W. Tozer, in his now classic book *The Knowledge of the Holy*, lamented a spiritual condition in the American churches that "has existed in the church for some years and is steadily growing worse." The condition of which he spoke (in 1961) was "the loss of the concept of majesty from the popular religious mind. The Church has surrendered her once lofty concept of God and has substituted for it one so low, so ignoble, as to be utterly unworthy of thinking, worshiping men." This loss of the sense of the majesty of God was accompanied, continued Tozer, with the "further loss of religious awe and consciousness of the divine Presence. We have lost our spirit of worship and our ability to withdraw inwardly to meet God in adoring silence. . . . It is impossible to keep our moral practices sound and our inward attitudes right while our idea of God is erroneous or inadequate."[1]

Tozer's words were to prove prophetic of things to come. About a decade later, J. I. Packer in *Knowing God* was also calling the attention of the evangelical churches to this loss of the sense of the greatness and majesty of the biblical God. This experiential grasp of the majesty of God is "knowledge which Christians today largely lack: and that is one reason why our faith is so feeble and our worship so flabby." Modern

---

[1]A. W. Tozer, *The Knowledge of the Holy: The Attributes of God; Their Meaning in the Christian Life* (Harrisburg, Penn.: Christian Publications, 1961), pp. 6, 7.

Christians, continued Packer, "though they cherish great thoughts of
man, have as a rule small thoughts of God." The God of the Bible,
while personal like us, unlike us is great; "the Bible never lets us lose
sight of His majesty, and his unlimited dominion over all his
creatures."[2]

Things were little different when, in 1985, Robert Webber again
called attention to the trivialization of the sense of God in much contemporary worship. The evangelical churches, by and large, still did
not get it. Our churches, observed Webber, "are characterized by a feeling of overfamiliarity, an inappropriateness in the approach to God.
The sense of transcendence and otherness and holiness of God seems
to be missing. A kind of secularization has taken place."[3] This loss of
the sense of the holiness and transcendence of God was evident, according to Webber, in many popular praise choruses. These choruses
often are not directed at God, or focused on the cross of Christ, but
rather they "concentrate on personal experience and self-realization.
They participate in the narcissism of our culture. . . . Our religion has
followed the curvature of a self-centered culture."[4]

The title of this chapter, "God, the Church and the Self," is an attempt to connect this book's overall purpose—the renewal of evangelical worship—with the deficiencies in the popular evangelical understandings of God, as highlighted by Tozer, Packer and Webber. But
why the concern for *reality* in evangelical worship? This chapter works
with the assumption that the renewal of contemporary worship calls for
a return to the first principles and foundations of the worship experience, beginning with an examination of the fundamental nature and
essential being of the *participants* involved in worship: God, the church
and the self. The problem in many contemporary evangelical worship
services that is being addressed in this chapter could be stated this way:
*Your "God" is too "light"; your vision of the church is too low; your view of
your self is too high, and consequently, your worship is too shallow.*

"Who's really here? What are we here for, and are we all clear about

---

[2]J. I. Packer, *Knowing God* (Downers Grove, Ill.: InterVarsity Press, 1973), pp. 73, 74.
[3]Robert E. Webber, *Worship Is a Verb* (Waco, Tex.: Word, 1985), p. 16.
[4]Ibid., pp. 16-17.

why we are here, and what we should expect?" Lack of clarity in perceiving the nature of the participants—God, church, self—and the activity in which they propose to engage—worship—will alter the nature of the experience. Clarity of understanding and a focused intentionality are essential for a deep and richly satisfying experience, whether the activity in question is having a serious conversation with a friend, making love to one's spouse or seeking the presence of God on Sunday morning.

Perhaps an analogy drawn from professional sports can help to clarify this point: consider the final game of the NBA championships. When the Boston Celtics and the Los Angeles Lakers came out onto the court for the opening tip-off, all the participants were quite clear about the nature of the activity and the participants. The Celtics had a *team* mindset and were quite aware of the difference between a pregame practice and the real thing; the Celtics knew that their fundamental engagement was not with the fans or the officials or the sponsors or the sports writers or plans for the next season—but with the Lakers, right now. In contrast (according to the thesis of this chapter) in many contemporary worship experiences, the participants are not fully and clearly aware of or expecting the *real presence of the Holy God in the midst of the assembly,* or of their deep identity as "team"/body of Christ, or of their true and deep individual identities as children of God and members of the mystical body of Christ prior to and during the worship event. This false consciousness inevitably impedes a deeper experience of communion with God; we need a new mindset for worship.

This focus on *reality* (ontology) also reflects the belief that in our modern and postmodern cultural context, reality isn't "what it used to be,"[5] and any traditional biblical or Christian worldview can no longer be taken for granted, or even assumed to be understood, much less believed, by most Americans. The challenges of scientific naturalism and

---

[5]The allusion is to Walter Truett Anderson, *Reality Isn't What It Used to Be* (San Francisco: HarperOne, 1992). At the heart of the postmodern sensibility, according to Anderson, is a growing suspicion and awareness that "all belief systems—all ideas about human reality—are socially constructed," p. 3.

atheism that deny the reality of God altogether; the commonsense realism of everyday life that tells us that what we can't see is not fully real; the new situation of religious pluralism in which the biblical God is only one of many gods on offer in the religious shopping mall; and the multiple, socially constructed virtual realities of the Internet and cyberspace all force the church to be more self-conscious about its own worldview and understanding of reality. This chapter will attempt to propose a more adequate understanding of the reality and weight of God, the church and the self that can provide a deeper foundation for Christian worship in the face of the competing ontologies of scientific naturalism, religious pluralism and the virtual realities of cyberspace.

THE ONTOLOGY OF GOD: EVANGELICAL IDOL

Dan Kimball, a youth minister trained at Willow Creek Community Church and Saddleback Church in Orange County, California, began to notice the different temperaments showing up in the younger generation of students attending his meetings. Students who once had been impressed by the fast-paced programming, dramas, media clips and topical messages were showing less interest. "The special effects in the video games they were used to went far beyond what we could offer," noted Kimball. "Their lives were fast paced as it was; coming to church for yet another fast-paced experience was losing its impact."[6] No longer could Kimball simply announce to the students "God loves you"; now they were asking, "By the way, which God are you talking about?"[7] Religious pluralism and diverse understandings of "God" in America are no longer merely the topics of academic discussion, but increasingly are felt realities as Americans rub shoulders with people of other religions and encounter a bewildering variety of belief systems in the workplace, schools and popular media.[8]

In order to effectively refocus evangelical worship practices, it is nec-

---

[6]Dan Kimball, *The Emerging Church* (Grand Rapids: Zondervan, 2003), pp. 14-15.
[7]Ibid., p. 15.
[8]On religious pluralism in modern America, see Diana L. Eck, *A New Religious America: How a "Christian Country" Has Now Become the World's Most Religiously Diverse Nation* (San Francisco: HarperSanFrancisco, 1997; 2002); and "The Pluralism Project at Harvard University" (copyright 1997-2010) <www.pluralism.org>.

essary for believers to be more self-consciously aware of the various background theories of reality such as scientific naturalism and postmodern virtuality that influence both religious and nonreligious people in their perceptions of the divine.

To return to the question posed by the young person in Dan Kimball's youth group, "By the way, which God are you talking about?" it is helpful to face the fact that there has probably never been a period in American history when more notions (or open denials) of God were on offer to the public. Is this "God" the Judeo-Christian God of the Bible that is now being vociferously denied and denounced by the new atheism of bestselling authors such as Richard Dawkins, Christopher Hitchens, Sam Harris and Daniel Dennett?[9] Is it the Allah of an Osama bin Laden or Muslim extremist that would seek to impose shariʻa law on the entire world? Is it the Krishna of the *Bhagavad-Gita* and the Hindu pantheon? Or perhaps the bodhisattva Kwan Yin before whose image a devotee in a Buddhist temple in Los Angeles lights an incense stick and offers a prayer?[10] Is it the impersonal Force of Luke Skywalker in the Star Wars series?[11] Is it the Goddess of Wicca or Neo-Pagan feminism?[12]

Are we talking about one of the many paths to enlightenment being offered for sale at the Kripalu Center for Yoga and Health in Stockbridge, Massachusetts? Some 30,000 guests make their way each year

---

[9]See, for example, Richard Dawkins, *The God Delusion* (New York: Houghton Mifflin, 2006); Christopher Hitchens, *God Is Not Great: How Religion Poisons Everything* (New York: Warner Books, 2007); Sam Harris, *Letter to a Christian Nation* (New York: Bantam Books, 2006); Daniel C. Dennett, *Breaking the Spell* (New York: Penguin, 2007). For a Christian response to the "new atheism," see John F. Haught, *God and the New Atheism* (Louisville: Westminster John Knox, 2008).

[10]There are now said to be more than 300 Buddhist temples in Los Angeles, making it home to the greatest variety of Buddhists in the world: cf. Eck, *A New Religious America*, pp. 148-51.

[11]According to the "U.S. Religious Landscape Survey" conducted in 2008 by the Pew Forum on Religion & Public Life <http://religions.pewforum.org/reports>, while 92 percent of the American public profess a belief in "God," for 25 percent, this means an "Impersonal force," for 60 percent, a "Personal God," and 7 percent replied "Other/don't know."

[12]"A poll conducted by the Covenant of the Goddess, a national organization, estimates 768,400 Witches and Pagans in the U.S." (cited in The Pluralism Project at Harvard University; copyright 1997-2010 <www.pluralism.org/resources/statistics/index.php>). On the modern revival of goddess worship, see Cynthia Eller, *Living in the Lap of the Goddess: The Feminist Spirituality Movement in America* (Boston: Beacon Press, 1995), and Philip G. Davis, *Goddess Unmasked: The Rise of Neopagan Feminist Spirituality* (Dallas: Spence Publishing, 1998).

to this New Age retreat center, which offers some 700 workshops and seminars each year. The phones are ringing constantly in the center's business office on the second floor; at the end of the day, it is a matter of business and marketing. According to Kripalu's president, Ila Sarley, "We're constantly re-examining. . . . What are the needs? What we are really looking at is what will someone pay to take a vacation to do."[13]

Or could the God in question mean the god of Liberal Protestantism who is concerned for justice and compassion, but never intervenes miraculously in the natural order? Or could it mean the Jesus of Dan Brown's *Da Vinci Code*, or the Prosperity God of a televangelist who promises health and wealth to all who believe and send in their contributions? Is it the cessationist God of some conservative Protestant groups who is holy and righteous, but somewhat distant from the world, who ceased performing miracles with the passing of the apostolic age?[14] To state the obvious, these questions hardly scratch the surface of the gods for sale in America today; this is pluralism with a vengeance, and serious Christians need to be clear about the nature and identity of the deity they intend to worship when they enter the church on Sunday mornings.

We now turn to consider two background theories of the real that impact Christian worship: scientific naturalism and postmodern virtuality. The assumption here is that these ontologies—or assumptions about the nature of reality—have a powerful impact on the believer's consciousness or preunderstanding even before he or she walks through the door of the church. Bringing these ontologies to the level of conscious awareness can help the worshiper to take corrective actions against their potentially harmful spiritual effects.

What is here being termed scientific naturalism refers, of course, to the modern scientific revolution that began with the work of Galileo, Newton, Descartes and Boyle in the seventeenth century and remains a dominant cultural influence to the present day. Modern science and

---

[13]Andy Newman, "It's Not Easy Picking a Path to Enlightenment," *New York Times*, July 4, 2008 <www.nytimes.com/2008/07/03/>.

[14]For a cessationist perspective, see B. B. Warfield, *Counterfeit Miracles* (Edinburgh: Banner of Truth, 1972 [1918]).

technology are the basis of the worldview that has come to be known as modernity; it is a worldview in which the natural world not only can be known, measured and predicted, but perhaps even more importantly, manipulated and controlled for human interests. Scientific naturalism may be said to have two expressions, one atheistic and the other deistic. In its atheistic form, matter is the final reality, and God has no ontological reality whatsoever, being a construct of the human imagination, a matter of wish fulfillment. Mao Tse Tung's aphorism, "Political power grows out of the barrel of a gun" is a crass expression of the political implications of this form of scientific naturalism.

In its more seemingly benign form—deism—the ontological reality of God is not denied, but God is *distant* from the world and not immediately involved in the external events of everyday life. In both its atheistic and deistic forms, scientific naturalism expresses an ontology in which God is either unreal or distant,[15] and in which humans are in control of their world. Material objects are more real than spiritual or mental objects, and that which is evident to the senses is the basis of knowledge. The dominant image or metaphor of modernity's ontology is the clock or a machine. Everyday commonsense experience reinforces these assumptions of scientific naturalism: stones appear to be more real than angels; God is not objectively present with us; that which cannot be easily measured or controlled is less significant for human interests. This worldview of scientific naturalism is conveyed by the elite universities, presupposed in the courts, and is the basis of much of the media, business community and economic life. The Christian living under the conditions of scientific modernity is constantly exposed to a process of mental conditioning that denies or calls into question the believer's fundamental conviction: God, not matter, as the ultimate reality. The message of modernity is, in effect, We are in control; we can make it happen. Such a mindset is inimical to bibli-

---

[15]Henri Nouwen has made the following observation about the implicit image of God held by most modern Christians: "Most of us distrust God. Most of us think of God as a fearful, punitive authority or *as an empty, powerless nothing.* Jesus' core message was that God is neither a powerless weakling nor [merely] a powerful boss, but a lover, whose . . . desire is to give us what our hearts most desire" (*Here and Now: Living in the Spirit* [New York: Crossroad, 1994], p. 22, emphasis added).

cal faith and healthy Christian worship.

Under these conditions the modern believer tends to divide the world into zones of the natural and the supernatural—and then, according to Charles Kraft, "we largely disregard the supernatural. Our focus is squarely on the natural world, with little or no attention paid to the supernatural world."[16] For example, a modern believer's instinctive reaction to a medical emergency is typically not, "Let's pray," but "Call the doctor."[17] Modernity tends to see the universe as a vast machine, operating according to natural laws without reference to God or supernatural forces. "If we do admit the existence of such beings," notes Kraft, "we tend to regard them as having little, if any, influence on the 'normal' processes according to which the universe and all within it operate."[18] Modernity can make God marginal or peripheral in the believer's day-to-day consciousness.[19] Biblical faith teaches not a dualism of natural and supernatural, but a view of a triune God who created the world, became physically present in it by the incarnation and remains present by the Spirit.

The ontology of scientific naturalism provided the intellectual foundations for the Industrial Revolution and modern industrial capitalism. In practice, the scientific knowledge and control of the natural world, and the harnessing of new forms of energy provided by fossil fuels, unleashed a period of material productivity unprecedented in human history. The new understanding of the laws of matter made it possible to produce material objects—consumer goods—in hitherto undreamed of abundance. If, at the philosophical level, scientific naturalism made the claim, "Matter is the ultimate reality," modern industrial capitalism

---

[16]Charles H. Kraft, *Christianity with Power: Your Worldview and Your Experience of the Supernatural* (Ann Arbor, Mich.: Servant, 1989), p. 27.

[17]The point being made here is not to diminish the proper place of medical care in Christian faith, but simply to draw attention to the instinctive priorities and what they seem to presuppose.

[18]Kraft, *Christianity with Power*, p. 28.

[19]This is a fundamental insight from the field of the sociology of knowledge. See, for example, Peter Berger and Thomas Luckmann, *The Social Construction of Reality* (Garden City, N.J.: Doubleday, 1967), p. 154: "Subjective reality . . . is always dependent upon specific plausibility structures . . . the specific social base and social processes required for its maintenance." What this book calls the "ontology of scientific naturalism" and the "ontology of postmodern virtuality" both in their own ways diminish the sense of the reality of God in the modern world.

made the promise, "The acquisition of an abundance of material objects is not only possible, but desirable, and can be the focus of human activity." A worldview dominated by scientific materialism can reinforce a lifestyle of consumerism.

The point of these observations is not to deny the great benefits produced by modern science and industrial capitalism. Michael Novak is probably correct in his claim that industrial capitalism has, in the aggregate, created great social good and lifted more people out of poverty than any other socioeconomic system.[20] The point is rather to call attention to the great spiritual dangers posed to Christian faith and worship by these dominant forces of scientific naturalism and industrial capitalism.

In the book of Deuteronomy Moses sternly warns the people, prior to their entrance into the promised land, that when their goods increase and their gold and silver is multiplied, "then your heart will become proud and you will forget the LORD your God, who brought you out of Egypt . . . it is he who gives you the ability to produce wealth" (Deut 8:14, 18). Humankind's power to exercise control over nature and to produce material wealth can, in fact, lead to forgetfulness of God. The very success of the scientific method can turn people's attention from the reality of the unseen God to the pursuit and acquisition of material objects, by which people seek to define their status and significance.

Many centuries later John Wesley was to make a similar observation about the tendency of riches to deflect people's attention from God: "I do not see how it is possible, in the nature of things, for any revival of true religion to continue long. For religion must necessarily produce both industry and frugality, and these cannot but produce riches. But as riches increase, so will pride, anger, and love of the world in all its branches."[21]

---

[20]See Michael Novak, *The Spirit of Democratic Capitalism* (New York: Simon & Schuster, 1982).

[21]Cited by Alan Wolfe, "And the Winner Is . . . The Coming Religious Peace," *Atlantic Monthly*, March 2008, p. 3 <www.theatlantic.com/doc/200803/secularism>. In this article Wolfe provides global data on national wealth and religiosity; in general, the more affluent societies (e.g., Western Europe, Scandinavia) are less religious than poorer countries (Africa, India, the Middle East). The United States is something of an exception to this pattern.

The other competing ontology to be considered is postmodern virtualism. If modernity is a sensibility and way of imagining reality stemming from the scientific and industrial revolutions, then postmodernity expresses a sensibility produced by the digital and information revolutions. Postmodern virtualism is the world of computers, the Internet, video, high-definition TV, cinema, satellite radio, Al Jazeera, CNN, smart phones, email, text-messaging, blogs, iPods, Google, Facebook, Twitter and all the appurtenances of a digital lifestyle.

Modernity produced a quantum leap in humankind's ability to produce material objects; postmodernity and the digital technology revolution have produced a quantum leap in humankind's ability to produce, transmit and transform data, information and images. Modernity enabled human beings to dramatically reshape the physical environment; postmodern virtualism is all about producing the images and representations in terms of which people define their identity and significance. A modern economy based on material production is being supplemented and transformed by an economy based on the production of simulations and the play of images.[22] The cacophony of lights, sound and images in New York's Times Square is an example of such a world fabricated from the play of images. The sensibility of postmodern virtualism can be called one of "image over reality, surface over depth, style over content, signifier over the signified."[23]

In such an environment the boundary between the real and the virtual or socially constructed becomes blurred and even insignificant.[24] A

[22]The terminology is from Jean Baudrillard, *Simulation and Simulacra* (1994), cited in Douglas Kellner, "Jean Baudrillard," in *The Blackwell Companion to Major Social Theorists*, ed. George Ritzer (Malden, Mass.: Blackwell, 2000), p. 741.

[23]Christopher Horrocks, *Marshall McLuhan and Virtuality* (Duxford, U.K.: Icon Books, 2000), p. 28.

[24]Jean Baudrillard, *Simulacra and Simulations* (Ann Arbor: University of Michigan Press, 1994), has spoken of a postmodern "hyperreality" in which real objects have been effaced or superseded by the simulations of digital and electronic technology. Baudrillard's influential commentaries on these and other aspects of postmodernity are limited by his lack of engagement with real, "hard" science, and by his lack of any transcendent perspective from which to critique the postmodern sensibility. A better guide here is Albert Borgmann, *Crossing the Postmodern Divide* (Chicago: University of Chicago Press, 1992), esp. pp. 82-97, "Hyperreality." Borgmann's observations are even more timely, given the continued advances in digital technology since 1992 (e.g., high-definition TV, Xbox video simulations such as the bestselling Guitar Hero, and the like) in which the simulations are more compelling than the real.

trip to Disneyland is not a trip to a "fake" world but rather to a better, and in some sense, more real world than the "real" world. "I don't want the public to see the real world they live in while they're in the park," Walt Disney remarked, "I want them to feel they are in another world." The point of the Disneyland experience, according to Peter Steeves, is not that Disneyland is a copy of our world, but rather that our world is a copy of Disney's.[25]

Disneyland is an example of a socially constructed (virtual) reality that can be for its inhabitants—at least for a time—more real and engaging than ordinary life. For a teenager playing a massively multiplayer online game such as World of Warcraft, or someone inventing a new personal avatar and online identity in Second Life, the virtual world and identity can be more interesting and compelling than ordinary reality.[26]

Walter Truett Anderson has argued that this notion of social construction is the key to understanding the postmodern sensibility. Viewed in this light, the central claim of the postmodern-virtual sensibility is that "all belief systems are socially constructed"—that is, all religions, theologies, laws, governmental systems, national boundaries and works of human culture generally. According to Anderson, not only the fact of human beings socially constructing their world, but also the consciousness of this fact is at the heart of the postmodern sensibility.[27]

Again, the point of these observations is not to simply rail against modernity and postmodernity and call for a Christian escape into some romantic, premodern vision of the past; the point is to raise awareness of the threats posed by these outlooks to the integrity and depth of the

---

[25]H. Peter Steeves, "A Phenomenologist in the Magic Kingdom: Experience, Meaning, and Being at Disneyland," in *The Things Themselves: Phenomenology and the Return to the Everyday* (Albany: State University of New York Press, 2006), pp. 147-79 at pp. 157-58.

[26]Martin Ramstedt has noted how that for many online simulation gamers and practitioners of neo-Pagan spiritualities, it is the case that "more and more people apparently find it unimportant whether something is literally or metaphorically true . . . the real success of 'virtual reality' has also contributed to the blurring of boundaries between the realms of the 'factual' and the metaphorical" ("Metaphor or Invocation: The Convergence Between Modern Paganism and Fantasy Fiction," *Journal of Ritual Studies* 21, no. 1 [2007]: 1-15 at p. 12).

[27]Walter Truett Anderson, *Reality Isn't What It Used to Be* (San Francisco: HarperSanFrancisco, 1990).

Christian experience of worship. Like modernity, the world of post-modern virtualism perpetuates the illusion of human control over our total environment, and can distract people from their true and most real end: the triune God of Scripture. Both competing ontologies—the ontologies of modernity and postmodernity—can function as idols for the Christian in our current historical context, and both can deflect, distract and seduce the Christian's heart affections from an undivided allegiance to the one true God.

Postmodern life can be a life of constant digital distraction, a never-ending experience of life in Vanity Fair.[28] Postmodernity can flood the mind and imagination of the modern Christian with a never-ending cascade of glittering images, deflecting the believer's attention from the invisible and eternal realities of heaven. The power of digital technology can perpetuate the Enlightenment myths of humanity's unlimited power to control and create their own world; true worship only begins when one surrenders his or her autonomy and control, and waits receptively in the presence of God for God to speak, to act and to love.

THE ONTOLOGY OF GOD: YOUR GOD IS TOO LIGHT

We now return to consider the ontology of God, that is to say, some of the fundamental characteristics of God's reality that especially need to be refocused and emphasized in the context of a renewal of evangelical worship. For the purposes of this discussion, the following characteristics or attributes of God will be highlighted: God as *"heavy,"* God as *holy,* God as *joyful,* God as *beautiful,* God as *relational* and God as *available.* An existential grasp of each of these aspects of God's being is important for a richly biblical and satisfying experience of worship.

To say that the God of the Bible is "heavy" is to draw an intentional contrast with the weightlessness of God in much of contemporary cul-

---

[28]In John Bunyan's Vanity Fair "all sorts of vanity" were sold all year long: "at this Fair are all such merchandise sold, as houses, lands, trades, places, honours, preferments, titles, . . . lusts, pleasures, and delights of all sorts" (*The Pilgrim's Progress,* ed. Roger Sharrock [New York: Penguin, 1987], p. 79). The world of postmodern virtualism could be said to be "Vanity Fair to the max." According to one recent research study, the average American worker gets an average of 156 emails each working day, and switches attention to a different task, on average, every three minutes (Maggie Jackson, "Creativity Can Thrive, If You Keep the E-mail in Check," *Boston Globe,* July 13, 2008, p. G1).

ture and church life.[29] To say that God is heavy is to recognize the intensity and the density of the reality of the divine being, in comparison with which the things of creation are but wisps or vapors or dreams. Such a notion is reflected in a biblical text such as Psalm 97:5, which states that "the mountains melt like wax before the LORD, before the Lord of all the earth." When God the Almighty appears on earth, Mount Everest melts like wax in the presence of the intensely concentrated and burning reality of the Creator's being. The stars and countless galaxies, in their mind-boggling number and size, that are the work of God's hands, will at the end of time "all wear out like a garment. . . . they will be discarded" (Ps 102:26). At the end of time the heavens and the earth will be shaken (Hag 2:6) and "the stars will fall from the sky" (Mt 24:29). In the ontology of Jesus, this physical world has a limited shelf life: "Heaven and earth will pass away, but my words will never pass away" (Mt 24:35). On Judgment Day, when the massive reality of God's great white throne appears, the earth and sky will flee from his presence (Rev 20:11).[30]

A universe that has endured now for some fourteen billion years will perish when its end is decreed by the eternal, self-existent One who made it. Like the dancing electrons on the screen of a video game that disappear when the message "game over" appears and the power plug is pulled—so God the Creator will finally pull the plug on this world, announce "game over," and summon humankind before the great white judgment throne. The whole creation can be thought of as God's holographic projection, dancing points of light projected on the screen of space and time, which can dissolve in a moment with a click of God's mouse. The modern person has large thoughts of him or herself and small thoughts of God, yet as James reminds us, one's life, in comparison to the eternity and intense reality of God, is like "a mist that appears for a little while and then vanishes" (Jas 4:14).

---

[29]The phrase the "weightlessness of God" is drawn from David Wells, *God in the Wasteland* (Grand Rapids: Eerdmans, 1994), p. 88.

[30]As John Zizioulas has pointed out, Christian and biblical ontology is *eschatological* in nature: only at the end will the temporary nature of the present world become apparent, when the intensity of God's eternal being is manifested (*Remembering the Future: An Eschatological Ontology* [Edinburgh: T & T Clark, 2008]).

The image of black holes from modern astronomy has captured the popular imagination: an infinitely dense concentration of matter from a collapsing star that radiates such a strong gravitational field that not even rays of light can escape from its surface. The God of the Bible is not an ontological black hole, so to speak, but rather a "white hole" of infinitely dense and concentrated reality that can spew forth a universe at the moment of the big bang creation. Neutron stars, stars that have collapsed catastrophically but that have not yet reached the black hole state, are said to have such a dense concentration of neutrons at their core that all the molecules in Mount Everest could be concentrated in a space the size of a teaspoon. This image of an intensely and densely concentrated star suggests the analogy of God as a "neutron star" of being—more intensely and densely real than anything in our ordinary human imagination and experience.

The point of suggesting these images and analogies is to provoke the evangelical imagination to a reversal of the commonsense ontologies of scientific naturalism and postmodern virtualism, in which human beings and human creations are heavy and central, and in which God is lightweight, peripheral or even nonexistent. Before true worship can begin, the worshiper must be aware of the infinitely weighty reality of the One in whose presence he or she dares to stand. To paraphrase Anselm's famous formulation in his ontological argument, God is that than which nothing more *real* can possibly be conceived; God is the fundamental and defining source and creator of everything else that exists.

This notion of the weightiness of God as the truly, densely, intensely and profoundly *real* is an expression of what has been traditionally in Christian theology called the aseity of God. God is the self-existent One, whose existence is necessary, eternal and dependent on no one or nothing outside himself. Such a notion of the divine reality is reflected in the classic and enigmatic words spoken to Moses at the burning bush: "Take off your sandals, for the place where you are standing is holy ground. . . . *'I am who I am'*" (Ex 3:5, 14). As Jeffrey Niehaus has observed, in this text the divine name is a statement of God's aseity, "of the fact that he is unconditional, essential being. Theophanic radiance [the flames] and power communicate to the natural senses what it means thus purely *to be*."[31]

The intensely real God of Sinai is not for sale; the true and living God, who is who he is and not who we might wish him to be, cannot be manufactured, marketed, bought, sold or controlled: "I am who *I* am."

In his commentary on the enigmatic words "I am who I am," John Durham writes that this phrase indicates the "'is-ness' of the God of Israel." This "is-ness" has the sense of "active presence"; this divine presence and reality is not "a bare 'is' but a living force, vital and personal. In no situation is he an ornamental extra; in every situation he is the key active ingredient."[32] When Moses met God on Mount Sinai at the burning bush, it was God, not Moses, who was the center of attention; so it is in true worship that the central focus is not the preacher or the praise band or the people, but the mighty One who chooses to be present with his covenant people.

The reality of God's aseity or eternal, necessary self-existence is the foundation for the Christian doctrine of creation *ex nihilo*. God is eternal and has always existed, but the universe is not eternal, and there was a time when it began to be. The universe, at the moment of the big bang creation event, was not made from preexistent matter, but space and time, together with matter and energy, began to be when God Almighty decreed, by an act of free and sovereign will, that they exist. The doctrine of creation *ex nihilo*[33] expresses a Christian understanding of God in which the power of the Creator is unlimited and absolute; nothing exists prior to the divine act of sovereign creation; nothing ex-

---

[31]Jeffrey J. Niehaus, *God at Sinai: Covenant and Theophany in the Bible and Ancient Near East* (Grand Rapids: Zondervan, 1995), p. 188. My colleague Gary Parrett has remarked that in Ex 3:14 God is saying to Moses, in effect, "I am not who you may think I am, or who you may wish that I am; I am *who I am*, and you need to adjust your thinking accordingly."

[32]John I. Durham, *Exodus*, Word Biblical Commentary (Waco, Tex.: Word, 1987), p. 69. Durham states that "I AM WHO I AM" also connotes the sovereignty and freedom of God in his self-disclosure: "By revealing himself as 'I AM WHO I AM' the Lord had in effect said, 'Yes, I have committed myself to you to be actively present with you, but I am not at your unfettered disposal. My active presence is mine and mine alone to exercise as when and under what conditions I choose" (p. 70). People must give up any notions of having the power to control God or their relationship with God.

[33]The historical development of this doctrine in early Christianity is traced in Gerhard May, *Creatio Ex Nihilo: The Doctrine of 'Creation out of Nothing' in Early Christian Thought*, trans. A. S. Worrall (Edinburgh: T & T Clark, 1994).

52

WORSHIP AND THE REALITY OF GOD

ists eternally apart from God that could frustrate or ultimately resist the divine purpose to redeem the people of God. The doctrine of creation *ex nihilo* implies that physical laws, indeed even space and time, are not in themselves eternal or self-existent, but only begin to be—and continue to be—as an act of the divine will.

The doctrine of creation *ex nihilo* is also a forceful reminder of the fundamental contingency of the created order, an insight emphasized in the theology of William of Ockham. As Ockham observed, "A creature . . . exists in such a manner that it does not necessarily exist";[34] it could be otherwise, or its behavior could be subject to change. "Ockham never loses sight of this basic Christian idea," writes Philotheus Boehner, "so radically opposed to the necessitarian view—that there is no inherent necessity for anything in this world to be what it is."[35] This is to recognize that the laws of physics are not logically necessary; they could be otherwise.[36] The God of Christian theism could have created a world in which the sky was green and water boiled at 125 degrees centigrade, or one in which the strength of gravity was different from its present value, or a stillborn universe with only hydrogen and helium atoms and not stars and galaxies at all. The practice of science implicitly recognizes this fundamental contingency of nature by insisting not merely on a comprehensive, internally consistent mathematical theory, but on the empirical verification of the theory: the scientist must rise from the study and look and see to find how nature has actually chosen to be.

This fundamental contingency is a characteristic not merely of individual existing things or particular physical laws, but of the world as a whole: the universe as a whole need not exist. In the classic observation of Heidegger, the most fundamental question of metaphysics is pre-

---

[34]William of Ockham *Summa totius logicae* 3.2.100.27, in *Philosophical Writings,* trans. P. Boehner (New York: Bobbs-Merrill, 1964), p. 106.

[35]Ibid., p. xix.

[36]Note, for example, the unanswered question posed by physicist Alan H. Guth: "[Even] If the creation of the universe can be described as a quantum process, we would be left with one deep mystery of existence: What is it that determined the laws of physics?" *The Inflationary Universe: The Quest for a New Theory of Cosmic Origins* (Cambridge, Mass.: Perseus, 1997), p. 276. Guth recognizes that the laws of physics are not logically necessary or self-evident, but are contingent on some conditions or factors other than themselves.

cisely this: Why are there beings at all, and why not rather nothing?[37]

This fundamental contingency of the universe has been recognized from a scientist's point of view by Stephen Hawking at the close of *A Brief History of Time*. Even if science achieves a "theory of everything," a unified set of equations that unifies all physical laws, there still remains, says Hawking, a very basic question: "What is it that breathes fire into the equations and makes a universe for them to describe. . . . Why does the universe go to all the bother of existing?"[38] The equations themselves do not answer the question of why there should be a universe for the equations to describe; mathematical equations can describe an existing world, but equations do not cause that world to exist.

Under the spell cast by certain images of Newtonian science, modern Protestant theology forgot or abandoned this crucial insight concerning the contingency of the natural order. The doctrine of creation *ex nihilo* pointed to the radical discontinuity of the beginning of the world from the present world system; things have not been eternally as they are now.

The upshot of the foregoing discussion is that, from the perspective of a biblical ontology, Spirit is more enduringly and powerfully real than matter, and invisible things are more enduringly and powerfully real than the visible. That is to say, God is more real than Mount Everest or the floor on which I am standing. This is not to say that matter is unreal or illusory, but only to point to the fact that matter and the material objects that I can touch, taste, see and measure are not ultimate, eternal or self-defining realities; only the triune God of the Bible is the ultimately real. This ontological awareness is the one presupposed in Pauline statements such as, "we fix our eyes not on what is seen, but on what is unseen. For what is seen is temporary, but what is unseen is eternal" (2 Cor 4:18), or, "this world in its present form is passing away" (1 Cor 7:31). It is on the basis of such an ontology that Paul can remind the believers in Colosse to "set your hearts on things above, where Christ is seated at the right hand of God. Set your minds

---

[37]Martin Heidegger, "What Is Metaphysics?" *Basic Writings* (New York: Harper & Row, 1977), p. 112.
[38]Stephen Hawking, *A Brief History of Time* (New York: Bantam, 1988), p. 190.

on things above, not on earthly things" (Col 3:1-2). While not denying the importance of earthly things, Paul reminds them that the eternally weighty realities are the unseen, spiritual and heavenly realities where Christ is enthroned at the right hand of God—realities that can be perceived with the eyes of faith, and not by the eyes of sense or by the scientific method.

This ontological paradigm shift and recognition of the weightiness of God means that a new "epistemology of faith" is needed for biblical worship; those who worship God in Spirit and in truth need to focus, with the eyes of faith, not on the human participants or leaders in worship, but on the unseen Living One who is truly present in the assembly, and who is the central and defining reality of every meeting in the church.

The God who is the central reality in biblical worship is not only a "heavy" God but also, preeminently, the holy God. "Holy, holy, holy is the LORD Almighty; the whole earth is full of his glory" (Is 6:3). The revelation of the thrice-holy God, which has echoed over the centuries in the liturgies of the church and which continues now in heaven and into eternity (Rev 4:8: "Day and night they [the living creatures] never stop saying: 'Holy, holy, holy is the Lord God Almighty, who was, and is, and is to come'"), shattered Isaiah's sense of self-sufficiency ("'Woe to me!' I cried. 'I am ruined! For I am a man of unclean lips, and I live among a people of unclean lips, and my eyes have seen the King, the LORD Almighty,'" Is 6:5), and changed his life forever.[39]

The Holy God whose exalted glory was glimpsed by Isaiah is the awesome God of the Sinai theophany, who called his covenant people into his presence in the midst of thunder, lightning, thick clouds and trumpet blasts, such that the people trembled in fear (Ex 19:16), even as the mountain itself trembled violently (Ex 19:18), signifying the "lightness" of the mountain's being in the presence of the overwhelming density and heaviness of the being of the great I AM Creator God Al-

---

[39]Significantly, a deeper encounter by Isaiah with God in worship (Is 6:1-4) preceded Isaiah's new call to mission (Is 6:8-9: "Who will go for us"), rather than mission preceding worship. See also Acts 13:1-3, where the launching of Paul's great mission to the Gentiles arises from the context of worship: "While they were worshiping the Lord and fasting, the Holy Spirit said, 'Set apart for me Barnabas and Saul.'"

mighty. So it is in new covenant worship that the people of God are in the presence of the living and Holy One, not at the foot of Mount Sinai, but at the heavenly Zion (Heb 12:22-24) in the presence of multitudes of angels in joyful assembly, praising their redeemer God together with the saints triumphant, doing so with reverence and awe (Heb 12:28), being fully conscious that the Holy One in whose presence they are is indeed a "consuming fire" (Heb 12:29).

Rudolf Otto, in his classic study *The Idea of the Holy,* documented how in premodern and traditional cultures the sense of the holy—of the "aweful," the "numinous," the fascinating yet at the same time terrifying sense of the powerful presence of the "wholly Other"—was the primordial and deepest feature of the religious experience and attitude.[40] "Holiness, then," according to Melissa Raphael, "contains within itself a sui generis category that is peculiar to religion and defines the essence of religion: the *sensus numinis*—the sense of the divine."[41] In the presence of the Holy One, Abraham realizes that he is but "dust and ashes" (Gen 18:27). This sense of the holy defined the boundaries between the sacred and the profane, the earthly and the heavenly, and the time of this world and the eternity of the world to come.

It is noteworthy that in the history of great revivals of religion, such as the Reformation and the Great Awakening, it has been the preaching of the cross and of the need for repentance that has been the source of true and lasting conversion and spiritual growth.[42] The preaching of the cross and the discovery of the depths of human sin themselves are grounded on the bedrock biblical truths of the holiness and majesty of God, throwing the sin of man and woman into sharpest relief. If the biblical Abraham were to visit some of the cozy and comfortable seeker-driven worship services of the present day, he might well say of them what he said to Abimelech, the pagan ruler of Gerar: "There is surely

---

[40]Rudolf Otto, *The Idea of the Holy* (New York: Oxford University Press, 1931).

[41]Melissa Raphael, *Rudolf Otto and the Concept of Holiness* (Oxford: Clarendon, 1997), p. 9.

[42]For vivid accounts of the powerful movements of the Spirit and the conviction of sin observed during the Wesleyan revival in July of 1759 in Everton, England, see John Wesley, *Journal,* vol. 4 (London: Epworth, 1938), pp. 33-343; for Edwards's accounts of the Great Awakening, see *A Faithful Narrative* (1738), *Distinguishing Marks of a Work of the Spirit of God* (1741) and *Some Thought Concerning the Revival* (1742) in *Works of Jonathan Edwards,* ed. C. C. Goen, vol. 4 (New Haven, Conn.: Yale University Press, 1972).

no fear of God in this place" (Gen 20:11).

Changing social conditions and structures since the time of the Enlightenment have made it more difficult for modern men and women to have a sense of a God who is majestic, who is holy, who is "high and lifted up," because modernity has produced a flattening of all social hierarchies. "No high king; no high God." The seventeenth century saw the ending of traditional notions of the divine right of kings; Charles I could be called to account by the democratic will of Parliament and beheaded like anyone else. In our present media-saturated environments, the constant glare of public exposure (CNN, talk radio, the Blogosphere, Internet, YouTube, etc.) tends to undermine the credibility and stature of traditional high-status leaders, whether preachers, presidents or politicians. As Joshua Meyrowitz has observed, modern media erase the boundaries between private and public behaviors, and move the (private) "back stage" to the (public) "front stage"; the "increased exposure of great people undermines their ability to look 'great.'"[43]

David Wells is surely correct when he writes that it is time for the evangelical churches "to recover the biblical emphasis on the holiness of God."[44] Without such a vision of the burning holiness of God, "worship loses its awe, the truth of his Word loses its ability to compel, obedience loses its virtue, and the church loses its moral authority."[45] Such a compromised church is in danger of valuing "self-image over character" and "pluralistic religious equality over the uniqueness of Christian faith."[46]

The evangelical churches today need to fight hard to retrieve a sense of the holiness of God. Recovering such a vision of the holiness of God in today's religious and cultural climate may be very difficult indeed, and yet not impossible. Such a recovery begins, at least in part, with minds like that of Jonathan Edwards, that are saturated in the images of Scrip-

---

[43]Joshua Meyrowitz, *No Sense of Place: The Impact of Electronic Media on Social Behavior* (New York: Oxford University Press, 1985), pp. 167-69. On this leveling effect of modern electronic media, see the section "Blurring of High and Low Status Situations," pp. 160-67.
[44]Wells, *God in the Wasteland*, p. 137.
[45]Ibid., p. 136.
[46]Ibid.

ture rather than in the profanities of the popular electronic media.

Joy is another attribute of the divine being that is crucial for authentic biblical worship.[47] "Joyful, joyful, we adore thee, God of glory, Lord of love; hearts unfold like flowers before thee, opening to the sun above": the words of Henry van Dyke set to Beethoven's "Ode to Joy" reflect the biblical joy of God's people and God's creation rejoicing in the divine presence, goodness and love. Joy was a central characteristic of the early Christian communities (cf. Acts 2:46-47), rejoicing in the reality of the resurrection and the experience of the presence of the risen Christ in worship and table fellowship. Jesus rejoices in his worship and praise of the Father, in the communion of the Spirit (Lk 10:21, "at that time, Jesus, full of joy through the Holy Spirit, said, 'I praise you, Father . . .'"), and purposes, in his farewell discourse, to share this joy with us as his disciples (Jn 15:11, "I have told you this so that my joy may be in you and that your joy may be complete").

From the beginning of creation, the Wisdom and Word of God was the Father's companion and coworker (cf. Jn 1:1-3); "I was filled with delight day after day, *rejoicing* always in his presence, rejoicing in his whole world and delighting in mankind" (Prov 8:30-31). The God of the old covenant rejoices in his people and delights in them (Zeph 3:17, "The LORD your God is with you [divine presence], he is mighty to save. He will take great delight in you, he will quiet you with his love, he will rejoice over you with singing"). God not only loves his people; he likes them and enjoys having them in his presence. This remarkable text in Zephaniah, apparently the only canonical text of Scripture in which God is depicted as singing with joy, finds its fulfillment in the new covenant, with God the Father rejoicing in the redemption and return of his lost children. The good shepherd rejoices in finding the lost sheep (Lk 15:5), and calls his neighbors to rejoice with him ("Rejoice with me; I have found my lost sheep," Lk 15:6); the woman rejoices when she finds her lost coin (Lk 15:9); the father of the prodigal

---

[47]It is indeed striking that in traditional systematic theology textbooks, joy, while mentioned as a fruit of the Spirit, is not listed as an attribute of God. But systematically, joy can be produced in human experience because its source and fundamental ground is in the being and nature of God himself.

rejoices at the return of his son and says, "Let's have a feast and celebrate" (Lk 15:23). Indeed, in Christian faith, heaven is a happy place;
God the Father and God the Son have smiling faces[48] and share with
the Holy Spirit their eternal, unending, inner-trinitarian joy with all
the redeemed family of God. God smiles at his Son and smiles at his
adopted sons and daughters. John of the Apocalypse sees and hears a
vision of the heavenly worship in which the joyous praise of the redeemed is so loud and raucous that it is like the roar of a mighty Niagara Falls: "Then I heard what sounded like a great multitude, like the
roar of rushing waters . . . shouting, 'Hallelujah! For the Lord God
Almighty reigns. Let us rejoice and be glad and give him glory!'" (Rev
19:6-7).

Joy is a fundamental characteristic of the inner being of the Trinity;
the Father rejoices in the Son, and the Son rejoices in the Father, in the
communion of the Holy Spirit, now and forever. We as the redeemed
people of God are on a journey into the joy-filled heart of the triune
God. We see, by the eyes of faith, not the incredible lightness of being,
but rather the incredible joyfulness of being, for joy is hardwired into
the heart of the universe. The eternal joy of the Trinity is recycled back
to God in the joyous praise and worship of all God's children.

Beauty is another fundamental characteristic of God that, like joy, is
a crucial element of rich and satisfying biblical worship. The psalmist
invites us to "Worship the LORD in the beauty of holiness" (Ps 96:9
KJV). David's heart desire is to be in God's presence and to contemplate
his intrinsic beauty and loveliness: "One thing I ask of the LORD, this
is what I seek: that I may dwell in the house of the LORD all the days of
my life, to gaze upon the beauty of the LORD and to seek him in his
temple" (Ps 27:4). God is beautiful: this core truth of God's being is
reflected in God's acts of creation, redemption and new creation. The
end and consummation of God's work is pictured in the stunning

---

[48]The images of God in the church and in the Christian's imagination can have powerful
impacts for good or for ill in personal piety and worship. The crucifix in Roman Catholic
churches, portraying a dead and suffering Christ, and the icons of "Christ Pantocrator" in
Orthodox churches, portraying a powerful but very somber Jesus, do indeed portray profound
biblical truths—but not the whole truth; the joyfulness of the inner life of the Trinity is missing in these images.

beauty and brightness of the new Jerusalem, the bride of Christ (Rev 21–22), which itself consummates and intensifies the artistic beauty reflected in the wilderness tabernacle and in Solomon's temple, both graced with the beautiful light of the Shekinah Glory cloud of the divine presence. The streets of gold and the precious stones and jewels that adorn the new Jerusalem, the church of the new creation, are images of the intensity and density of the beauty of the new creation, a beauty that is rooted in the being of the triune God who is the source of all goodness, truth and beauty.[49] It is then a good, right and fitting thing that worship should reflect God's beauty in music, liturgy, architectural setting and the visual arts. It is an encouraging development that many evangelical churches seem to be now discovering a new appreciation for beauty and the visual arts as an enhancement to their historically word-oriented traditions.

Undergirding these divine attributes is the fundamental reality of the relational and personal character of God's being. The modern revival of trinitarian theology,[50] and especially the work of the Orthodox theologian John Zizioulas,[51] has directed the attention of the church to the trinitarian reality of persons in relation as the ultimate ontological categories—the categories "more real than which none greater can be conceived." Scientific naturalism (and significant strands of Western philosophy since the pre-Socratics) have asserted that matter and energy (and natural selection) or some impersonal category of being are the final explanatory principles by which all reality is to be understood;[52] Chris-

---

[49]On beauty as a fundamental characteristic of the Trinity, see David Bentley Hart, *The Beauty of the Infinite: The Aesthetics of Christian Truth* (Grand Rapids: Eerdmans, 2003), esp. pp. 155-77. I wish to thank my colleague Adonis Vidu for pointing me to this reference.

[50]For an overview and introduction to this important trend, see Colin Gunton, *The Promise of Trinitarian Theology* (Edinburgh: T & T Clark, 1991); Catherine LaCugna, *God for Us: The Trinity and Christian Life* (New York: HarperCollins, 1991); Jürgen Moltmann, *The Trinity and the Kingdom* (Philadelphia: Fortress, 1993); and Roger Olson and Christopher A. Hall, *The Trinity* (Grand Rapids: Eerdmans, 2002).

[51]See John Zizioulas, *Being as Communion: Studies in Personhood and the Church* (Crestwood, N.Y.: St. Vladimir's Seminary Press, 1993), especially chap. 1, "Personhood and Being"; and Zizioulas, *Communion and Otherness* (New York: Continuum, 2006). In this latter work Zizioulas develops the trinitarian theology proposed in *Being as Communion*, emphasizing the "otherness" of Father, Son and Holy Spirit in the triune God as a paradigm for personal and social communion that preserves rather than denies differences.

[52]Similarly, in advaita Hinduism, Brahman is the ultimate ontological category, and in Bud-

tian theism, to the contrary, says that persons in holy, loving relations are the final and ultimate realities of the universe, from which all things real are derived. The laws of physics, chemistry and biology are not the ultimate categories; God as Father, Son and Holy Spirit define ultimate reality for the Christian. The trinitarian reality of persons-in-relation as highest reality has profound implications (to be further developed below) for the Christian understanding of the being of the church and of the self. Given the ontological primacy of the Trinity, loving relationships among people are not merely instrumental to some other purpose or task (such as evangelism), but are valuable for their own sake, as reflective of and participating in the inner life of the triune God.

The good news is that the glorious community of persons—Father, Son, Holy Spirit—is not only fundamentally relational, but also *available*. The whole *telos* or purpose of creation, redemption (incarnation, cross, resurrection, ascension) and new creation is to invite redeemed persons into the communion and friendship of the inner life of the Trinity, in a never-ending and ever-deepening experience of the divine love and ecstasy (cf. Eph 3:19, "to know this love that surpasses knowledge—that you may be filled to the measure of all the fullness of God"). The generosity, joy and overflowing divine hospitality of the triune God, inviting us to the joys of the wedding feast, is now enjoyed in worship here on earth and finally consummated in heaven in the new creation.[53]

THE ONTOLOGY OF THE CHURCH:
HIGH, HEAVY AND THEANTHROPIC

"What comes into our minds when we think about God is the most important thing about us," was the provocative assertion made by

---

dhism, Nirvana plays this role; both are impersonal in nature.

[53]The new ontology of God, church and self being proposed in this chapter implies a new epistemology distinct from that of scientific naturalism or postmodern virtualism—a new epistemology based on Spirit, Word, faith and a renewed Christian imagination. The outlines of such a faith-based epistemology, together with appropriate epistemic practices that can undergird the renewal of worship, will be suggested in chapter five, "From Ontology to Doxology." This new epistemology of worship will shift the focus of the visual field from the visible to the invisible, from earth to heaven, and from the human preacher and participants to the risen Christ who is invisibly but really present in the power of the Spirit in the midst of the worshiping assembly.

A. W. Tozer in the previously cited book, *The Knowledge of the Holy.*[54] In a similarly provocative way, Dan Kimball has suggested that "what comes into our minds when we think of the word *church* is the most important thing shaping how we function as a church."[55] How we worship will reflect certain notions of what we believe the church *is*, that is, certain understandings of the being or "ontology" of the church.[56]

In the ordinary understanding of most Christians, *church* is first of all a building, a place where we go on Sundays to engage in certain activities. Even the Protestant Reformers could define the church in terms of its activities, that is, "where the Word is truly preached and the sacraments rightly administered." Darrell Gruder in *The Missional Church* has noted how the terminology of church shapes people's expectations. "Popular grammar captures it well," observes Gruder. "You 'go to church' much the same way you might go to a store. . . . You 'belong to a church' as you would a service club with its programs and activities. . . . Both members and those outside the church expect the church to be a *vendor of religious services and goods.*"[57]

More reflective Christians know that the church is first of all a people and not a building, but the fundamental nature or being of the church is rarely an object of conscious reflection. This latter circumstance reflects a long-standing tendency in Christian history to take the church for granted. From the time that Cyprian wrote *The Unity of the Catholic Church* in A.D. 251, it may have been more than a thousand years—1378—before a Christian theologian wrote another treatise devoted specifically to the doctrine of the church, Wycliffe's *The Church.*[58] The doctrine of the church did not form a separate theme in Christian theology until the fifteenth century, and the first edition of Calvin's *Institutes*

---

[54]Tozer, *Knowledge of the Holy*, p. 9.

[55]Kimball, *Emerging Church*, p. 92.

[56]I am deeply indebted in this section of the chapter to Simon Chan, *Liturgical Theology: The Church as Worshiping Community* (Downers Grove, Ill.: InterVarsity Press, 2006), esp. to chap. 1, "The Ontology of the Church," pp. 21-40.

[57]Cited in ibid., p. 93, emphasis in original.

[58]Kevin Giles, *What on Earth Is the Church?* (Downers Grove, Ill.: InterVarsity Press, 1995), p. 213. Giles attempts to remedy past "ecclesiological deficits" in systematic theology by proposing a trinitarian doctrine of the church.

(1536) had no separate chapter on the church.[59] It is fair to say that in the evangelical tradition, the doctrine of the church has been a Cinderella doctrine, neglected in favor of the more glamorous issues of preaching, evangelism and mission. Consequently, the being of the church, as the context of worship, has suffered inattention and neglect.

We need some reflection on the ontology or fundamental being of the church. The significance and weight of a human activity depends greatly on the context in which the activity takes place. A higher and weightier view of worship flows from a higher and weightier view of the church. To illustrate: both the boys kicking a soccer ball around in a city park and the teams of Spain and the Netherlands in the final game of the World Cup are playing soccer, but the latter is a much more intense and weighty expression of the game. A support staff entering data on laptop computers in the local high school and a support staff working on laptops on Air Force One with the president of the United States on board are engaged in similar activities, but the latter staff has greater weight and authority. The White House is not just a building on Pennsylvania Avenue in Washington, D.C., but that place where the president is personally present—a center of command and control and authority. The "real church" is not just a collection of people on Sunday morning—but an assembly where the risen Christ is present.

Three of the fundamental images of the church in the New Testament[60]—the family of God (the Father), the body of Christ (the Son) and the temple of the Holy Spirit—call attention not only to the trinitarian and pneumatic nature of the church, but also to the presence of the living, triune God as its defining and characteristic mark. Throughout the Bible it is assumed that the initiative in true worship is God's, and of particular significance for understanding the divine initiative is the reality of the divine presence, in connection with the ark and mercy seat, the cloud and fiery pillar in the wilderness, the tabernacle, and the temple as places of manifestation of the glory of God.[61] The *ecclesia*, the

---

[59]Wolfhart Pannenberg, *Systematic Theology*, vol. 3 (Grand Rapids: Eerdmans, 1998), pp. 21-22: "Excursus: The Place of Ecclesiology in the Structure of Dogmatics."

[60]Cf. Paul Minear, *Images of the Church in the New Testament* (Philadelphia: Westminster Press, 1960).

[61]C. E. B. Cranfield, "Divine and Human Action: The Biblical Concept of Worship," *Interpre-*

assembly of the living God, the true church, is that entity constituted by those people elected and called by God, assembled by his authority in his presence to experience and respond to his presence in the worship-event. In biblical thought, the presence/*parousia* of the true and living God unmasks and overturns the commonsense metaphysics of self-enclosed naturalism. When Yahweh appears on the Day of the Lord, "the mountains melt like wax before him"—the apparent solidity of a Mount Everest disappears like smoke in a hurricane, like shadows of the night before the rising sun—before the intense ontic reality of the triune God, whose ontic density places the lightness of material being in its proper perspective.

The personal presence of God in the ecclesia, by virtue of his covenant promises, his Word, sacraments and Spirit, invests the ecclesia with an ontic weight that does not obtain with merely human organizations and assemblies.[62] In practice, it seems that ordinary evangelical Protestant concepts of the church reflect notions that are more sociological than theological, more functional and pragmatic than "mystical" and ontological, more Pelagian[63] than Pauline and pneumatic—that is, an eviscerated ecclesiology in which the church is viewed as a voluntary human organization gathered for certain activities: worship and praise, instruction and motivation, and friendship.

The ecclesia of the New Testament is in fact a theanthropic (divine-human) reality, considered ontologically; that is to say, its reality can only be partially described in terms of material, sociological, psychological, anthropological and historical categories; these latter categories

---

tation 12 (1958): 385-98 at 386; the entire article is worthy of careful study.

[62]A high ontology of the church is presented, from an Orthodox perspective, by Sergius Bulgakov, *The Bride of the Lamb* (Edinburgh: T & T Clark, 2002), 253-68, based on his reading of Eph 1:4-11 and the biblical images of the bride of Christ and the temple of the Holy Spirit: "The Church . . . is a union of divine and creaturely principles, their interpenetration without separation and without confusion" (p. 262). In terms of the present reflections, the church could be seen to represent a unique theanthropic ontology grounded in the eternal mind and purpose of God (cf. Eph 1:4).

[63]The term "Pelagian" has been suggested by James Torrance as a characterization of much Protestant worship, in the sense that, in practice, it seems to be performed in merely human energy, as though true worship in "Spirit and in truth" (Jn 4:24) did not require the presence and energy of the Spirit himself (*Worship, Community and the Triune God of Grace* [Downers Grove, Ill.: InterVarsity Press, 1997], pp. 20, 92, 117).

can be useful in describing aspects of the church, but they fail to capture its defining essence. The ecclesia is a sui generis entity in the universe, among the ensemble of all entities constituting the real, for it is essentially that class of individuals among the species *Homo sapiens*, from the beginning of time, chosen and designated to subsist, exist and have their identity and purpose defined and grounded by a real ontic bonding with the triune God, mediated by Word, Spirit and sacrament. The ecclesia *is* the family of God the Father; the ecclesia *is* the body of Christ the Son; the ecclesia *is* the temple of God the Holy Spirit—where the word *is* receives full ontic weight. This real presence of the triune God and his ontic-covenantal bonding with his people was manifested experientially in the Pauline assemblies of the New Testament era, as the cry "Abba" expressed the sense of the personal presence of the Father, the cry "Maranatha" the vivid awareness of the risen, exalted and returning Son, and the Spirit was palpably felt in the manifestations of the charisms exercised by each one (1 Cor 14:26). In the New Testament all churches are "charismatic" in the sense of being constituted by the Holy Spirit.

The evangelical Protestant tradition has been characterized as generally having a low ecclesiology; the New Testament, however, has a high and ontically weighty ecclesiology, because it has a high Christology.[64] The church is "high" because Christ is high: seated at the right hand of the Almighty, as *kyrios* invested with universal and plenipotentiary authority, appointed as "head over everything *for the church,* which is his body, the fullness of him [Christ] who fills everything in every way" (Eph 1:22-23).[65] The glory/*kabod*/heaviness of the glorious Son flows into the ecclesia, the beloved bride of the Son, who fills his church with his Spirit, his love, joy—and ontic weight. At the end of this filling, this "pleromafication" of the church, it will be visibly re-

---

[64]On the high ecclesiology in Paul, especially in the prison epistles, see Lucien Cerfaux, *The Church in the Theology of St. Paul* (New York: Herder, 1959), pp. 289-383, "The Church Heavenly."

[65]Paul Minear notes that the ecclesiology of the New Testament, the image of the church as the body of Christ, is "high," for it is "as high as the new humanity, as the resurrection body of Christ, as the Holy City, which comes down out of heaven. . . . [It] dwarfs to hill-like proportions the highest of the high churches" (*Images of the Church in the New Testament* [Philadelphia: Westminster Press, 1960], p. 259).

vealed as the massive, beautiful and intensely real entity depicted in the imagery of the new creation (Rev 21–22)[66]—a reality in which the beauty and value of the present age takes a quantum leap upward into an unimaginable future.

It is essential, then, for the people of the ecclesia to have an ontology of the church "from above," constituted by an awareness and recognition of its theanthropic, trinitarian and pneumatic character, rather than an ontology of the church "from below," driven by functional, empirical and pragmatic categories, all of which are prone to be held captive by the impoverished doxological imagination of modernity and its consumerist and entertainment-driven concerns.

A number of distinctions can be made with regard to the church's aspects and manifestations. The church preexisted in a conceptual sense in the eternal mind and plan of God before matter, energy, space and time were created by God *ex nihilo* in the big bang creation event: "he [the Father] chose us [the church, the body of Christ, temple of the Spirit] in him [in relation to the Son] before the creation of the world" (Eph 1:4).[67] As foreseen and intended in the pretemporal consciousness and purpose of the Holy Trinity, the church already had ontic reality, for any entity conceptualized and willed by the eternal God has reality even prior to its historical and physical creation.[68] This conceptual reality is then actualized as historical and empirical reality as God calls, converts and assembles his chosen people through the Abrahamic, Mosaic and new covenants and the regenerative power of the Spirit in the *ordo salutis* (Rom 8:29-30). This historical and empirical church, consti-

---

[66]The massive dimensions of the new Jerusalem/ecclesia—a cube measuring 1,400 miles long, wide and high (Rev 21:16)—and the gold, silver and precious stones that image its nature—all point to the intensification, magnification and ontological "weightiness" of the value, beauty and being of the church as theanthropic reality.

[67]The laws of physics, chemistry and biology, the fundamental physical constants, are "friendly to life" ("cosmic coincidences") because God created the physical world and its laws for the purpose of creating humanity and with the church in view as his final purpose.

[68]Theologically, in terms of the knowledge of God, it is usual to distinguish between those things that are known by God as logical but merely hypothetical possibilities (e.g., a world in which John Wilkes Booth did not shoot Abraham Lincoln), and those things foreknown by God as to become actual, because of the determination of the divine will that it become actual (e.g., that Jesus would die on the cross in Jerusalem). The latter has more ontic weight than the former; a set of symbols such as "2+2=5" has no coherent meaning, is not known as such by God or other rational agents, and hence has no ontic weight.

tuted with a theanthropic, pneumatic and trinitarian ontology, then subsists in either its gathered or scattered state. When the church gathers itself together intentionally as a church, in the name of the Lord Jesus (1 Cor 5:4; cf. 1 Cor 14:23-25), as an assembly of God for the worship of God, then God himself is present, and the church can experience its full theanthropic and ontological weight—the transcendent Christ is then immanently and really present in the midst of the assembly, investing it with his own reality, authority and weightiness.

An analogy may help to illuminate this distinction between the church as gathered and scattered, with the gathered church being understood as having greater ontological weight and depth. Twelve persons called and selected to be on a federal grand jury spend weeks hearing evidence and argument in a complex case involving terrorism and national security. At the lunch breaks, the members of the jury are strictly charged not to discuss the case with one another in the cafeteria; they are, so to speak, off duty. Though still a jury ("scattered"), they do not have the full authority invested in jury members as a jury until they are officially gathered again into the courtroom by the federal authority that called and constituted them in the first instance. In like manner, the ecclesia can be thought of as scattered during the other six days, but when gathered on resurrection day, the day of the Lord, when the Lord himself is present in the Spirit, then they are invested with the ontological weight and powerful presence of the Lord himself, and their action—worship—is accordingly invested with the greatest weight and significance.

THE ONTOLOGY OF THE SELF: TRINITARIAN, ECCLESIAL AND DOXOLOGICAL

How does the typical evangelical Christian understand himself or herself when coming to church on Sunday? What constitutes such a person's core identity, and upon what fundamental view of reality—or ontology, as it were—is that sense of identity based? Raising such questions may seem somewhat academic or pedantic, but they are very relevant to this book's project of raising foundational questions about the nature of an activity such as Christian worship.

In other areas of human life and activity, it is quite evident that being clear and self-consciously aware of one's true identity is essential for functioning successfully in that activity. Kobe Bryant of the Los Angeles Lakers may be a husband, a father, a businessman or investor during the off season, but when he steps out onto the court for an NBA conference title game, he is intently focused on his identity as a team member of the Los Angeles Lakers. Forgetting this essential reality—even for a few minutes—and being distracted by the next business deal, family problems or a future commercial endorsement could have catastrophic effects, making the difference between victory and defeat. Are evangelical Christians equally clear about their core identities during the act of worship?

A bewildering variety of ways of understanding the self are on offer in modern and postmodern America today. Some of these possibilities are not likely to be immediately germane for an evangelical believer, but are still worth noting, given the religious pluralism in the surrounding culture. For a person practicing certain forms of Hinduism or its New Age variants, atman or the soul is identical to Brahman, the impersonal Absolute; the message is, in effect, "You are 'God'"; you simply need to understand and experience, through study, meditation and spiritual practices, that primal metaphysical reality. The point is for my self or soul to experience union with or absorption by the Absolute. For a Theravada Buddhist, on the other hand, the self is an illusion to be deconstructed by insight, meditation and spiritual practice. The self has no final ontological reality, but is like a candle flame that is to be blown out and extinguished in the attainment of Nirvana.

Today's evangelical believer, while most unlikely to be committed to any such Eastern view of the self, is much more likely, however, to be influenced by some version of an Enlightenment or postmodern view of the self. Modern philosophy since Descartes, Kant and Locke has seen the human being as an autonomous self who can set his or her own standards for truth and morals, apart from tradition, Scripture or church. Kant exemplified this modern "turn to the subject" in his famous "Copernican revolution" in epistemology. Heretofore, asserted Kant, mankind had assumed that the foundations of knowledge were to be found in the mind's conformity to an antecedent reality external to the self. On the contrary, Kant's project in the *Critique of Pure Reason* was to argue that knowledge was in fact based on the conformity of the external world to the presumably a priori categories of the human mind. For John Locke, the autonomous self found expression in a social contract theory of government that saw human institutions and governments as having no a priori, transcendent bases, but as being socially constructed by the voluntary agreements and contracts of individuals.

The rise of the Romantic Movement in the nineteenth century reacted against the rationalism of the Enlightenment philosophers, but not against its basic premise: the autonomy of the self. Not reason but depth of feeling was seen to be the core of the self, and this form of romanticism came to expression in what has been termed by Robert Bellah as expressive individualism.[69] "I want to be 'me,' and I want you to recognize and appreciate my definition of 'me,'" could be seen as the heart cry of this romantic version of the self—whether expressed on *American Idol*, Facebook, Twitter, YouTube or some other social networking site.

This modern self of expressive individualism appears in therapeutic or consumerist versions and blends almost seamlessly into postmodern versions of the fragmented, socially constructed self. The therapeutic self of our highly psychologized society has been documented in studies such as Martin Gross's *The Psychological Society* (1979) and Philip Rieff's *The Triumph of the Therapeutic* (1987).[70] This therapeutic turn in our culture is associated with an ethics of subjectivity and with expressions such as doing "what feels right," "following your heart," "having the courage to be yourself" and cultivating "emotional intelligence."[71] This therapeutic self is easily integrated with a consumerist self defined by its consumption of images, experiences and services; by its possessions, lifestyle habits and corporate logos. "I shop, therefore I am; I

---

[69]Robert Bellah, *Habits of the Heart: Individualism and Commitment in American Life* (Berkeley: University of California Press, 1985).

[70]Martin L. Gross, *The Psychological Society* (New York: Random House, 1979); Philip Rieff, *The Triumph of the Therapeutic* (Chicago: University of Chicago Press, 1987).

[71]Paul Heelas and Linda Woodhead, *The Spiritual Revolution: Why Religion Is Giving Way to Spirituality* (Malden, Mass.: Blackwell, 2005), p. 80.

possess the stylish brands, therefore I am socially significant."[72]

These therapeutic and consumerist versions of the modern autono-mous self are so entrenched in our American culture that they inevita-bly shape the expectations for worship that we bring to church on Sun-days, unless we consciously and intentionally take steps to counter them. Robert Webber is probably near the mark when he warns that evangelicalism, "following the Enlightenment culture, asks, What is in it for me? Its approach to worship is self-focused. It focuses on . . . self-help or empowerment."[73]

These tendencies forming the modern autonomous self are magni-fied by the digital imagery and Internet technologies that produce what Kenneth Gergen has called the postmodern saturated self.[74] Pulled in a thousand different directions by a never-ending cascade of images, messages and voices that saturate the mind and compete for attention, this fragmented self can live in a virtual world of fantasy and make believe, and can construct a new self at will: "a TV producer, a ball club manager, a 'whole new me,' a Master Chef, a video creator, a blogger, a flaming cloud in Second Life. . . . As a gay person, you are re-creating and reinventing institutions like marriage. . . . You see through institu-tions . . . and co-opt them and use them for what you want."[75] This saturated self is also a self of fractional relationships, in which various pieces of me are shared, quite provisionally, among a bewildering vari-ety of people, shifting relationships and partial commitments.

Various writers have suggested that these conditions of postmodern virtualism tend to reinforce the narcissistic tendencies of the self. In his

---

[72]James B. Twitchell has argued that advertising and the creating of "brands" has the social function of conferring social status and meaning on the individual: "Branding is the central activity of creating differing values for such commonplace objects and services as flour, bottled water . . . denim jeans . . . air travel. . . . Giving objects their identity, and thus a perceived value, is advertising's unique power . . . by adding value to material, by adding meaning to objects, by branding things, advertising performs a role historically associated with religion" (*Adcult USA: The Triumph of Advertising in American Culture* [New York: Columbia University Press, 1996], pp. 12-13). I wish to thank my son, Nathaniel Davis, for pointing me to this reference.
[73]Robert E. Webber, "The Crisis of Evangelical Worship," in *Worship at the Next Level*, ed. Tim Dearborn and Scott Coil (Grand Rapids: Baker, 2004), p. 91.
[74]Kenneth Gergen, *The Saturated Self* (New York: Basic Books, 1991).
[75]Grant McCracken, *Transformations: Identity Construction in Contemporary Culture* (Blooming-ton: Indiana University Press, 2008), pp. xvi, xxi.

book *Mediated: How the Media Shapes Your World and the Way You Live in It,* Thomas de Zengotita, a cultural anthropologist, suggests that our media-dominated culture is one of "living in a world that is made up of a 'flattering field of represented options,' a world of images, polls, surveys, focus groups, *American Idol,* of voting someone 'off the island,' of having my consumer preferences scanned at the check-out line, of having Amazon analyze my reading preferences . . . ad infinitum."[76] This postmodern, mediated self is constantly flattered with the impression that its consumer preferences are the constant center of someone's attention, that they really matter.

Gregory Jones, the former dean of Duke Divinity School, was introduced into the world of Facebook by his teenage children, and quickly developed his list of 181 online "friends." While it is a plus to expand our social networks, such virtual friendships have their limitations, noted Jones. "We may have multiple social networks and thousands of acquaintances and still find ourselves profoundly lonely. . . . We are not likely to turn to Facebook when a loved one is dying, for guidance in vocational discernment, or for the joys and warmth of physical embrace."[77]

Similarly, Perry Glasser, a faculty member in the writing program at Salem State College, has noticed the ubiquity of the Internet, Facebook, cell-phone and text-messaging culture among his twenty-something students, and he asks if all this technology is changing a generation's sense of self. "The electronic network flatters every yuppie wannabe with the same delusional lie," he writes. "You are the hub of a great ever-changing network. The heavens may wheel, but we remain fixed at the center. . . . This most photographed [Facebooked] generation in history is by many measures the most narcissistic. Social networking sites present a huge, electronic refrigerator door with no judgmental parent exerting critical judgment."[78]

While observations such as those above might be dismissed as the cranky reactions of an older and less techno-savvy generation, never-

---

[76]Thomas de Zengotita, *Mediated* (New York: Bloomsbury, 2005), p. 255.
[77]L. Gregory Jones, "My Facebook Friends," *Christian Century,* July 15, 2008, p. 35.
[78]Perry Glasser, "The Dance of the Bees," *Boston Globe,* April 24, 2008, p. A15.

theless, they do raise the question of how our digitally saturated culture is shaping the expectations and perceptions of those who come to church on Sunday mornings. Has the self sitting in the pew been fundamentally reshaped by the gospel—or does it bear the marks of the narcissistic forces of the therapeutic and consumerist culture in which it lives? Such questions deserve to be placed in the spotlight of a consciousness formed not just by culture, but by the weightier realities of the biblical God and the church of the new creation.

To return, then, to the question, Who is the believer at church on Sunday morning? What is his or her core identity and essential being? The answers of Enlightenment modernism or contemporary postmodernism that see human beings as some form of self-defining, self-constructing autonomous individuals simply will not do from the perspective of the New Testament and the realities of true worship in the church of the new creation. "If anyone is in Christ, they are a new self, a new creation; the old self is gone, the new self has come" (2 Cor 5:17, paraphrased). Believers, when they walk through the door of the church, should do so with a consciousness that they are adopted sons and daughters of God, through faith in Jesus Christ, in the communion of the Holy Spirit, living members of the living body of Christ—and chosen from eternity for the specific purpose of enjoying communion with God (Eph 1:4).

The new Christian self is no longer an autonomous, individualistic self, but a trinitarian and ecclesial self: this, from the moment of conversion, is the worshiper's fundamental ontological reality and true self-understanding. The believer has been baptized by the Spirit into the body of Christ (1 Cor 12:13), and is, from that time forward, a living member of Christ the true vine (Jn 15:5) and mystically united to him. The Christian's personhood is trinitarian in the sense that, according to the promise of Jesus, all three persons of the Trinity come to dwell in the heart of the believer: "I will ask the Father, and he will give you another Counselor *to be with you forever.* . . . If anyone loves me, he will obey my teaching. My Father will love him, and *we will come to him* and make our home with him" (Jn 14:16, 23).

This new Christian self or personhood is also trinitarian in the sense that it reflects, in a finite and analogous way, the perichoretic nature of the inner-trinitarian life: persons dwelling in one another, enjoying communion in intimate personal relationships of holy love, and yet forever distinct, not being absorbed into the other's person.

The believer is really, truly, factually, ontologically united in communion with all three persons of the triune God, Father, Son and Holy Spirit. This truth of the believer's new state of being precedes and is the proper foundation of any particular act of worship. As Eric Mascall has stated, from the fact of the mystical union it follows that "the Christian should be defined not in terms of what he himself does, but of what God has made him to be. Being a Christian is an ontological fact, resulting from an act of God."[79] And as Herman Ridderbos has astutely noted, the mystical union, being "in Christ," is not just an occasional reality in certain sublime spiritual moments; rather it is, in Pauline and New Testament teaching, "an abiding reality *determinative for the whole of the Christian life*. . . . we have to do here with the church's 'objective' state of salvation."[80] We are as really connected to Christ and to other believers by the bond of the Holy Spirit as teenagers, texting one another on their cell phones, are connected to one another by the invisible signals broadcast from the nearest cell tower.

Commenting on the reality of the believer's mystical union with Christ in his Ephesians commentary, Harold Hoehner notes that "we are no longer dead in our trespasses. Rather we are alive in the heavenlies with Christ [Eph 2:6]. . . . This corporate solidarity is a reality now, but in the future its reality will be enlarged as we fully bond with our Savior, with new bodies and without sin."[81]

At the risk of belaboring the point, it should be said again that being fully conscious of one's true identity can make a real difference in the quality of one's relationships and experiences. For example, a new son-

---

[79]E. L. Mascall, *Christ, the Christian, and the Church* (London: Longmans, Green, 1946), p. 77.
[80]Herman Ridderbos, *Paul: An Outline of His Theology* (Grand Rapids: Eerdmans, 1975), p. 59, emphasis added.
[81]Harold W. Hoehner, *Ephesians: An Exegetical Commentary* (Grand Rapids: Baker Academic, 2002), p. 336. On Christ's corporate solidarity with believers, Hoehner also cites Thomas G. Allen, "Exaltation and Solidarity with Christ: Ephesians 1:20 and 2:6," *Journal for the Study of the New Testament* 28 (October 1986): 103-20.

in-law, just married into his wife's family, can still, for a period of time, feel like an outsider at family gatherings. But when he really internalizes the awareness that "I am not an outsider; I am part of this family"—and when his wife's family see him this way as well and act accordingly—then, and only then, does he feel and experience the closeness and enjoyment that flows from this new perception of the family relationships. As Christians we are no longer outsiders or "slaves," but friends, and beloved sons and daughters, welcomed and accepted into the Father's household.

The new-creation self is also an ecclesial self, defined and constituted by its membership in the body of Christ. The believer is mystically united to Christ, the head of the body, but also mystically united, through baptism and the bond of the Holy Spirit, to the other members of the body. "Make every effort to keep the unity of the Spirit through the bond of peace. There is one body and one Spirit . . . one Lord . . . one God and Father of all, who is over all and through all and in all" (Eph 4:3-6). As J. K. S. Reid has written, as believers we have our true identity, our true selves, at all times and in all activities, in our mystical union with Christ; because "we are grounded in him . . . it shifts the centre of gravity from the individual to the church."[82]

The new-creation self, the recognition and consciousness of which is the basis for new covenant worship, is in fact a new way of being a human being. As the apostle Paul stated in Ephesians 2:15, it was Christ's purpose in his life, death and resurrection, to "create in himself one new man out of the two," a new way of being human that transcends the old boundary markers of race, social class and nationality. So it is that, being mystically united with Christ in his living body, "there is neither Jew nor Greek, slave nor free, male nor female, for you are all one in Christ Jesus" (Gal 3:28). The modern or postmodern self may see itself as self-constructed or socially constructed, but the Christian sees himself or herself as divinely reconstructed in and by Christ and the Spirit.

This new-creation self, this new way of being human, is meant to

---

[82]J. K. S. Reid, *Our Life in Christ* (Philadelphia: Westminster Press, 1963), p. 94.

transform the predominant "I" consciousness into a "we" consciousness.
In some African Christian cultures this corporate consciousness is expressed in sayings such as "I am because we are"; in the modern Anglican Church of Kenya it is said in the eucharistic liturgy, "We are because He is."[83] These sayings express the spirit and the reality of Paul's
theology of the body and the new creature in Christ.

This new way of being human implies that our core identity on Sunday mornings (or any other day of the week) is no longer that we are
(American) citizens; we are conscious that our real citizenship is in
heaven (Phil 3:20); our consciousness is no longer captivated and absorbed by matters of earthly politics, economics, spending, consumption, trips to the mall or Hollywood and Internet entertainment, but
rather is focused on the unseen but more lastingly real world of heaven
above (Col 3:1-2), where Christ is enthroned at the right hand of God.
My fundamental identity is no longer defined by my job ("I am a software engineer at Microsoft"), but rather by the confession "I am in
Christ."

The new-creation self is in fact a doxological self in the sense that
the Christian realizes that he or she was created for worship: we were
created and redeemed that we "might be for the praise of his glory"
(Eph 1:12). The Christian realizes that worship is not just incidental
and preparatory to some other activity (such as mission or evangelism),
but rather, worship is intrinsic and central to the purpose for which
God created the universe and humanity: that we might "glorify God
and enjoy him forever" (Westminster Shorter Catechism, Q. 1). Worship in the Spirit and in truth is the highest act of a human being, the
act in which we are most truly human, and the highest act of the church.
At its best, Sunday morning can be the high point and culmination of
a believer's week. There is no more meaningful or enjoyable experience
for a redeemed human being than to be in the divine presence, sensing
God's glory and experiencing God's love.

In conclusion, then, renewal in evangelical worship involves a new

---

[83]Martha Giltinan, "Greetings from Mother Martha," in Vine and Branches: News of the Family of Christ Church of Hamilton and Wenham, June 2008 <http://vineandbranchescchw
.wordpress.com/2008/06/15/greetings-from-mother-martha/>.

consciousness, a new mindset, a new ontological way of thinking about God, the church and the self. In this new mindset, God is seen, by the eyes of faith, as weighty, as holy, as joyful, as beautiful, as relational and as available—that is, really present. The church is seen as high and "heavy," as a unique theanthropic reality; and the self is seen as a trinitarian, ecclesial and doxological self that is made to glorify God and to enjoy him forever. The implications of such an ontology for the worship of the church will be developed in the chapter to follow.

3

Reality in Worship

THE REAL PRESENCE OF GOD
ON SUNDAY MORNING

The observation that John Calvin wanted the Eucharist to be celebrated weekly in Geneva, but that he was prevented from doing so by
the town council is relatively well known among Reformed theologians
and historians of liturgy.[1] It is also a curious fact of American church
history that many American Presbyterian churches, even very conservative ones, have not followed Calvin in his eucharistic theology, either
in terms of his desire for weekly observance or in his doctrine of Christ's
real spiritual presence through the Holy Spirit on the occasion of the
Eucharist.[2] Many of these churches, and much of the American evangelical tradition from the nineteenth century to the present, have been
closer to Zwingli than to Calvin on the matter of the presence of Christ
in the sacrament.[3] Churches in this Zwinglian memorial tradition ob-

---

[1]These circumstances have been studied recently, for example by Laurence C. Sibley, "The
Church as Eucharistic Community: Observations on John Calvin's Early Eucharistic Theology (1536-1545)," *Worship* 81, no. 3 (2007): 249-67.

[2]For Calvin's understanding of a real though spiritual presence of Christ at the Eucharist see
Institutes 4.17.3-10: the "secret power of the Holy Spirit towers above all our senses. . . . the
Spirit truly unites things [the glorified body of Christ in heaven, and the believer on earth]
separated in space." On Calvin's eucharistic theology, see Hughes Oliphant Old, *Worship That
Is Reformed According to Scripture* (Atlanta: John Knox Press, 1984), and *The Patristic Roots of
Reformed Worship* (Zurich: Theologischer Verlag, 1975); Brian A. Gerrish, *Grace and Gratitude:
The Eucharistic Theology of John Calvin* (Minneapolis: Fortress, 1993); Kilian McDonnell, *John
Calvin, the Church, and the Eucharist* (Princeton, N.J.: Princeton University Press, 1967).

[3]Even Charles Hodge, that stalwart proponent of the Reformed theology of Old Princeton,

serve the Eucharist in obedience to Christ's commandment, but often there seems to be an underlying feeling that it is a marginal practice that, if not quite superfluous, lacks the emotional and imaginative impact that can be found in a compelling sermon. This sensibility asks the question, What do I "get" in the Lord's Supper that I can't get in a good sermon? What's the point of doing this? It seems that in many evangelical Protestant churches no compelling responses to those inchoate doubts are being provided to those who gather (monthly or quarterly) at the table.

The purpose of this chapter is not to provide further analysis of Calvin's view of the real spiritual presence of Christ in the Eucharist (see further chap. 4), but rather to use it as a point of departure for reflection on the larger issue of the *real presence of God* as the central reality in Christian worship. Furthermore, we will explore some of the possible reasons for the sense of the *absence* of God in many occasions of worship in contemporary American Protestantism.[4] We will first note some of the cultural influences stemming from the Reformation, the Enlightenment and nineteenth-century revivalism that have contributed to a thinning and flattening of the Protestant evangelical doxological imagination[5] and to the impoverishment of the theology and practice of worship. Next, we will explore the ontology of worship and its context. Third, we will examine the fourfold pattern of biblical worship and the historic elements of Christian worship. And finally, we will explore a modern cyberspace analogy of worship as an online simulation game and some recent research in the area of ritual studies for the purpose of

---

could view Calvin's understanding of the Lord's Supper as "an uncongenial foreign element" in Reformed theology, *Princeton Review* 20 (1848): 227-78, cited in Sibley, "The Church as Eucharistic Community," 65n.54. The Zwinglian memorial view has been called, perhaps unfairly, a "real absence" view: Christ is really not present with the worshiping congregation, but only being recalled to mind.

[4]Would a sociologist of religion visiting a typical Protestant worship service—on either side of the modernist-fundamentalist divide in modern Protestantism—find clear evidence that the participants believe and act as though they were conscious of actually being in the presence of the living God?

[5]The term "doxological imagination" is proposed as a semantic reminder that worship involves humans not only at the cognitive-logical level, but also engages or should engage the imagination (visual sense), the emotions, the will and the body: worship understood as a holistic and embodied human activity.

stimulating a richer and more robust (but biblically grounded) evangelical sense of imagination in worship.[6]

REFORMATION, ENLIGHTENMENT, REVIVALISM AND DOXOLOGICAL POVERTY

In their different ways the Protestant Reformation of the sixteenth century, the scientific revolution of the seventeenth century and the philosophies of the seventeenth- and eighteenth-century Enlightenment, and the revivalism of nineteenth-century evangelicalism contributed to the impoverishment of the Protestant doxological imagination and practices of worship. The Protestant Reformation delivered essential spiritual and theological benefits, of course, in the recovery of the biblical gospel of justification by faith through faith in Christ alone, the translation of the Scriptures into the vernacular, administration of the Eucharist in both kinds, congregational singing and so forth. These gains need to be maintained, recognized, respected and further implemented in any proposals for the renewal of Christian worship.

At the same time, however, we can ask if the Reformation had unintended detrimental consequences for subsequent Protestant practices of worship. For example, did Protestant rejections of the Roman Catholic doctrine of transubstantiation overreact in the direction of "real absence" memorial views? Did the Reformation emphasis on the preaching of the Bible[7] contribute to a neglect of the role of the sacraments in Christian worship? Did the Protestant (especially Cromwellian) "stripping of the altars" and iconoclasm contribute to an impoverishment of the religious imagination, especially in regard to the heavenly realities of the saints and martyrs, angels and archangels, and "all the company

---

[6]The term "ontology of worship" is introduced to call attention to the fact that all human activities and practices presuppose some ontology, i.e., a background theory of what is real. This book claims that much contemporary worship operates on the basis of a thin and flattened ontology that has been impoverished by the impact of scientific naturalism, the practices of revivalism and inadequate biblical understandings of worship. Consequently, many worship events lack robust "ontic weight."

[7]Queen Elizabeth I considered four sermons a year quite enough for the English church, and viewed preaching with some suspicion; the Puritans understandably wanted weekly if not daily opportunities for the people to hear the Bible preached (James Hastings Nichols, *Corporate Worship in the Reformed Tradition* [Philadelphia: Westminster Press, 1968], p. 91).

of heaven" of the invisible church triumphant? Week by week the faithful in medieval churches could see, in the artistic representations of the
saints and angels, visual reminders of spiritual realities that transcended
the ordinary. Did this Protestant iconoclasm[8] leave the Protestant
evangelical tradition more impoverished, and perhaps less equipped
than the Catholic and Orthodox[9] traditions, which in their different
ways are more visual, to respond appropriately to the new postmodern,
media-driven, image-saturated sensibilities of emerging generations?[10]
Such questions are, of course, easier to pose than to answer, and will
not be pursued at greater length in this essay, but they do deserve the
consideration of serious students of contemporary worship practices.

It is generally recognized that the Enlightenment and the scientific
revolution of the seventeenth century constituted a watershed in the
religious sensibilities of Christians in the West,[11] with a major impact
on both Protestants and Catholics and theological conservatives as well
as liberals.[12] Across the religious spectrum the impact of the new scien-

---

[8]In a fascinating and perceptive study, *Image as Insight: Visual Understanding in Western Christianity and Secular Culture* (Boston: Beacon, 1985), Margaret Miles notes that sixteenth-century
Protestant iconoclasm was experienced by many Protestants not as destructive, but as liberat-
ing, in the sense that images and frescoes of the saints, the Virgin, Christ as Pantocrator, and
so forth, were felt to be a religious representation and justification of ecclesiastical hierarchy
and authority: hierarchies on earth were a reflection of hierarchies in heaven (chap. 5, "Vision
and Sixteenth-Century Protestant and Roman Catholic Reforms," pp. 95-125). For further
insights on the generally low estimation of the visual arts in English and American Protestantism, see John Dillenberger, *The Visual Arts and Christianity in America: The Colonial Period
Through the Nineteenth Century* (Chico, Calif.: Scholars Press, 1984), with many illustrations
and examples.

[9]On the significance of icons as understood in the Orthodox tradition, see Leonid Ouspensky
and Vladimir Lossky, *The Meaning of Icons* (Crestwood, N.Y.: St. Vladimir's Seminary Press,
1982).

[10]See Tex Sample, *The Spectacle of Worship in a Wired World* (Nashville: Abingdon, 1998), for observations on the pervasive impact of the new digital technologies—sound, light, image, rock
music beat—on the sensibilities of post–World War II generations. For contrasting views on
digital technology in worship, see Marva Dawn, *Reaching Out Without Dumbing Down* (Grand
Rapids: Eerdmans, 1995) [critical], and Len Wilson and Jason Moore, *Digital Storytellers: The
Art of Communicating the Gospel in Worship* (Nashville: Abingdon, 2002) [pro-technology].

[11]The Orthodox churches, largely hidden from the West because of the cultural dominance of
Islam and Soviet communism, are only now fully encountering the challenges of modernity
represented by the Renaissance, the Reformation, the Enlightenment, the scientific revolution
and the historical-critical attacks on biblical authority.

[12]Among the many studies in this area, see Bernard J. Cooke, *The Distancing of God: The Ambiguity of Symbol in History and Theology* (Minneapolis: Fortress, 1990), esp. chap. 9, "Modernity,
Science, and Religion." See also Peter Gay, *The Enlightenment: An Interpretation*, 2 vols. (New

tific view of the world—the clockwork universe of Newton[13]—tended to push religious sensibility and imagination away from mystery toward morality, and away from a sense of the immediate presence of God in the world (and in the worship-event) toward a deistic sense of a distant God far removed from the immediacies of the present.

This moralizing tendency in Enlightenment religion was exemplified, for example, in Kant's *Religion Within the Limits of Reason Alone* (1793), where he spoke of three kinds of "illusory" faith: "faith in miracles . . . faith in mysteries . . . faith in means of grace."[14] "Means of grace" such as the Eucharist could only be justified, on Kant's view, not as mysterious means of experiencing the presence of the divine, but only as pedagogical tools for the inculcation of moral behavior. The sacraments and Christian worship generally needed to be demystified to be made more acceptable to Enlightenment sensibilities. The Christian God may have acted in the past, but is now only known in memory.

At the risk of oversimplification, it might be helpful to posit significant points of contrast between the cosmological imaginations of three historical eras and religious sensibilities: the biblical/premodern, the Enlightenment/modern and the postmodern. In any given culture today all three sensibilities may coexist and be present to various degrees, and the boundaries between these sensibilities may not be sharply drawn either synchronically or diachronically. Nevertheless, these distinctions can still provide worthwhile points for reflection. The point here is that the dominant cosmological imagination of a given culture provides the background ontology ("what is real?") for the religious practices of a given community, even where that community may formally dissent from the prevailing worldview.

In the biblical/premodern imagination, the notion of a cosmic hier-

---

York: Knopf, 1966-1969); and Paul Hazard, *The European Mind: The Critical Years, 1680-1715* (New Haven, Conn.: Yale University Press, 1953).

[13]On the historical origins of this mechanistic imagery in modern science, see E. J. Diksterhuis, *The Mechanization of the World Picture* (New York: Oxford University Press, 1969).

[14]Cited in James F. White, *A Brief History of Christian Worship* (Nashville: Abingdon, 1993), p. 144.

archy or the "Great Chain of Being"[15] may be proposed as the dominant image. Reality is hierarchical in nature, with the earth and human beings below, and the heavens and the saints and the Virgin and the angels and the Holy Trinity above. The world below is in principle open to the transcendent world above (cf. Gen 28:10-22, Jacob's dream at Bethel), and God is religiously available through the sacraments, the prophetic and biblical word, dreams, visions and other supernatural interventions in human history. The human social and ecclesiastical hierarchies below mirror the heavenly hierarchy above. Spiritual realities above (especially the Holy Trinity) have greater ontic weight than the transient material realities below. Premodern cultures had religious sensibilities in which a sense of the holy and of certain places as holy (where the divine presence had manifested) were generally part of the cultural fabric—a sense of what Rudolf Otto called the feeling of the "numinous," which is largely missing in many contemporary (and, especially, seeker-driven) worship settings.[16]

The scientific revolution of the seventeenth century presented, and still presents, a massive challenge to the biblical and premodern religious sensibility. Reality is no longer imaged as hierarchical, and certainly not with the triune God at the top of a metaphysical hierarchy, but as naturalistic, nongeocentric and de-centered. Heaven above and hell below are discarded as pre-scientific mythological notions, together with their disembodied inhabitants. The clockwork universe can serve as a master image for this sensibility, and the only real fish are those that can be caught in the nets of logical demonstration, mathematical formulae and the empirical results of the scientific method: all the rest is "sophistry and illusion," in the famously dismissive words of Hume. God, if still accorded reality, is existentially distant and for practical purposes lacks ontological weight, or alternatively, in a more consistently naturalistic point of view, is merely a construct of human imagination and the evolutionary history of the race, an epiphenomenon of material forces and processes.

---

[15]The classic study here is Arthur O. Lovejoy, *The Great Chain of Being* (New York: Harper & Row, 1936).

[16]Rudolf Otto, *The Idea of the Holy* (New York: Oxford University Press, 1931). Abraham's characterization of the Canaanite city of Gerar (Gen 20:11) seems sadly apt for many contemporary worship gatherings in the West: "There is surely no fear of God in this place."

Mathematics—which, as Galileo noted, was the true language of science, and a crucial instrument for humanity's control and domination of nature—replaces the pictorial, narrative imagination with the quantitative: the real is that which can be quantified, measured and expressed in a mathematical formula such as $E=mc^2$.[17] The dominance of mathematical formulae in the scientific mindset devalued the final and formal causes of Aristotle in favor of the material and efficient causes of scientific investigation, and also devalued the narrative and pictorial ways of knowing of the biblical and premodern sensibilities.

Orthodox theologians and biblical scholars labored mightily and often successfully during the modern period to defend the Bible and the Christian faith from the assaults of Enlightenment materialism and atheism. But the fact remains that at the subliminal level, the unrelenting pressures of modernity can be absorbed in one's mother's milk, reinforced as it is by the pervasive influence of those strategic institutions that control the image production of a culture and constitute the gatekeepers of acceptable definitions of the real and the dominant ontology: the elite universities (and especially, the faculties of the hard sciences), the federal judiciary, the public schools, the major media outlets and the entertainment industries.[18] Christian churches need to constitute in their practices—especially in their practices of worship—alternative plausibility structures that can embody and experience the presence of the divine in a way that directly challenges the suffocating naturalism of the dominant culture. It is important to defend belief in God and the supernatural theologically and apologetically, but this cognitive strategy, in order to have lasting impact, needs to be embodied within a believing community that expects to experience and is actually aware of experiencing the reality and presence of the God of the Bible in its worship.

---

[17]Einstein's famous formula states that matter and energy are, in principle, convertible, and that a quantity of matter m would release the enormous amount of energy represented by the amount of matter m multiplied by the speed of light c multiplied by itself—the principle of the atomic bomb.

[18]The secularization of these institutions has been examined in George Marsden and Bradley Longfield, eds., *The Secularization of the Academy* (New York: Oxford University Press, 1992); Richard John Neuhaus, *The Naked Public Square: Religion and Democracy in America* (Grand Rapids: Eerdmans, 1984); Stephen L. Carter, *The Culture of Disbelief: How American Law and Politics Trivialize Religious Devotion* (New York: Basic Books, 1993).

The postmodern sensibility is, of course, no one unified set of ideas, but rather a sensibility that is pervasively felt in our culture as an alternative to the Enlightenment and scientific naturalism. For our purposes here, the phrase the "re-enchantment of nature," for example, provides a point of departure for discussion. This sensibility is expressed in the imaginative worlds of *Star Wars* and *Lord of the Rings* and *Harry Potter*, in the efflorescence of Eastern and New Age religions, the "Green" movements of ecology and eco-feminism, the invention of neo-Paganism and the revival of the religions of pre-Christian Europe, and the neo-romantic and Gothic worlds of simulation games and virtual worlds such as Myst, World of Warcraft and Second Life.

In this post-Enlightenment and postcolonial sensibility, mystery, magic and ritual return with a vengeance to challenge modernity's rationalisms. Orthodox Christian churches should not capitulate epistemically to this new sensibility, but neither should they ignore it, for the new imaginative landscape—in some ways closer to the biblical world than to that of the Enlightenment—provides an opportunity to connect with cultural streams that are now seeking a sense of the transcendent. Will postmodern seekers be able to find in the worship events of the American churches the sense of the reality and presence of God that the consumerist and entertainment-driven expressions of modernity have failed to provide?[19] Can evangelical churches retrieve from their own theological traditions the elements of mystery, of sacrament, of the immanence of the Spirit in nature, of humanity's connection with the earth, and the deeper resonances of ritual action to connect with this postmodern sensibility? A positive answer seems to require the recovery of a more robust theology of worship than that practiced in many churches today.

To round out this first section of this chapter, we note that the revival tradition of eighteenth- and nineteenth-century America, so for-

---

[19]In 1977 Paul Vitz, noting the cultural shift under way, wrote that the "search for transcendence of the self is now firmly begun . . . the country is full of holy men—Sri Chinmoy, Maharishi, . . . Baba Ram Dass . . . but where are the Christian holy ones? Where are the Christian mystical messengers to our pagan universities and suburbs?" (*Psychology as Religion: The Cult of Self-Worship* [Grand Rapids: Eerdmans, 1977], pp. 134-35). The "emerging church" movement can be seen as one attempt to respond to this shift in sensibility.

mative for the evangelical Protestant heritage, did not escape the flattening impact of the Enlightenment on worship practices and sensibilities. In the drama and excitement of personal conversion experiences in the revival meeting setting, the momentum of the religious meeting typically reached its climax in the sermon and the invitation to a decision for Christ, not in an invitation to an encounter with the presence of Christ in the Eucharist. Revivalism arguably contributed, however unintentionally, to the further marginalization of the Lord's Supper in American evangelicalism: the real focus was on the sermon, not on the bread and the wine. This frontier style[20] of worship pushed American evangelicalism in the direction of simpler, more casual, less liturgical and more speaker-oriented styles of worship—a trajectory that can be traced from Whitefield to Finney to Billy Graham to Bill Hybels and Willow Creek at the present.

In its weakest and crassest expressions, the frontier model of worship could focus the consciousness of its participants on the magnetic personality of the revival speaker rather than on the glory of the risen Christ, invisibly but truly present in the assembly in the power of the Spirit. The frontier model of worship had the unintended consequence of shifting the attention of the audience from the name of Jesus (heavenly *Kyrios*, "Lord," Acts 2), invisible in heaven, to the big-name speaker, visible on the earthly stage.[21]

As Gordon Lathrop has astutely noted, if, in the Finneyite version of frontier worship, "the whole purpose of the church is to bring individuals to such a decision [of conversion] . . . then, from the classic Christian point of view, if decision-making is the central matter, *the meeting will not really be around God,* no matter how orthodox or trinitarian a theology may be in the mind of the speaker."[22]

---

[20]On the impact of the "Frontier Tradition" of worship on the American churches, see White, *Brief History of Christian Worship,* pp. 160-61.

[21]And, more recently, at times to the big name band in emulation of rock star celebrity concerts.

[22]Gordon W. Lathrop, "New Pentecost or Joseph's Britches? Reflections on the History and Meaning of the Worship Ordo in the Megachurches," *Worship* 72 (1998): 522-23, emphasis added. The entire article is worthy of careful reading. Lathrop finds the antecedents of today's seeker-driven megachurch worship services in Finney's pragmatically driven new measures and revivalism.

The stage had been set for an unintended shift from God-consciousness to celebrity-consciousness as the tacit preunderstanding of the evangelical attendee at worship events. The loss of the sense of the presence of the sacred in the evangelistic event can lead to a state of affairs where the attendees are more aware of the (celebrity) speaker and their own subjective feelings than of the objective presence of the Holy One.

THE ONTOLOGY OF WORSHIP: IS GOD REALLY AMONG US, OR NOT?

This section now focuses specifically on the ontology of worship. This terminology is used in order to call attention to the following claim: all theologies and practices of worship presuppose certain ontologies or background theories of what is considered real. Further, eviscerated or thin background theories of the real will produce thin or eviscerated expressions of worship. We argue here that the ontologies or background theories of the real that underlie the worship practices of most Protestant evangelical churches have been substantially weakened and thinned out by the relentless pressures of scientific naturalism and by the frontier traditions of worship stemming from revivalism. This thinning of worship has not been adequately recognized or challenged from the perspective of a robust evangelical and biblical theology of worship.[23]

This reflection on the ontology of worship will be in four parts: first, observations regarding ontology in general; second, observations on the ontology of worship with respect to the context of worship, that is, the location of the church's worship-event in space, in time, and in relation both to the heavenly realm and to the lower creation; third, observations on the fourfold structure of biblical worship; and fourth, reflections regarding the event character of worship looking at the ontological nature of games and play as specific forms of human activity that suggest, by way of metaphor and analogy, fruitful insights about the ontic quality of the worship-event. These latter reflections will be in-

---

[23]Substantive Protestant treatments of the theology of worship include J. J. von Allmen, *Worship: Its Theology and Practice* (New York: Oxford University Press, 1965) [Reformed], and Peter Brunner, *Worship in the Name of Jesus* (St. Louis: Concordia, 1968) [Lutheran].

formed by perspectives drawn from the sociology of knowledge, cultural anthropology, studies of symbol and ritual, and concepts drawn from information science and computer technologies.

ONTOLOGY: GENERAL CONSIDERATIONS

First, with regard to a general ontology or background theory of the real, a five-level ontology is here presupposed, with historic Christian and biblical theism assumed as normative. This schema distinguishes five levels or realms of the real: Level 1 is the triune God, Father, Son and Holy Spirit—where the Son is recognized as the eternal Logos, incarnate, crucified, risen, now enthroned at the right hand of the Father as cosmic Lord of the universe and of the church. The Holy Trinity, as eternal, uncreated and necessarily existent, has the greatest ontic weight of any level, and is the source and ground of all else that constitutes temporal and created realities. This ontic density of God, a "neutron star" of trinitarian Being, will be visibly manifested on the day of the Lord and the Last Judgment, as John described: "earth and sky fled from his presence" (Rev 20:11). The relative insubstantiality of the seemingly solid physical universe will then become apparent.

As the ground and starting point of any proper biblical and Christian ontology, the self-grounded reality of the Holy Trinity shows that the ultimately real is personal and not impersonal in nature, and that, more specifically, the ultimately real is found in persons in relationship—not in an abstract and impersonal Being,[24] or in the material objects for sale at the mall, or in the images and simulated experiences of the world of digital media.

Level 2 is the spiritual or heavenly world: angels, archangels, principalities, powers; Satan, demons; saints, martyrs, the invisible church triumphant. Entities in level 2 are created, not eternal realities, and are understood to have such personal attributes as consciousness, intelligence and will.[25] These entities of the invisible, heavenly church have

---

[24]This critical insight has been advanced vigorously in trinitarian theology by John Zizioulas, *Being as Communion: Studies in Personhood and the Church* (1985; reprint, Crestwood, N.Y.: St. Vladimir's Seminary Press, 1993); see also his subsequent work, *Communion and Otherness* (Edinburgh: T & T Clark, 2007).

[25]The eclipsing and neglect of the spiritual world in the modern church is noted by the Episco-

largely faded from the Protestant imagination in worship since the seventeenth century.

Level 3 is the human being, *Homo sapiens,* considered, in Christian and biblical theism, to be created in the divine image for relationship with the Trinity, but then fallen and subsequently redeemed (or redeemable) in Jesus Christ. The designation Level 3 suggests that *Homo sapiens* occupies something of an intermediate position in the schema of reality, being capable of conscious awareness of and interaction with entities in the other four levels.

Level 5 consists of material (but subhuman) entities: animate, inanimate, sentient, nonsentient (e.g., rocks, trees, great blue whales, bald eagles, dinosaurs, stars, black holes, electrons, Mount Everest and golden retrievers). Here are the entities generally associated with the biblical concept of the creation or nature. These entities of creation, celebrated in the Psalms, have likewise largely faded from evangelical worship in the modern period.[26]

Level 4 consists of entities occupying the realms of the *symbolic* and *cultural*—a broad variety of humanly produced cultural artifacts such as a song by the Beatles such as "Eleanor Rigby"; the Constitution and Bill of Rights; cave paintings in Lascaux, France; a recipe for apple cobbler or blueberry muffins; Einstein's theory of special relativity; traffic laws for the Commonwealth of Massachusetts; software for a computer game such as Myst V; a performance of Shakespeare's *Macbeth;* the books in the Library of Congress; the iPod and iPhone; eBay; Google; Microsoft Office; the rules governing major league baseball; the rite of the Latin Tridentine Mass—and so forth, ad infinitum. The point here is that *Homo sapiens*—or biblical humankind as the image of God—is a

---

pal priest Charles Jaekle, *Angels, Their Mission and Message* (Harrisburg, Penn.: Morehouse, 1995), p. 2: "I, for one, cannot recall one sermon on that subject that I ever preached, or heard anyone else preach, in all my years within the Christian church. . . . Further, I cannot recall even once, in all my entire theological education . . . any discussion having to do with angels or the church's historic angelologies."

[26]The New Testament scholar Richard Bauckham has drawn attention to the "living creatures" in the heavenly worship of Revelation 4; these creatures "are priestly representatives of all creatures . . . humans find themselves not set over but alongside other creatures, caught up with them in the common worship of their common Creator . . . [Rev 4 points to] . . . the renewal of all creation in the coming Kingdom of God" ("Creation's Praise of God in the Book of Revelation," *Biblical Theology Bulletin* 38, no. 2 [Summer 2008]: 55-63 at 62).

symbol-using creature who has the power to make and shape his own world through symbolic creativity and invention. A person rarely if ever relates to the natural world immediately, without symbolic mediation, but almost exclusively through symbolically shaped media: clothing, furniture, tools, instruments, and most crucially, though the symbols of language, mathematics, music and culturally learned and transmitted practices and experiences.[27]

The symbolic-cultural world is a world of information—that is, a patterned string of symbols that convey meaning, that can give structure and function to material objects and processes, and provide scripts for human performances and behavior. Information is embedded, for example, in the DNA of the double helix's genetic code in every living cell, in mathematical formulae, in the Code of Hammurabi, in the musical score of Beethoven's Fifth Symphony, in the lines of code that constitute the software of Microsoft Office or Google's search algorithms. The scientific community is, in fact, beginning to recognize information as a fifth form of natural reality—alongside space, time, matter and energy.[28] Level-4 realities can be recognized as having their own degree of ontic weight or reality—as do entities in levels 2, 3 and 5.

Today, this level-4 ontology of information-as-reality can be exemplified by the Google search engine and the software codes that drive it. One observer has noted that Google's hidden algorithms "have the power to make or break reputations, to shape public debates, and to change our view of the world."[29] The first ten citations provided by a

---

[27]Cultural anthropologists have defined culture as systems of symbols—law, religion, music, myth, rituals, scientific theories—that give meaning and identity to a social group and define their place in the larger scheme of the universe; see Clifford Geertz, *The Interpretation of Cultures* (New York: Basic Books, 1973); Amos Rapoport, "Spatial Organization and Built Environment," *Companion Encyclopedia of Anthropology* (London: Routledge, 1994), pp. 460-502.

[28]Hans Christian von Baeyer, "Information as Physical Reality: A New Fundamental Principle Proposed by Anton Zeilinger," Foundations of Information Science (2005), abstract available at <http://www.mdpi.org/fis2005>; von Baeyer, "In the Beginning Was the Bit," *New Scientist* no. 2278 (February 17, 2001). Zeilinger, an Austrian physicist and specialist in quantum mechanics, has proposed that information theory can provide a way of unifying the worlds of classical and quantum physics; cf. Anton Zeilinger, "A Foundational Principle for Quantum Mechanics," *Foundations of Physics* 29 (1999): 631-43.

[29]Drake Bennett, "Stopping Google," *Boston Globe*, June 22, 2008, p. K2.

Google search tend to become "knowledge" in our current world; these intangible lines of computer code have the power to reshape our world. Google's economic clout—one measure of the real—is attested by its 15,000 employees and by a market capitalization as big as Coca-Cola and Boeing combined.[30]

This five-level ontological schematic is relevant in several ways as a hermeneutical device for reflecting on the ontology of worship. With regard to levels 1 and 2—the triune God and the inhabitants of the heavenly realm—various influences have conspired to colonize and domesticate the doxological imagination of Protestant evangelicalism. Much popular evangelical preaching is effectively unitarian, focusing on Christ to the neglect of God the Father and God the Holy Spirit, and further, this Christ is generally imaged as the historical Jesus, dying on the cross, with little discourse (except perhaps at Easter) on Christ as the presently risen, living, reigning and returning Lord—the Lord who is religiously available in the here-and-now through the Spirit in Sunday worship. The real presence of the risen Christ in the power of the Spirit with the assembly (1 Cor 5:4, "When you are assembled in the name of our Lord Jesus . . . and the power of our Lord Jesus *is present*"), is the church's "nuclear option" available every Sunday. But the church has largely forgotten this option and generally does not seriously invoke it ("in the name") with full understanding. Here are acres of diamonds in the midst of the evangelical church waiting to be rediscovered. The risen Lord is Reality-Definer, Reality Greater than Which None Can Be Conceived, a weightier and more compelling "high definition" reality than anything that Richard Dawkins or Stephen Hawking or Steve Jobs or Pixar Studios can conceive or simulate.

When Saul of Tarsus met the risen Christ on the road to Damascus, he experienced a massive reality encounter and ontological shock that changed his life and understanding of reality forever. In every true worship assembly the Damascus Road reality can be available to impact and transform the believing church by faith (1 Cor 14:25, "God is really

---

[30]Ibid.

among you!"), because in New Testament faith, every Sunday is resurrection day.

Level-2 religious imagination was also stripped by Reformation and Puritan iconoclasm, removing from the churches the weekly visual reminders of the saints, the angels, the Virgin, the martyrs and all the "company of heaven." The unremitting foreground and background pressures of scientific naturalism tended to make the imaginative intensity of angels and demons and the heavenly world recede in the modern evangelical mind, despite the continued affirmation of these realities at the formal and theological levels.[31]

Level-5 realities—the creation, the world of nature, the animal world and the biosphere—are generally underrepresented in the evangelical worship imagination as well. Reference to creation often comes in creation-evolution controversies, not with respect to the intrinsic value and beauty of creation, itself to be redeemed (Rom 8:21-22) in its eschatological trajectory toward a glorious new creation (Rev 21–22). This trajectory of creation toward the glorious new creation is largely underrepresented in the church's hymnody, preaching and doxological imagination generally.

Level-4 realities—the world of symbols, words, rituals, cultural artifacts and so forth—can also, curiously, be underrepresented in the evangelical doxological imagination, even though the evangelical Protestant tradition is a very word-oriented tradition, a tradition of the Book. Some of the possible reasons for this defect, rooted in a thin theology or ontology of culture, will be suggested below in the discussion of the ontology of the game and of play. In another respect, however, and more importantly—the level-4 realities of the virtual world of digital entertainment are overrepresented in the contemporary mind and threaten the shelf space of the evangelical imagination with a hostile takeover, so to speak, crowding out the angels and archangels and saints and prophets and apostles and martyrs with the images of the shopping mall, the movies, television, video games and the Internet.

---

[31]This generalization needs to be somewhat qualified in light of the Pentecostal and charismatic revivals since 1900 and the recent growth of the Southern Hemisphere church, which gives greater prominence to the reality of the spirit world and the demonic.

THE ONTOLOGY OF THE CONTEXT OF WORSHIP: KINGDOM SPACE, KINGDOM TIME

In chapter two the theme of the ontology of the church itself was considered; this section will reflect on ontology of the context of the church and its worship, specifically, the peculiar and ontologically distinct nature of the space and time within which the worship-event takes place. The claim here is that, according to the theology of the New Testament, space and time themselves are altered and no longer ordinary space and ordinary time—because of the resurrection and exaltation of Jesus as Lord, the irruption of the age to come, and the outpouring and presence of the Holy Spirit.

As to the nature of time in authentic biblical worship, the assembly acts not in ordinary time, but in what can be called kingdom time—for with the advent of the Messiah, the ontic reality of the heavenly kingdom has begun to enter into ordinary time and history: "the kingdom of heaven is drawing near." The believing church experiences the presence of the risen Christ in the power and presence of the Spirit, and lives between the "already" and the "not yet." The believing church is the end-time assembly of the Lord upon whom the end of history as we know it has already come (1 Cor 10:11). The powers of the future age to come (Heb 6:5) are already being experienced as present in the gathered assembly. The great events of the redemptive past—the exodus, the crossing of the Red Sea, Sinai, the cross, the resurrection—are remembered not just notionally and informationally in a Zwinglian sense, but are made spiritually present (cf. Deut 5:2-3: "the LORD our God made a covenant with us at Horeb . . . with all of *us* who are alive here *today*").[32] By the believing assembly's mystical and covenantal personal bond with the Lord through word, sacrament and Spirit, the assembly experiences sacred "time travel," reexperiencing with the Lord and his people the power of the saving events of the past, as well as tasting the reality of the future new creation in the "down payment" of the Holy Spirit.

---

[32]Cf. Edward P. Blair, "An Appeal to Remembrance: The Memory Motif in Deuteronomy," *Interpretation* 15 (1961): 43, 47: In the Bible "If one remembers in the biblical sense, the past is brought into the present with compelling power. . . . The patriarchs and the prophets become our contemporaries."

This unique, sui generis time in authentic New Testament worship can be called "ancient-future time" or "kingdom time." The members of the believing assembly, chosen from eternity (Eph 1:4), are seen by God as mystically present at the exodus, at the Last Supper, at the cross, at the empty tomb, at Pentecost—for these events were preordained with each member in mind as mystical beneficiaries and participants.

Sacred past and promised future are ontologically and not merely metaphorically present in the worship-event. This experience of the past and the Spirit-mediated experience of the future are constitutive for authentic Christian worship according to the New Testament. Not *chronos,* ordinary clock-time, but *kairos,* redemptive time, is the real time during which the worship-event takes place.[33] In the "already" of the kingdom, the powers of the future are already beginning to be experienced (Heb 6:5) as the church gathers by faith in the presence of the risen Christ, who is actually present through the Holy Spirit.

Similarly, the spatial context of Sunday worship—whether cathedral or house church—is not ordinary space, but is transformed, spiritually,[34] into sacred, kingdom space. This term is meant to evoke the image of an assembly caught up in real worship "between heaven and earth." In the liturgy the assembly is invited to "Lift up your hearts . . . we lift them up unto the Lord." John of the Apocalypse is "in the Spirit" on the Lord's day (Rev 1:10), and is lifted into the midst of the heavenly worship (Rev 4–5; 19) where he sees the Lamb on the throne in the midst of countless angels and the church triumphant. John's vision of heavenly worship is not unique to the New Testament; the writer of Hebrews reminds his readers that in worship they come into the presence of the heavenly Zion and thousands of angels in festive assembly (Heb 12:22-24).

Paul reminds the Corinthians that in their assembly they worship in

---

[33]Cf. Paul Hoon, *The Integrity of Worship: Ecumenical and Pastoral Studies in Liturgical Theology* (Nashville: Abingdon, 1971), p. 131: "worship transforms time into its own time—'sacred time' or 'liturgical time.' . . . Wherever two or three are gathered, there *am* I. The action of worship is grounded in the past action of the Word yet contemporizing and futurizing itself."
[34]That is, in view of the *epiclesis,* or prayer of invocation for the Lord to be present in the Spirit with the worshiping assembly when it consciously and intentionally gathers *as a church.*

the presence of the angels (1 Cor 11:10). The apostle teaches that each believer is seated spiritually and mystically in the presence of Christ in the heavenly places (Eph 2:6); the believers have been united by the Spirit with Christ in his resurrection and exaltation.[35] As analogy for this being seated with Christ in the heavenlies, one might think of the Holy Spirit as the broadband, high-speed connection for a real-time teleconference meeting in which Christ and the heavenly realm are brought into the presence, via a high-definition flat-panel screen on the wall, of the worshiping church on earth. Christ is present to the church on earth (Mt 18:20; 28:20; 1 Cor 5:4), and the church is present to Christ in heaven (Eph 2:6; Heb 12:22-24); both conditions are simultaneously true through the bond of the Holy Spirit as connector of heaven and earth.

In the Spirit, the believing local church on earth, resting under the Shekinah Glory (Is 4:5-6) is being transformed, like Moses on Mount Sinai, by beholding the glory of God in the face of the risen, glorified Christ (2 Cor 3:18), with whom they are seated in the heavenlies. The standpoints of John, of the writer of Hebrews and of Paul should not be viewed as extraordinary but as the normal experience of the church in worship; its self-consciousness during worship can rightly be termed heavenly and pneumatic ("in spirit and in truth," Jn 4:24).

While biblical, Christian worship is "heavenly" in that its sense of space is not limited to earth but keenly aware of heavenly realities, it can also be said to be "earthly" in that, like the psalmist, it can invite the lower creation—the sea creatures, the animals, mountains, hills, fruit trees and all cedars (Ps 148) to join in the praise of the glorious God, in anticipation of the renewal of all creation at the end of history (Rom 8:21-22). The praises of God's people for God's redemption of humanity do not forget God's work to redeem and transform the lower creation. It is fitting, then, for the physical space in which the assembly gathers for worship to symbolically, visually and liturgically enrich the Christian's imagination with images of the heavenly court and of a creation waiting for full redemption.

---

[35]Thomas G. Allen, "Exaltation and Solidarity with Christ: Ephesians 1:20 and 2:6," *Journal for the Study of the New Testament* 28 (1986): 103-20.

Many premodern religions have a sense of a sacred space that is largely lacking in many evangelical communities living under the conditions of modernity. As Mircea Eliade has noted, in traditional religions, "space is not homogeneous; it experiences interruptions, breaks in it; some parts of space are qualitatively different from others . . . the religious experience of the nonhomogeneity of space is a primordial experience . . . the manifestation of the sacred ontologically founds the world" and gives it a center.[36] Moses takes off his shoes at the burning bush because the place where he is standing, where Yahweh chooses to reveal himself, is holy ground.[37] This is what Rudolf Otto in his classic study, *The Idea of the Holy,* called the sense of the "numinous" or the "aweful" *mysterium tremendum.* The loss of this sense in much contemporary worship is a mark of the alienation of such worship from the biblical realities.[38]

Traditional Protestant religious sensibility may find the notion of sacred or special space troubling. Is it not the case, it might be asked, that in the context after A.D. 70, after the resurrection and ascension, after the destruction of the Jewish temple, now all places are equally sacred and equally profane? Is it not the case that the church is now called to worship God not merely in Jerusalem or Mount Gerizim (Jn 4:23-24) but "in spirit and in truth"? This is indeed the case, but this objection misses a crucial point in texts such as John 4:23-24 and 1 Corinthians 14:23-25 ("if the whole church comes together . . . 'God is really among you!'"), namely, that when the assembly gathers in the name of Jesus and the Lord is present in the power of the Spirit (worshiping "in Spirit," Jn 4:24) then that location is a special location not in virtue of the building or room per se, but because the Lord himself is actually present. Air Force One becomes a special airplane; it be-

---

[36]Mircea Eliade, *The Sacred and the Profane: The Nature of Religion* (New York: Harper & Row, 1957, 1961), pp. 20-21.

[37]Since the sixth century the Greek Orthodox monks at St. Catherine's Monastery in the Sinai peninsula have remembered Mount Sinai as a special place, where God revealed himself to Moses in the burning bush.

[38]David F. Wells has called attention to the loss of the sense of the holiness of God in evangelicalism in *No Place for Truth* (Grand Rapids: Eerdmans, 1993), p. 300, and to the sense of the "weightlessness" or inconsequentiality of God in modern culture in *God in the Wasteland* (Grand Rapids: Eerdmans, 1994), p. 88.

comes for that time the White House because the president of
the United States of America is actually on board and personally in
command.

To briefly recapitulate, then, this discussion of the ontology of the
context of the church's worship, when the church worships "in spirit
and in truth," ordinary space and time become kingdom space and
kingdom time. The earthly assembly is lifted up to heaven, seated with
Christ in the heavenlies (Eph 2:6), in the presence of the angels and the
church triumphant (Heb 12:22-23), and the powers of the age to come
can be experienced *now* in the act of worship (Heb 6:5; 1 Cor 5:4).

A sports analogy may help to make the foregoing a bit more concrete. It could be said that Fenway Park in Boston both is and yet is
not the same baseball park in February and in late October. On a cold
February afternoon during the off season, Fenway Park is still Fenway Park, though deserted, quiet and forlorn. Late in October, with
the Yankees in town, bottom of the ninth, two outs and a full count,
bases loaded, the Red Sox down by one run and the American League
championship on the line, a capacity crowd, bright lights, emotion
running at fever pitch—then, for this "kairos," Fenway Park is no
ordinary place and this is no ordinary time, but a magical and intense
moment that the fans might remember for the rest of their lives and
recount to their children after them. Because of the participants in
the game and the historic nature of the event, here is a parallel universe that for those moments and for these fans is more intense and
real than ordinary life.

The skeptical reader at this point may be tempted to ask, So what?
Why all this talk about "special space" and "special time" on Sunday
morning? What difference does it really make? The point of this way of
looking at worship is to provide a perspective from which the spell of
modernity and postmodernity can be broken, the imaginations dulled
by habit and tradition reinvigorated, and worship again be recognized
as the truly extraordinary experience that the New Testament describes.
We can be like the prisoners in Plato's allegory of the cave,[39] chained to

---

[39]Plato *The Republic* 7.514a-520a, trans. Benjamin Jowett (New York: Modern Library, 1941).

our places with eyes focused on the shadows dancing on the walls, who need to break those chains and rise upward to rediscover the brightness of the risen Sun of Righteousness in our midst.

THE FOURFOLD PATTERN OF BIBLICAL WORSHIP

Because the living God, the risen Christ and the Holy Spirit are present in the midst of the assembly, true worship takes place in kingdom space and kingdom time, where ordinary space and time are altered by the massive reality of the Creator and Redeemer of space and time,[40] where earth is lifted up to heaven, and the future impinges on the present. The meeting space is spiritually energized and charged by the presence of the Spirit, the Shekinah Glory; ordinary time is suffused with the power of the past redemptive events of the incarnation, cross and resurrection, and anticipates the revelation of the Christ who is to come and who will usher in the new creation. Before exploring in the final section of this chapter some cyberspace analogies from the world of online gaming and virtual reality that might help us to reimagine the real presence of God in Christian worship, we will now reflect on the historic fourfold pattern of worship and how the various elements of historic worship can mediate the presence of God to us as his people.

Liturgical scholars are in general agreement that for at least the first fifteen hundred years of the history of the church, Christian worship followed a basic fourfold pattern: gathering, ministry of the Word, ministry of the table, dismissal.[41] This fourfold pattern is reflected, for example, in the events of the inauguration of the Sinai covenant as described in chapters 19 and 24 of the book of Exodus: God, through Moses, calls the people to assemble in his presence at the foot of Mount Sinai (Ex 19:10-25); God descends in power and glory on Mount Sinai,

---

[40]To cite an analogy from modern physics, according to the understanding of gravity and space in general relativity, a massive object like the Sun actually bends space around it by the strength of its gravitational field, like a rubber sheet stretched across the head of a drum being bent by a bowling ball placed at its center. In biblical imagery, when God shows up, "earth and sky fled from his presence" (Rev 20:11).

[41]Marva Dawn, *How Shall We Worship?* (Wheaton, Ill.: Tyndale House, 2003), pp. 100-105; see also Dom Gregory Dix, *The Shape of the Liturgy* (London: Continuum, 1945, 2005). For historical examples of Western liturgies and orders of worship, see Bard Thompson, *Liturgies of the Western Church* (Philadelphia: Fortress, 1961).

speaks to the people, and the people respond by pledging obedience to the covenant (Ex 24:3); the covenant is ratified with blood sacrifices (Ex 24:8), and then Moses and representatives of the people are invited up to the mountain to enjoy a fellowship meal in the presence of God and to see the divine glory (Ex 24:9-11). By implication, the meeting of God with the people is ended (dismissal); Moses then ascends to the top of Sinai and spends forty days and nights in the cloud, in the presence of God (Ex 24:18).

The fundamental reality in this account is the *awesome presence of God* to his people; it is God who has "called the meeting" at his own initiative, not the people; true worship is seen to be a believing and obedient response to God's prior word of revelation in the context of the covenant established by God: *I will be your God, and you will be my people, and I will dwell among you.* God is the central actor in biblical worship, not the people; the people assemble at God's command, and they respond to his actions and directive words.

Early Christian worship originated in the context of Judaism and the synagogue, and the "ministry of the Word" continued the Jewish practices of the reading of Scripture, homily and prayer. This ministry of the Word, rooted in Judaism, was culminated in the Eucharist, the ministry of the table, in which the believers, in response to the Lord's command to "do this in remembrance of me," met the risen Christ, in the power of the Spirit, at the Communion table, continuing the table fellowship they had enjoyed with him during his earthly ministry.

Despite the wishes of Protestant reformers such as Luther and Calvin, who wished to restore the New Testament and early church practice of frequent Communion, most post-Reformation Protestant churches did not celebrate weekly Communion, for a variety of reasons (examined in chap. 4 below). In the evangelical traditions of revivalism and frontier worship since the time of Charles Finney, the fourfold pattern has been collapsed to a threefold pattern, without Communion, and with the central focus on the preacher and evangelistic preaching. The unintended result of this collapsing of the historic fourfold pattern into a threefold revival pattern was to shift the focus of the assembly's attention from the unseen God to the very visible revival speaker, and to the musicians who were to "warm up" the people for the speaker's message.

Consider now the elements that have historically been present in Protestant worship services built around the preaching of the Word: a call to worship, prayer of invocation, prayer of confession, opening hymn, reading of Scripture, offering, creed, pastoral prayer, sermon, closing hymn, benediction. The order of these elements has varied considerably, of course, in the many Protestant traditions, and not all elements have been present in a given service, but the overall pattern has been typical. What has tended to happen in the evangelical tradition since the rise of revivalism in the nineteenth century, and increasingly with the predominance of contemporary worship styles since the 1970s, is the collapsing of the above elements into an essentially three-part structure: an opening time of "worship" led by a praise band; the "teaching time" consisting of a topical (or expository) message from the Bible; and third, some form of response to the message. Even the terminology of "worship time" as descriptive of the praise choruses is problematic; this points to a loss of an awareness that the entire meeting of the covenant people with God constitutes the act of worship.[42]

Many evangelical and charismatic contemporary worship services include no call to worship as a distinctly identifiable element of worship, this often being replaced by an informal and cheery greeting such as "Good morning, we are glad you are here." There is usually no prayer of invocation that acknowledges and invites God to be present;[43] his-

---

[42]A sympathetic and carefully nuanced appraisal of contemporary "praise and worship" style services is presented by Sarah Koenig, "This Is My Daily Bread: Toward a Sacramental Theology of Evangelical Praise and Worship," *Worship* 82, no. 2 (March 2008): 141-61. I agree with Koenig that the understood purpose of the praise songs is for the worshiper to experience an intimate sense of the love of God, present through the Holy Spirit, and would readily grant that such a presence is in fact experienced. I am concerned, however, that this style of worship, if elements such as a call to worship, invocation and confession of sin are omitted, tends to minimize the worshiper's awareness of the *holiness* of God. The "praise and worship" format does not clearly express a sense of the presence of God understood *corporately;* the focus is rather on the individual's subjective consciousness. Koenig also acknowledges (p. 160) the problematic nature of the praise songs, in effect, being a "sacrament," an occasion for the divine presence, that can displace the Eucharist in the worship life of these churches.

[43]In a biblically grounded call to worship, it is God who is issuing the call to worship through the human worship leader; it is God "who is calling this meeting," and we as his people are responding to his call to meet with him in worship. The entire worship service is authorized by the authority of God; the meeting is special because it is "in his name," signifying both the authority and presence of God.

toric hymns of the church are replaced with praise choruses; the reading of Scripture is abbreviated or collapsed into the preacher's message;[44] pastoral prayer for the needs of the people and the world is shortened or omitted altogether; there may be no confession of sin; and there may be no real benediction to close the service.[45]

What is going on here, and what is wrong with this picture? The short answers to these questions are that contemporary evangelical Christians have lost their awareness of the *presence of the living and holy God* as the central reality of all true worship. And contemporary evangelicals, reflecting the influence of modern and postmodern culture, have shifted their focus in worship from the *objective* to the *subjective*, from the invisible God who is at the center of the event, to the visible preachers and praise leaders who are leading the events on stage, and to their own subjective feelings and desires. Human actions have now come to occupy the center stage on Sunday mornings, and God is pushed to the margins. Do we hear God's call: "I am really here among you; will anyone acknowledge my presence, and enter into communion with me?"

Modern evangelicals need to rediscover the biblical truth that in true worship it is God, not us, who is the central reality and the central actor. The New Testament scholar C. E. B. Cranfield was right on the

---

[44]Gary Parrett and Steve Kang have observed in this regard: "Often many churches that pride themselves on being 'Bible churches' actually feature the least amount of Scripture in their services. There may well be a fine expository sermon based upon a few verses of a biblical passage. But are those the only verses of Scripture the congregation will hear read on this particular Lord's Day?" Gary Parrett and Steve Kang, *Teaching the Faith, Forming the Faithful: A Biblical Vision for Education in the Church* (Downers Grove, Ill.: InterVarsity Press, 2009), p. 391. The further problem with a "how-to," topical sermon based on a small snippet of Scripture is that the listener is not placed into the larger framework of the biblical metanarrative, but rather, the biblical story is made to fit into an all too often worldly American narrative of how to achieve happiness, success and self-fulfillment. This way of using the Scripture does not challenge the listener to look at the world from a radically different biblical perspective, and it fails to give the listener a critical vantage point from which to distance himself or herself from the influence of the surrounding culture.

[45]Not long before his death, James Montgomery Boice of Philadelphia's Tenth Presbyterian Church had noted with concern the disappearance of prayer, reading of Scripture, confessions of sin, historic hymns and expository preaching from many American evangelical worship services; see J. Ligon Duncan, "Does God Care How We Worship?" in *Give Praise to God: A Vision for Reforming Worship*, ed. Philip Ryken, Derek Thomas and J. Ligon Duncan (Phillipsburg, N.J.: Presbyterian & Reformed, 2003), pp. 18-20.

mark when he wrote, in an article titled "Divine and Human Action: The Biblical Concept of Worship," that "in each particular act of worship the chief actor is not man but God . . . his divine action consisting in the presence of Jesus Christ in fulfillment of his promise, 'Lo, I am with you always, even to the end of the age' (Mt 28:20) . . . his presence is an event, renewed again and again. . . . The risen and exalted Lord comes again and again in fulfillment of his promise to be with his church."[46]

Cranfield is not the only biblical scholar who has called attention to the real presence of God as the central reality of Christian worship. J. J. von Allmen has stated that the "Christian place of worship is the assembly in which Jesus Christ, God's temple, is present, in the power of the Spirit."[47] Larry Hurtado has noted that for the earliest Christians "the worship event was not merely a religious exercise by the participants, an opportunity to re-affirm their beliefs and to engage in ritualized behavior; it was an occasion for the manifestation and experience of divine powers . . . expectations were characteristically high that in the worship setting God would be encountered in demonstrative fashion."[48]

Ralph P. Martin has written that the hallmark of early Christian worship, for which other religions of the time could provide no true parallel, was the vivid sense of "the presence of the living Lord in the midst of His own. . . . All the components of divine service were calculated to lead the worshippers to an awareness of His presence."[49] New Testament worship, according to Martin, "stands within the 'magnetic field of the Holy Spirit.'"[50]

If this vivid sense of the divine presence characterized the early church, why can it not be so today? Is it not still true that "Jesus Christ is the same yesterday and today and forever" (Heb 13:8)? Is it not still

---

[46]C. E. B. Cranfield, "Divine and Human Action: The Biblical Concept of Worship," *Interpretation* 12 (1958): 387.

[47]Allmen, *Worship: Its Theology and Practice*, p. 242.

[48]Larry Hurtado, *At the Origins of Christian Worship* (Grand Rapids: Eerdmans, 1999), pp. 56-57. By way of contrast, the expectations of worshipers on Sunday mornings today are typically low.

[49]Ralph P. Martin, *Worship in the Early Church* (London: Marshall, Morgan & Scott, 1964), p. 130.

[50]Ibid., p. 131.

true that Christ is not dead, but alive now and forevermore? Has the Holy Spirit been taken from the church, or is Christ's promise still true (Jn 14:16) that the Counselor will be with the church forever?

From the beginning of creation, when the Spirit of God was brooding over the waters (Gen 1:2), through the wilderness wanderings when the Shekinah Glory inhabited the tabernacle, and later the temple of Solomon, until the incarnate glory came to his people in the flesh (Jn 1:14), God has been coming to his people, seeking them, that he might dwell with them, that they might behold his glory. Isaiah foresaw a time when all God's people would be gathered on Mount Zion and would be covered by the Shekinah Glory (Is 4:5-6). Now, after the resurrection, ascension and Pentecost, God's people can boldly enter into the glory cloud (cf. Heb 10:19, "we have confidence to enter the Most Holy Place"; Heb 12:22, "You *have come* to Mount Zion, to the heavenly Jerusalem") each and every Sunday morning when gathered to worship the living God in Spirit and in truth.

When God's people lose Isaiah's vision of the burning holiness of God, confessions of sin disappear on Sunday morning. Intercessory prayers disappear when affluent, comfortable American Christians have diminished awareness of their true spiritual need. The public reading of Scripture disappears when human preachers presume to control the texts and the agendas of the meeting. All these developments reflect the replacement of a God-centered focus in contemporary worship with a more human-centered one.

On the contrary, when God is recognized as the central reality on Sunday morning, and when God, not the human being, is seen to be the central actor, to whom all must respond, then the elements of worship can be seen in a different and truer light. In the call to worship we realize that the meeting is no merely human meeting, planned and controlled by our human agendas, but a special meeting called by God, on his divine authority, for his purpose of meeting with his people. In the call to worship God himself is speaking through the human worship leader.[51] We are called to lay aside our personal agendas, to realize

---

[51]God himself, of course, is the real worship leader; God is both the recipient and the primary, active leader of worship. My wife and I were visiting a church in the District of Columbia

where we are and what we are to be doing, to focus our attention on the unseen God, and to yield to him our full awareness and attention.

In a prayer of invocation we acknowledge that, without the divine presence, our Sunday meetings can be a merely human performance; we pray that the God, who is truly (metaphysically) always present, will on this occasion, freely, graciously and powerfully make his presence known and felt.

In the public reading of Scripture—ideally, lessons from both the Old and New Testaments, and perhaps a psalm as well—we listen for God's voice speaking through the text that he himself has inspired and can now illuminate to our understanding. We hear the divinely inspired words without human commentary before we hear the human commentary in the sermon. Taking seriously the public reading of Scripture is a way of acknowledging the freedom of God to speak to us directly apart from the human preacher. We recognize that we, as humans, are not in control and not lords and masters of the Word of God.

In the prayers and hymns and offerings we respond as God's people to God's words and God's presence, reflecting the fundamental rhythm of worship: God's revelation; our response. At the end of the service, as we are dismissed to serve God in the world, the worship leader pronounces the benediction. The benediction is not just a way of ending the meeting, or a time for final announcements or a summary of the sermon, but an action in which God himself, speaking through the human worship leader, pronounces his favor on the people. A biblical benediction is, in effect, a summary of the gospel: "and now may the love of God, and the grace of our Lord Jesus Christ, and the fellowship of the Holy Spirit be with you all, Amen." These words, heard in faith, actually impart grace to the hearer. Like a mother giving her child a kiss at the door before the child leaves for school, God says to his children as they leave the meeting, "I love you and will be with you as you go."[52]

---

recently, and the bulletin for that Sunday—which otherwise had a very biblical and traditional order of worship, began with a notation that "We call ourselves to worship." No, we do not "call ourselves" to worship; we respond when God calls us to worship: we are not in control!

[52]It is noteworthy that according to Luke, the final act of Jesus as he ascended to heaven was to pronounce a benediction on his disciples: "While he was *blessing* them, he left them and was

Consequently, then, many evangelical churches today with contemporary worship services need to rethink both the elements of worship they include in their services and what these elements really mean. What is needed is a paradigm shift—a shift in spiritual perception—as to how these elements function: a shift in focus from the visible human actors on the stage to the invisible God who acts through them and who is at the center, not the periphery of the worship-event. This is a shift in focus from the visible realities of earth to the invisible but more deeply real things of heaven; a shift from illusions of the human management and control of the worship service to a receptive attitude that waits expectantly in the presence of God for the sovereign God to graciously act and speak.

THE ONTOLOGY OF THE WORSHIP-EVENT: CYBERSPACE ANALOGIES

To close this chapter on the ontology of worship itself we will use the analogies of game or play. The analogies of game or play and the illustrations from the realms of cyberspace and online gaming that follow are not intended to suggest that worship is merely entertainment or recreation or fantasy. The point is to reflect on some contemporary realities that might give some freshness to the Christian imagination and so enrich the experience of worship. With Martin Ramstedt we note that for many people today, "Cyberspace . . . has nowadays turned into a salient metaphor for a realm of transcendence or 'soul space' where the limitations and constraints of the physical world do not apply."[53] Exploring the metaphorical analogies suggested by cyberspace is simply another way of thinking about the nature of transcendence and the biblical heaven—the true "alternative reality."

As a point of departure, consider the definition of play offered by Johan Huizinga in his classic treatment of the subject, *Homo Ludens: A Study of the Play-Element in Culture:*

---

taken up into heaven. Then they worshiped him and returned to Jerusalem with great joy" (Lk 24:51-52).

[53]Martin Ramstedt, "Metaphor or Invocation? The Convergence Between Modern Paganism and Fantasy Fiction," *Journal of Ritual Studies* 21 (2007): 11.

Play is a voluntary activity or occupation executed within certain fixed limits of time and place, according to rules freely accepted but absolutely binding, having its aim in itself, . . . joy and the consciousness that it is different from "ordinary life."[54]

This definition of play—which can encompass games, sporting events such as baseball, a staging of Shakespeare's *Hamlet,* a performance of the *1812 Overture* by the Boston Pops in Symphony Hall, a computer simulation game such as Myst, and many other expressions of human culture, including liturgical worship—draws attention to the fact that such activities are socially constructed, rule-based activities[55] pursued for their own sake, usually for enjoyment and emotional intensity, and provide for their participants a sense of participating imaginatively in an alternative world that, for the duration of the game, is more interesting than everyday life. Such activities are, in practice, consciousness-altering events that are pursued, in large measure, for the purpose of experiencing such different states of consciousness. Participation in these games generally involves what the poet Samuel Taylor Coleridge called the "willing suspension of disbelief" in ordinary and customary perception, in order to enjoy a different state of awareness or a different way of looking at the world.[56]

Before considering this definition of play as a hermeneutical device or heuristic tool for reflection on the ontology of the worship-event, a possible objection should be acknowledged. Some readers may think that the comparison of Christian worship to "play" is demeaning to the biblical understanding of worship and trivializes it. It is true that in our

---

[54]Johan Huizinga, *Homo Ludens* (London: Routledge, 1998), p. 26.

[55]Other human activities, such as a courtroom trial or commuting to work, are socially constructed and rule-based, but are generally not pursued as ends in themselves for inherent enjoyment, but as means to other human ends—i.e., the pursuit of justice or earning a living. The logical structures and semantics of socially constructed "institutional facts" such as marriage, money and contracts have been analyzed by the philosopher John Searle in *The Construction of Social Reality* (New York: Free Press, 1995), esp. chap. 2, "Creating Institutional Facts."

[56]The phrase was coined in Coleridge's *Biographica Literaria* (1817), recalling his collaboration with Wordsworth in the *Lyrical Ballads* (1798). Coleridge was making the point that good poetry can help the reader of the poem to see and experience the world in a fresh way, and can even "excite a feeling analogous to the supernatural, by awakening the mind's attention from the lethargy of custom": in "Suspension of Disbelief," *Wikipedia* <http://en.wikipedia .org/wiki/suspension-of-disbelief/> (accessed November 12, 2007).

current (American) cultural context, the words *game* and *play* tend to evoke images of the trivial and the superficial, of frenzied and over-hyped events in professional sports, of TV game shows that can embody the consumerist, entertainment-oriented and often competitive and violent elements of the culture.

All this being acknowledged, Huizinga has pointed to the game as a serious subject for cultural reflection and analysis because games are expressions of *Homo sapiens'* distinctive capacities for imagination and symbolic thought. The human capacity to envision and build a structure like the Eiffel Tower and the activity of a colony of beavers building a dam in a mountain stream differ essentially in that while the beavers build a structure by instinct, with little or no symbolic mediation, the human builder can, by an act of imagination, see a state of affairs that transcends the immediate environment, and construct that vision through the use of tools and symbols. The human's powers of visual imagination and manipulation of symbols (verbal, mathematical, visual) are constitutive of the human *qua* human, and distinguish humanity from the lower animals.[57]

It should also be noted that in our ordinary, day-to-day existence, we as human beings rarely if ever encounter nature in a pure, unmediated state.[58] We move in a built environment in which human symbols, images, intentions and purposes have been impressed on material objects—the carpet on the floor, the light fixture in the ceiling, the car keys in my pocket, the MP3 file on the iPod (as well as the iPod itself), the Google homepage on my laptop, the food on the table, the clothing we wear, the traffic rules we (usually) observe, the National Anthem at Fenway Park, the language we speak, the textbooks in our schools, the movies we watch . . . ad infinitum. Even wilderness experiences—a hike in the remote regions of the Grand Tetons, for example—are still

---

[57]From the perspective of paleoanthropology, the emergence of clearly symbolic representations such as the beautiful cave paintings of Lascaux and elsewhere point to the emergence of culturally modern man, in distinction from earlier forms such as the Neanderthals, *Homo erectus* and the *Australopithecine*, whose behaviors and relationship to their environments did not seem to be mediated primarily by symbols.

[58]This has been pointed out perceptively by the cultural anthropologist Thomas de Zengotita in *Mediated: How the Media Shapes Your World and the Way You Live in It* (New York: Bloomsburg, 2005).

in fact symbolically mediated experiences by virtue of the images and words I have absorbed through my guidebook, the backpack on my back, the maps, my culturally inherited memories and expectations, and so forth. All this is to say that *Homo sapiens* is by nature a culture-forming creature and relates to the natural environment through the mediation of cultural worlds (law, religion, literature, music, rituals, images, traditions) that he himself has largely constructed through his own symbolic and imaginative capacities.

We now turn to a metaphorical and analogical comparison of a worship service and an online, multiplayer, interactive computer simulation game[59] such as World of Warcraft.[60] Millions of players around the world are involved in this popular simulation game, most of them clustered in the United States and Canada, Europe, Australia, South Korea and China. For those unfamiliar with such online simulation games, the imaginative landscape of World of Warcraft, set in the imaginary world of Azeroth, has a neo-Pagan, magical and Gothic ethos reminiscent of elements of *Star Wars*, *Lord of the Rings* and Harry Potter. Players are characters in opposing factions (the Alliance and the Horde), choose membership in different races (human, night elves, gnomes, orcs, undead, trolls, etc.), character classes (druid, hunter, paladin, priest, rogue, etc.), and professions (herbalism, mining, alchemy, enchanting, cooking, fishing, etc.), and engage in combat, fighting monsters, performing quests, building skills, interacting with other players (and nonplayer characters driven by artificial intelligence), and earning money, rewards and honor points. The online game universe of World of Warcraft is supported by an online virtual community with chat forums, places for the display and exchange of personal artwork, videos and comic-strip style storytelling.

World of Warcraft is an impressive contemporary example of a game

---

[59]In his insightful article, Martin Ramstedt notes that "Fantasy role-playing games provide an intense link between mythic and mythological stories on the one hand, and personal imagination on the other, by allowing players to literally become part of the story. . . . Cyberspace . . . has nowadays turned into a salient metaphor for a realm of transcendence or 'soul space.' . . . the real success of 'virtual reality' has also contributed to blurring the boundaries between the realms of the 'factual' and the metaphorical" ("Metaphor or Invocation?" pp. 11-12).

[60]The following descriptions are based on the article "World of Warcraft," *Wikipedia* <http://en.wikipedia.or/wiki/World_of_Warcraft> (accessed November 16, 2007).

as defined by Huizinga above: "a voluntary activity . . . executed within
certain fixed limits . . . having its aim in itself . . . and the consciousness
that it is different from ordinary life." It is also intriguing to look at this
enormously popular game as functioning, for some of its participants, at
least, as a substitute for religion. Warcraft projects a complex, mysterious
alternative world that appeals strongly to the imagination and emotions;
has a multilevel ontology of sentient beings that mimic the imaginative
worlds of religion and myth (angels, demons, etc.); has story lines of the
conflict of good and evil; provides a sense of community; and provides
opportunities for personal skill development and social recognition. The
presence of magical powers mimics the supernaturalism of the biblical
world and provides imaginative relief from the world of scientific naturalism and everyday life. It is no surprise that for the hundreds of thousands (millions?) of adolescents[61] around the globe who live in World of
Warcraft, this alternative world, supported by powerful computer servers
and software and sophisticated 3-D graphic animations, is emotionally
and imaginatively more compelling than the everyday realities of high
school algebra—or typical church services!

The concept of fantasy associated with games such as World of Warcraft, suggesting as it does frivolous and unproductive activities of an
escapist nature, may deflect attention from the significant cultural and
religious implications of this contemporary development in the cyber-
world. Fantasy is an expression of the power of humans to imagine, to
visualize a state of affairs different from the everyday world, and as such
is intrinsic to human nature and behavior. The imaginatively constructed
Gothic world of Warcraft is not utterly different from the imaginatively
constructed worlds of Dickens's *A Christmas Carol* or Shakespeare's *Macbeth* or *Beowulf* or Cinderella or the score for Beethoven's Fifth Symphony—though the literary quality and cultural level may vary from case
to case. Each of these can be viewed as level-4 socially constructed symbolic artifacts. Such cultural artifacts are real and have ontic weight to

---

[61]This is not to suggest or claim that all or the great majority of online gamers are adolescents,
   though many are; the author does not know precise user demographics. Anecdotal evidence
   and personal observation suggests, however, that such online gaming is heavily populated by
   Gen X and Millennial males.

the extent that they display internal structures and coherence, embody intentions, meanings and symbolic references, encode information, have stable existence over time, and have the power to shape and influence human behaviors and institutions. The information encoded in the software for a game such as Warcraft—or, for that matter, in Microsoft Office—has an objective existence that contrasts, say, with the more ephemeral and shadowy reality of my private dream last night ("I dreamed I was Elvis Presley") or a hallucination. The dream has some reality, insofar as it is an experience that affected me (privately), but it lacks the public, intersubjective, coherent and more enduring reality of entities here characterized as occupying ontic levels 1 through 5.[62]

Finally, to introduce a thought experiment of viewing a worship service metaphorically as an online, multiplayer simulation game, imagine that in the game of World of Warcraft, currently in progress, the players encounter a mysterious new player-avatar—a player of enormous knowledge, skill and wisdom—who in fact is an extraterrestrial being, a "Golem," from a highly advanced civilization in another very distant galaxy. A transcendent, godlike being has become immanent in the world of Azeroth, interacts with its participants and is really present to them through his avatar.

It is easy enough to complete the comparison: in authentic Christian worship, the risen, reigning, glorified and returning Christ is present to the worship participants through his "avatar"—the Holy Spirit.[63] In the game of Kingdom Life, the players/congregants are imaginatively (by

---

[62]Perhaps the ontological schematic of this chapter could be amended to include a level 6 of lesser realities such as dreams and hallucinations that are not in the category of nonbeing but lack the fuller degrees of reality recognized for the entities of levels 1-5.

[63]This analogy of Holy Spirit as "avatar" of the risen Christ in the midst of the worshiping assembly recalls an element frequently missed in many worship services: a consciousness of the real presence of Christ in the midst of the community. Cf. Ralph P. Martin, *Worship in the Early Church* (London: Marshall, Morgan & Scott, 1964), p. 130: "the hall-mark which stamped the assembling together of Christians (Heb 10:25) as something for which no other religion can provide a parallel, was *the presence of the living Lord in the midst of His own* (Mt 18:20; 28:20)." Cf. also Larry Hurtado, *At the Origins of Christian Worship* (Grand Rapids: Eerdmans, 2000), p. 50: "They [NT Christians] experienced their assemblies as not merely human events but as having a transcendent dimension. They sensed God as directly and really present in their meetings through his Spirit." Or to use another analogy, the risen Lord, through the power of the Spirit, projects himself, from the right hand of God in heaven, as a spiritual hologram into our worship space and interacts with us in real kingdom time.

faith) transported in the Spirit to a complex, transcendent world (the heavenlies) that is more intense and interesting than ordinary life; the time between game starts (invocation) and game over (benediction) is not ordinary time, but kingdom time. The church sanctuary/cyberspace is not an ordinary space, but a kingdom space, with the interpenetration of heaven and earth. The activity is participatory—both the players/congregrants and the triune God, Father, Son and Holy Spirit are "online," present and interacting in real time. The Bible, the sacraments and the liturgy are the software;[64] the church building, furnishings and musical instruments are the hardware; the mind of the triune God is the heavenly server that archives all the software and the history of its action.

This comparison could easily be misunderstood. The analogy is not intended to suggest that authentic worship is, so to speak, only a virtual reality or a simulation of a more real everyday reality. To the contrary, the notion in this analogy and thought experiment is that authentic Sunday worship, because of the *real presence* of Christ by the Spirit in the midst of the assembly, is more intensely real than ordinary life,[65] because the greater ontic reality and weight of the level-1 triune God is irrupting into the midst of the assembly and investing it with an "eternal weight of glory" (cf. 2 Cor 4:17). The ascended Lord is constantly filling the church with the fullness of his glorious reality (Eph 1:23), a present foretaste and anticipation of that final glorious "ontic density" that will be displayed in the church/new Jerusalem in the new creation—where its consummated beauty and weight will be revealed as unimaginably vast beyond its present earthly dimensions (Rev 21:16).

---

[64]Cf. Gerard Loughlin on the connection between the Christian narrative and its enactment and embodiment in liturgy and worship: "The participants' absorption into the story is made possible through their absorption of the story in and through its ritual enactment. They are not simply witnesses of the story, but characters within it" (*Telling God's Story: Bible, Church and Narrative Theology* [Cambridge: Cambridge University Press, 1996], p. 223, as cited in David Torevell, *Losing the Sacred: Ritual, Modernity and Liturgical Reform* [Edinburgh: T & T Clark, 2000], p. 10).

[65]In popular culture, stories of persons abducted by extraterrestrial beings—with life-transforming consequences—are generally viewed with great skepticism. To follow this science-fiction analogy, in the act of true worship, those assembled in the name of Jesus in the presence of the Spirit do in fact have a close encounter with an extraterrestrial being from a higher world—the risen Christ who is actually present in their midst.

The claim here advanced is that the act of true New Testament worship "in the Spirit" involves a process of real transformation of the believing church ("Christ *in you*, the hope of glory") in anticipation of the final, end-time of the "ontic weight-gain" divinely ordained by the triune God for his people. Human beings are still human beings; this is no form of pantheism; but true worship can be part of the process by which believers are being "transformed from one degree of glory to another" as they worship in the presence of the risen Lord (2 Cor 3:18).

To carry this analogy one step further, we could say that, from God's point of view, this world, the creation, is an online simulation for which God, the Director and Programmer, has written the code; we are artificial intelligence avatars or bots that have been given freedom and agency in the simulation called This Age. Gamers in This Age are living "in the matrix"; their brains and imaginations have been colonized by the Commander of the Evil Empire. Most of the gamers in This Age, however, do not realize that "Game Over" will soon be flashing on the screen. The Programmer is soon to pull the plug and call the gamers into his presence (the great white throne, Rev 20:11, "Earth and sky fled from his presence"), into final reality (the age to come), and administer a huge ontological shock: Judgment Day. "Hey, dudes; the game is over; it's now either wrath and eternal destruction or unending joy and bliss."

It will be left to the reader to reflect further on this thought experiment, metaphorically comparing Sunday worship and an online simulation. Hopefully, enough has been suggested to encourage additional efforts to restore to the Protestant evangelical doxological imagination some of the sense of mystery and transcendence, and especially the sense of awareness of the *real presence of Christ* in the worshiping assembly, that has been stripped away and weakened by the influences of Reformation iconoclasm, Enlightenment naturalism, revivalism's marginalization of the Eucharist, and the seductive powers of modern consumer and entertainment-oriented cultures. The following chapter will consider how evangelicals might rediscover a richer experience of the Lord's Supper and a more vivid sense of meeting the risen Christ at the table.

4

The Eucharist

MEETING THE RISEN
CHRIST AT THE TABLE

We had arrived a few minutes late for the 11 a.m. Sunday service at a community church in a shopping center in Denver, and the Communion service, which preceded the sermon, was already underway: Communion was a walk-up format where the people served themselves from tables placed in the four corners of the auditorium. A young mother, juggling her baby on her hip while serving herself, had not noticed that she had dropped the bread on the floor. I discreetly crept up behind her, rescued the bread from the floor and placed it back on the table. At the rear of the auditorium a teenage boy with a bored look on his face bent over a table near the wall and was licking the small plastic cup of grape juice with his tongue.

My wife and I, who attend a conservative Episcopal church near Boston with a beautiful liturgy, were frankly appalled at the casual—indeed, sloppy—way in which the Lord's Supper was being administered. A sense of the presence of the holy in the administration of holy Communion was not obvious that morning, from our point of view, at least. As we reflected on our experience that morning, which, by the way, had featured an outstanding exposition of John 15 and the cruciality of abiding in Christ, we were reminded of the somewhat marginalized place that Communion holds in the worship of many evangelical churches in America. While the Lord's Supper is observed in dutiful response to the Lord's command, for many Christians it seems to be a ritual that is performed without a deep sense of spiritual meaning or sense of the presence of the living Christ who meets his people around the table. Questions such as, why are we doing this? or, what do we get from Communion that we can't get in a good sermon? may be present in the minds of many.

This chapter argues that recovering a more meaningful and frequent experience of the Lord's Supper in the life of the evangelical church involves the rediscovery of a central reality in the worship of the New Testament and the early church: the *real personal presence of the risen Christ who meets his people in joyful fellowship around the table.* The point of recovering the New Testament and early church pattern of frequent Communion is not to argue for some additional ritual or sacramentalism in the life of the church. The point is rather to recover the vivid awareness of the resurrection of Jesus Christ—the living reality presupposed by the practice of the Eucharist—as the central, joyous fact for all true worship, every Sunday of the year.

I will argue this thesis in four steps: first, some church history will be traced to see how a sense of the real presence of Christ in the early eucharistic life of the church became, in much of Protestant evangelicalism, an experience of the real absence; second, aspects of the New Testament that highlight the reality of the real personal presence of Christ to the church will be examined. Third, some recent developments in ecumenical theology and the philosophy of language that shed fresh light on eucharistic understanding will be considered; and fourth, some practical advantages of a real personal-presence understanding and more frequent celebration of the Eucharist will be presented.

PROTESTANT JOURNEYS TO THE REAL ABSENCE: SOME HISTORICAL DETOURS

Some reflection on church history will help us to understand some of the factors that led from the early Christians' vivid experience of the real personal presence of the risen Christ who met them at (not on) the Communion table to the much later sense of the real absence in much of Protestant evangelicalism.

Before examining the church history, however, it will be helpful to reflect briefly on some reasons why a more theologically robust understanding of the Lord's Supper is important for Christian life and worship. It is of course true that the observance of the Lord's Supper is important in the life of the church because Christ specifically commanded "Do this in remembrance of me." The founder of the Christian church commanded that his life and work be remembered and taught not merely by the preaching of sermons or through Bible studies, but specifically by the observance of this ritual meal. This commandment alone is sufficient to make the Lord's Supper an essential and abiding element of the Christian's life and worship.

The Protestant liturgical scholar J. J. von Allmen has drawn attention to two other reasons for the essential place of the Eucharist in Christian worship. He observes that all Christian worship is based on the person and work of Jesus Christ, and that the work of Christ can be understood in terms of a "Galilean" phase that focused on the proclamation of the Word, and a "Jerusalem" phase that culminated in his atoning death on the cross. Balanced Christian worship reflects both the prophetic ministry in Galilee and its priestly culmination in Jerusalem; the preaching of the Word naturally culminates in and is completed by the commemoration of and personal appropriation of the benefits of the cross at the Communion table. "A liturgy without the Eucharist is like the ministry of Jesus without Good Friday."[1]

The celebration of the Lord's Supper is also an essential means for maintaining the difference between the church and the world, in a way that is not merely subjective, self-centered and moralizing, but based on the command and will of the Lord Jesus Christ. The invitation to come to the table is specifically for those who have made a personal commitment to Jesus as Savior and Lord and to the standards of his kingdom. According to Allmen, if today's churches have become too influenced by worldly standards and values, it is in part "because our sacramental life has become so atrophied."[2]

Two additional reasons for recovering a more central place for the

---

[1] J. J. von Allmen, *Worship: Theology and Practice* (New York: Oxford University Press, 1965), pp. 154-55.
[2] Ibid., p. 155.

Lord's Supper in evangelical worship could be added to those noted above. Historically, for more that 1500 years, the Eucharist was an integral and indeed the culminating feature of Sunday worship, and the Protestant tradition needs to reconsider its departure from this historic Christian practice. Perhaps even more crucially, there is also Martin Luther's observation that the Lord's Supper is crucial because it is a Christ-commanded way of remembering and summarizing the gospel itself. The words "this is my body" recall and crystallize the core realities of the Christian faith: the incarnation, cross and resurrection. Week by week the believing Christian cannot only be reminded of the fundamentals of the faith, but also actually experience the benefits of the work of Christ (forgiveness of sins, hope of eternal life), and further, the actual, real-time joy of friendship and communion with the risen Christ who is truly present through the Holy Spirit with his people at the table.

Church historians and liturgical scholars agree that the Lord's Supper was observed frequently in the New Testament and in the early church, and that there was a vivid sense of the presence of the risen Christ at these gatherings around the table. James F. White has noted that the Eucharist has since New Testament times been the "primary act of congregational worship," an act that "conveys the very heart of the gospel in dramatic form Sunday after Sunday."[3] Martin J. Heinecken has noted that in the New Testament period, in the celebration of the Lord's Supper "the risen, living, Christ was believed to be present. There is no intimation that this meal was to be only a reminder of either a past event or an absent loved one."[4] John Calvin stated that Christ did not ordain the Lord's Supper to be received only once a year, "and that, too, perfunctorily, as is now the usual custom." Commenting on the practice of the apostolic church as Luke describes it in Acts 2:42 (the believers "devoted themselves to the apostles' teaching and to the fellowship, to the breaking of bread and to prayer") he notes that it

---

[3]James F. White, "The Order of Worship: The Ordinary Parts," in *Companion to the Book of Worship*, ed. William F. Dunkle Jr. and Joseph D. Quillian Jr. (Nashville: Abingdon, 1970), pp. 11-30.

[4]Martin J. Heinecken, "An Orientation Toward the Lord's Supper Today," in *Meaning and Practice of the Lord's Supper*, ed. Helmut T. Lehmann (Philadelphia: Muhlenberg Press, 1961), pp. 180-81.

became "the unvarying rule that no meeting of the church should take place without the Word, prayers, partaking the Supper, and almsgiving. . . . That was the established order . . . and it remained in use for many centuries after."[5]

The New Testament scholar Norman Perrin notes that the "table-fellowship of the kingdom" was a central feature of the ministry of Jesus, and that a "remarkable sense of the fellowship between the early Christians and the risen Lord" was a prominent feature in primitive Christianity. The disciples' vivid and joyous experiences of table fellowship with Jesus "survived the crucifixion and provided the focal point for the community life of the earliest Christians."[6]

In his comprehensive article in the *Anchor Bible Dictionary*, Hans-Josef Klauck has drawn attention to the connection between the resurrection of Jesus—at the very core of New Testament faith and experience—and the celebration of the Lord's Supper. "Without the resurrection of Jesus and the experience of Easter on the part of the disciples," he notes, "there never would have been a regular practice of the Lord's Supper." The resurrection of Jesus was foundational to this practice, because the table of the Lord was "the place at which every believer who was temporally removed from the first Easter could gain the assurance of the *presence of the risen Lord.*"[7]

Similar points are made by the noted New Testament scholar Oscar Cullmann in his study of early Christian worship. The Lord's Supper was the natural climax toward which the early worship service moved and "without which it is not thinkable, since here Christ united himself with his community as crucified and risen and . . . actually builds it up as his body (1 Cor 10:17)." It is in the Lord's Supper that "Christ comes in the Spirit to his own."[8] According to Cullmann, "*The certainty of the Resurrection* was the essential religious motive of the primitive Lord's Supper. . . . When they assembled to 'break bread' they knew the Risen

---

[5]John Calvin, *Institutes of the Christian Religion,* trans. Ford Lewis Battles (Philadelphia: Westminster Press), 4.17.44, "The Lord's Supper Should Be Celebrated Frequently," p. 1422.
[6]Norman Perrin, *Rediscovering the Teaching of Jesus* (New York: Harper & Row, 1967), p. 107.
[7]Hans-Josef Klauck, "Lord's Supper," in *Anchor Bible Dictionary*, ed. David Noel Freedman, vol. 4 (New York: Doubleday, 1992), pp. 362-72 at 366, emphasis added.
[8]Oscar Cullmann, *Early Christian Worship* (Chicago: Henry Regnery, 1953), pp. 34, 20.

One would reveal His presence in a manner less visible but no less real than previously."[9]

This sense of being in the presence of the risen Christ during Communion is reflected in the oldest eucharistic prayer outside the New Testament, from the early third-century liturgy of Hippolytus of Rome: "Remembering then his death *and resurrection,* we offer this bread and cup to you, giving you thanks that you have made us worthy to stand *before you* and serve you."[10] These early Christians were aware of the presence of the risen Lord at the table; further evidence of this from the New Testament writings will be noted below. Though this vivid sense of the living, personal presence of Christ at the table was to diminish in later centuries (and be replaced by notions of a presence focused on the visible elements), there is no reason theologically why the church today cannot recover such an experience, for Christ is still alive and risen from the dead, the Spirit is still given to the church, and Christ continues to seek communion with his disciples around the table.

Various factors conspired in the patristic period to contribute to less frequent Communion and a diminished sense of the presence of the risen Christ in fellowship with the worshiping community. In the fourth century increasing numbers of half-converted people entered the churches, and preachers admonished the at times unruly crowds not to approach the table in an unworthy manner. John Chrysostom emphasized the sincerity of heart and purity of soul that was necessary for the worthy communicant: "With this, approach at all times; without it, never!"[11] The intended effect of such admonitions was to "fence the table" and guard it from the careless and unworthy, but the unintended consequence was to encourage the practice of noncommunicating attendance at the Eucharist. "Many people preferred to give up the reception of communion rather than to amend their lives," notes Paul Brad-

---

[9]Oscar Cullmann and F. J. Leenhardt, *Essays on the Lord's Supper* (Richmond: John Knox Press, 1958), p. 12. Cullmann notes further on p. 15, "His presence is understood to be as real as possible. He comes to participate in the meal and not to serve as food . . . this presence is at one and the same time that of Christ risen, of Christ living, and of Christ who is to come."

[10]In Herman Wegman, *Christian Worship in East and West* (New York: Pueblo Publishing, 1985), p. 46, emphasis added.

[11]Cited in Paul Bradshaw, *The Search for the Origins of Christian Worship* (New York: Oxford University Press, 2002), p. 220.

shaw; "many people . . . stayed until the time for communion and then left the church."[12] This practice of infrequent Communion persisted throughout the Middle Ages and continued to be the dominant reality on the eve of the Reformation.

Various scholars have drawn attention to other factors that altered the character of the eucharistic experience in the patristic and medieval periods. Krister Stendahl, for example, has argued that the piety of the Western church became dominated by an "introspective conscience" that reflected more the experience of Augustine (and later, that of Luther) than it did that of the apostle Paul or the New Testament generally.[13] This introspective tendency affected the reception of the Eucharist and was later compounded by the influence of the penitential disciplines of the Irish monks and missionaries whose manuals for self-examination came to dominate the practice of penance in the Western church.[14] The practical center for penance shifted from baptism, experienced once and for all, to the repeated preparation for the Mass. This mood of penitence and self-examination came to dominate eucharistic experience, replacing the more joyful experience of the New Testament and early church. The reality of a corporate celebration was being replaced by one of individualistic introspection and penitence—and this ethos was inherited by the Reformers and, to a great extent, not overcome by their attempted reforms.

Dietrich Ritschl has argued that with Augustine there is also a significant shift in the way in which the Western church thought of the resurrection of Christ.[15] The resurrection is now understood almost exclusively as an event in the past, and not as an event that still is experienced as a living reality in the church's eucharistic worship in the present. Ritschl believes that the pervasive influence of Augustinian categories in Western theology contributed to a loss of the sense of the continuing, active, personal presence of the risen Christ with the

---

[12]Ibid.

[13]Krister Stendahl, "The Apostle Paul and the Introspective Conscience of the West," *Harvard Theological Review* 56 (1963): 203.

[14]Ibid.

[15]Dietrich Ritschl, *Memory and Hope: An Inquiry Concerning the Presence of Christ* (New York: Macmillan, 1967), pp. xii, 6.

church, and to the later Protestant emphasis on the doctrine of justification by faith as the means of the individual believer's access to God and the benefits of Christ's redemption.

Other factors were at work during the medieval period to diminish the role of the laity and the quality of their eucharistic experience. Since the seventh century the popes had authorized the great monasteries in Europe to ordain larger numbers of their monks, and this practice led to private celebrations of the Mass as expressions of the monks' personal devotions. The idea soon became widespread that a layman, by giving a priest or monk a stipend for saying a Mass, could facilitate one's personal salvation or that of a departed family member.[16]

As the church moved from the patristic period into the Middle Ages, Latin ceased to be the living language of the people, and as a result the eucharistic liturgy was being recited in a language that the people could not understand. The words of institution were thought to be so powerful and holy that they should be protected against all possibility of profanation by the unholy, and as a result by around A.D. 1000 at the latest, it had become the custom for the priest to recite the eucharistic prayer in a soft whisper that could not be heard by the congregation.[17]

Architectural changes in the medieval period also tended to diminish the role of the laity in the Eucharist. The table was moved from its earlier more central location and placed on the back wall of the church. The bishop or priest who had once faced the people to celebrate the Supper now turned his back on them. Parts of the liturgy—the *Kyrie, Gloria, Sanctus*—that in earlier times had been said or sung by the people now became the province of the choir and clergy seated in separate choir stalls. The experience of the Eucharist had been transformed from one of frequent Communion—of actually receiving the elements—to one of being a spectator who saw the priest elevate the host for the purpose of adoration. Watching the priest consecrate the elements and elevate the wafer was supposed to confer spiritual benefits on those present, even without

---

[16]Joseph M. Powers, S.J., *Eucharistic Theology* (New York: Herder & Herder, 1967), p. 25; Theodor Klauser, *A Short History of the Western Liturgy* (London: Oxford University Press, 1969), p. 103.
[17]Klauser, *Short History*, p. 99.

personal reception. Popular belief held that one who beheld the sacred host in the morning would not become blind that day, would not become hungry or die that day and so forth.[18]

By the fourteenth and fifteenth centuries, as Gregory Dix has noted, popular eucharistic piety had become "more and more one-sided, treating the sacrament less and less as the source of the unity and of the corporate life of the church [cf. 1 Cor 10–11], . . . and more and more only as a focus of purely personal adoration of our Lord therein present to the individual. . . . Deprived of frequent communion and with a liturgy in Latin, private adoration was all that was left to the unlettered layfolk . . . with which to exercise their piety."[19]

The doctrine of transubstantiation was officially defined for the Western church at the Fourth Lateran Council in Rome in 1215 and expounded in that same century by Thomas Aquinas in his *Summa Theologica*,[20] but such understandings of the Eucharist focusing on a change in the elements had been gaining momentum since at least the ninth century. In the ninth century the monk Paschasius Radbertus, abbot of the Benedictine monastery of Corbie in France, wrote a treatise titled *The Lord's Body and Blood,* in which he defended a very realistic view of the sacrament. For Radbertus, after the words of consecration are spoken, the elements of bread and wine on the altar become the true body and blood of Christ; this true body and blood in the elements are identical to the natural body and blood of Christ during the Lord's earthly life and now in his body reigning in heaven.[21] The Jesuit scholar Tad Guzie has noted that Radbertus's treatise is the first historical document known to us that focuses directly on the physical elements of bread and wine; earlier patristic discussions by Augustine, Ambrose

[18]Joseph Jungmann, *Pastoral Liturgy* (New York: Herder & Herder, 1962), pp. 64-74, "The State of Liturgical Life on the Eve of the Reformation," at p. 71.

[19]Dom Gregory Dix, *The Shape of the Liturgy* (1945; reprint, London: Continuum, 2005), p. 249.

[20]The complex history surrounding the development of the doctrine of transubstantiation and its later history are reviewed by James F. McCue, "The Doctrine of Transubstantiation from Berengar through Trent: The Point at Issue," *Harvard Theological Review* 61 (1968): 385-430.

[21]See George E. McCracken, ed., *Early Medieval Theology,* Library of Christian Classics 9 (Philadelphia: Westminster Press, 1957), "Paschasius Radbertus of Corbie: *The Lord's Body and Blood* (selections), text, pp. 94-108, and introduction, pp. 90-93. According to McCracken, the work by Radbertus appears to be the first treatise in the history of the church devoted *exclusively* and specifically to the doctrine of the Eucharist.

and Chrysostom referred to the bread and the wine in the context of
the whole action of the Eucharist as a sacramental event. For Radbertus, on the other hand, "the starting point was no longer the action but
the *elements* out there on the altar table."[22] This focus on the elements
was a momentous shift that was to continue to set the parameters of
discussions of the "real presence" in subsequent centuries, and had the
unintended effect of contributing to a depersonalizing of Christ's presence—Christ now being conceived of as "in" the elements rather than
as a personal presence among his people. Radbertus's contemporary
Ratramnus, on the other hand, also a monk of Corbie, defended a more
symbolical understanding of the presence of Christ at the Eucharist in
his work *Christ's Body and Blood.*

The discussion and debate on the nature of the real presence continued
in subsequent centuries during the Middle Ages, and in the year 1059,
Berengar of Tours, who was thought to have held symbolic views of the
presence, was forced to recant these views and to sign a statement that
affirmed that the bread and the wine on the altar are, after the consecration, "not only a Sacrament but also the real body and blood of our
Lord Jesus Christ, and . . . these are held and broken by the hands of
the priest and are crushed by the teeth of the faithful."[23] Such a physi-
calist, even crude expression of the nature of the presence represented
what has been termed the triumph of the "Ambrosian" ("realistic") over
the "Augustinian" (spiritual, "symbolic") understandings of the Eucharist that had been present in the church since the patristic period.[24]

The doctrine of transubstantiation received its classic formulation in the
work of Thomas Aquinas in the thirteenth century. According to Aquinas,
using the metaphysical terminology of Aristotle, by divine power the "complete substance of the bread is converted into the complete substance of
Christ's body, and the complete substance of the wine into the complete
substance of Christ's blood . . . it can be called by a name proper to itself—

[22]Tad W. Guzie, S.J., *Jesus and the Eucharist* (New York: Paulist Press, 1974), pp. 60-61, emphasis in original.
[23]In Darwell Stone, *A History of the Doctrine of the Holy Eucharist*, vol. 1 (London: Longmans,
Green, 1909), p. 247.
[24]McCue, "Doctrine of Transubstantiation," p. 386.

'transubstantiation.'"[25] The exterior appearance ("accidents") of the bread
and wine are unchanged, but the inner reality ("substance") is changed
when the priest pronounces the words of institution; this real, though spiritual change, can only be discerned by faith, not by sight.[26]

This doctrinal understanding, localizing the "real presence" and focusing attention on the physical elements, was to have further ripple
effects in eucharistic piety and practice. This understanding led to the
practice of the elevation of the host after the consecration, a practice
prescribed by a synod in Paris in 1209 or 1215. At the moment of consecration, a bell was rung, the people were to kneel, strike themselves
on the breast and say a brief prayer. "Christ was shown to the faithful
in order to be adored; the . . . bread, that now was only exteriorly bread,
was no longer so much to be eaten as to be beheld and worshipped as
the body of Christ."[27] The consecrated hosts were set apart in separate
monstrances or tabernacles for adoration by the faithful at times other
than the Mass, and carried about in processions such as the feast of
Corpus Christi that also originated at this time.

As noted earlier, the eucharistic theology of the Middle Ages increasingly focused on the passion or the death of Christ. The joyous
awareness of the resurrection of Christ as a present reality was diminished, along with a recollection of his ascension and priestly interces-
sion. Consequently, as Gregory Dix has observed, there was little way
of entering into Christ's action except by some form of the "repetition"
of Christ's sacrifice, "however guarded, or by a mere mental remember-

---

[25]St. Thomas Aquinas, *Summa Theologiae*, 3A.73-78, *The Eucharistic Presence*, vol. 58, ed. William Barden, O.P. (New York: McGraw-Hill, 1964), 3A.75.5, p. 73.
[26]Ibid., pp. 110-11 note c. comments on the mode of Christ's presence: "Christ's body as localized is in one place only, namely in heaven. The same body which is localized in heaven is
really present in the Eucharist in a nonlocal way. Christ's body with its dimensions, with part
distinct from part, is present to the dimensions of the bread not as to a containing place, but as
substance is 'spiritually' equally present to all the parts of the dimensions that contain it. . . . It
is only as 'spiritually' contained that the extended body of Christ is related to the dimensions of
the bread." By these distinctions in scholastic philosophy, Barden, as a modern Catholic theologian in the Thomistic tradition, is attempting to protect the doctrine of transubstantiation
from a crudely physicalistic understanding that would limit the body of Christ to the physical
dimensions of the elements as "containers," but it is far from evident that such fine distinctions
are well understood by the laity who participate in the Mass.
[27]Wegman, *Christian Worship in East and West*, pp. 230-31.

ing of it, however vivid and devout."[28]

During the later Middle Ages there was also the paradoxical situation that though the Mass was celebrated with growing frequency, actual reception by the laity was diminishing in frequency. While there may have been as many as fifty masses a week in a typical parish church, reception of Communion by laypersons was reduced to about three times a year at the beginning of the medieval period and to about once a year after the thirteenth century.[29]

The Protestant Reformers reacted strongly against much of the eucharistic theology and practices of the medieval Roman Catholic church, notably, against the doctrine of transubstantiation; the withholding of the cup from the laity; the concept of the Mass as a "propitiatory sacrifice for the living and the dead"[30] that sped souls from purgatory; private masses; and infrequent reception of Communion by the people.

Martin Luther, ordained as a priest and Augustinian monk, while rejecting the doctrine of transubstantiation, was more "catholic" in his understanding of the Lord's Supper than either Zwingli or Calvin, insisting on a strong sense of the real presence of Christ—in both his human and divine natures—instrumentally conveyed to the recipient by the elements of bread and wine. Luther's view is commonly stated with words such as the body of Christ is "in, with, and under"[31] the bread, though for Luther, such "common everyday language" is a hu-

---

[28]Dix, *Shape of the Liturgy*, p. 625. The official Roman Catholic understanding of the Mass is that the priestly action at the altar is a "re-presentation" and *not* a literal "repetition" of the once-for-all sacrifice of Christ at Calvary.

[29]Theodore G. Tappert, "Meaning and Practice in the Middle Ages," in *Meaning and Practice of the Lord's Supper,* ed. Helmut T. Lehmann (Philadelphia: Muhlenberg Press, 1961), p. 83; see also, more extensively, Robert F. Taft, S.J., *Beyond East and West: Problems in Liturgical Understanding* (Rome: Pontifical Oriental Institute, 1997), pp. 87-110, "The Frequency of the Eucharist throughout History."

[30]For a comprehensive study of the Roman Catholic understanding of the Mass as a propitiatory sacrifice prior to and at the time of the Reformation, see Francis Clark, S.J., *Eucharistic Sacrifice and the Reformation* (London: Basil Blackwell, 1960).

[31]The term "consubstantiation" is frequently associated with the Lutheran view, but Luther himself never used this term, and some Lutheran scholars such as Herman Sasse have distanced themselves from this terminology: Hermann Sasse, *This Is My Body: Luther's Contention for the Real Presence in the Sacrament of the Altar* (Minneapolis: Augsburg, 1959), p. 161. This work by Sasse is one of the finest treatments by a Lutheran scholar of Luther's eucharistic theology in its late medieval and Reformation historical context.

man attempt to express the mystery of the belief "that Christ's body is truly present in the Supper." Were it not for the exigencies of ecclesiastical controversies, Luther would have been content to limit explanation to the simple words of Scripture, "this is my body."[32]

Luther was unwilling to separate the spiritual benefits of the Supper from the reception of the actual physical elements; for him, the elements were not merely "signs" or "seals," but the actual vehicles or carriers of the grace of God. For him the bread and the body are not changed into one another, but remain undivided and unseparated, so that like a red-hot iron in the fireplace, the iron remains iron and the fire remains fire, but the iron and the fire are inseparably united and permeate one another.[33]

This intimate, integral and mysterious union of the body and blood of Christ with the elements of bread and wine is a "sacramental union" effected by the power of God and by the Holy Spirit. As expressed in the later and authoritative Lutheran confession, the Formula of Concord (1584), "We believe, teach, and confess that the body and blood of Christ are taken with the bread and wine *[cum pane et vino]*, not only spiritually through faith, but also by the mouth . . . but after a spiritual and heavenly manner *[sed supernaturali et coelesti modo]*, by reason of the sacramental union *[ratione sacramentalis unionis]*.[34] Here the confession attempts to maintain a strong physical presence of the body of Christ as conveyed with the bread, while acknowledging that this presence is effected "spiritually" and is known not through the senses, but by faith in God's word.

For Luther, the Lord's Supper was not a peripheral part of the Christian life, but an epitome and summary of the gospel; this accounts for

---

[32]Martin Luther, "Confession Concerning Christ's Supper" (1528), in *Luther's Works*, vol. 37: *Word and Sacrament*, ed. Robert Fischer (Philadelphia: Muhlenberg Press, 1961), p. 166. This treatise ("Great Confession") is Luther's most comprehensive and mature statement of his eucharistic theology.

[33]Ernst Sommerlath, "Lord's Supper," *Encyclopedia of the Lutheran Church*, ed. Julius Bodensick (Minneapolis: Augsburg, 1965), 2:1339; the elements of the Supper are like a pipe through which grace flows or like a bridge over which the grace of God comes to us (p. 1337).

[34]*Formula of Concord* 7.6, "Of the Lord's Supper," in *Creeds of Christendom*, ed. Philip Schaff (New York: Harper & Bros., 1877), 3:139.

the vehemence with which he contended for his own view in the controversies with Zwingli and other reformers. A statement of his from
the "Great Confession" of 1528 merits extensive quotation on this
point:

> See, then, what a beautiful, great, marvelous thing this is, how every-
> thing meshes together in one sacramental reality. The words [of institu-
> tion] are the first thing, for without the words the cup and the bread
> would be nothing. Further, without bread and cup, the body and blood
> of Christ would not be there. Without the body and blood of Christ, the
> new testament would not be there. Without the new testament, forgive-
> ness of sins would not be there. Without forgiveness of sins, life and
> salvation would not be there. . . . See, all this the words of the Supper
> offer and give us, and we embrace it by faith. Ought not the devil, then,
> hate such a Supper and rouse fanatics against it?[35]

If Luther had been asked the question "Why should the Supper be
celebrated frequently?" he might well have been astonished; we can
imagine him saying, "Why then should the gospel be frequently
preached? Why should forgiveness of sins be frequently offered in the
church? Only the devil himself would promote infrequent communion
and neglect of the sacrament!"

Ulrich Zwingli, the reformer of Zurich, is generally remembered as
the advocate of the "memorial" view of the Lord's Supper. In his *Commentary on True and False Religion* (1525), Zwingli argued that the word
is in the words "this is my body" must be taken in the sense of "signifies"; the Lord's Supper is "nothing but the commemoration by which
those who firmly believe that by Christ's death and blood they have
become reconciled with the Father proclaim this life-bringing death,
that is, preach it with praise and thanksgiving."[36] The Supper is the
"thanksgiving and common rejoicing of those who declare the death of
Christ, that is, trumpet, praise, confess, and exalt his name above all
others."[37] Relying heavily on the sixth chapter of the Gospel of John,

---

[35]Luther, "Confession Concerning Christ's Supper," p. 338.
[36]Ulrich Zwingli, *Commentary on True and False Religion*, ed. Samuel McCauley Jackson and
Clarence Nevin Heller (Durham, N.C.: Labyrinth, 1981), pp. 224, 237.
[37]Ibid., p. 24. Though for Zwingli the Supper is indeed an occasion for the believer to "remem-

especially John 6:63 ("The Spirit gives life; the flesh counts for nothing"), Zwingli asks, "To eat the body of Christ spiritually, then, what is it but to trust in Christ?"[38] Faith, then—not the physical elements—is the essential means by which the believer feeds on Christ.

It was one of the great tragedies of the Reformation period that Zwingli and Luther were not able to resolve their differences on the Lord's Supper at the Marburg Colloquy in 1529.[39] These differences involved both different assumptions regarding biblical interpretation and different understandings of the nature of Christ's body in heaven. Zwingli was convinced that the word *is* in the text "this is my body" had to be taken figuratively; Luther, though well aware that the Bible was filled with figurative expressions, insisted that the text should be taken literally unless it could be shown to be contrary to some other article of faith—which for Luther, was not the case.[40] Zwingli argued that since the Scriptures clearly asserted that the body of Christ was now at the right hand of God in heaven, it could not be at the same time on earth, in the bread, on the Communion table. Luther replied that "the right hand of God is everywhere," and Christ is present in the sacrament by the power of divine omnipotence; the resurrection body of Christ is not limited to a local presence and was said to have passed through closed doors.[41] This matter of the relationship of the body of the ascended Christ in heaven to the church's spatio-temporal location on earth will be further considered in the third section of this chapter below.

Calvin's view of the Eucharist can be seen as something of a medi-

---

ber" the death of Christ, this is not the exclusive element in his eucharistic understanding. The Supper is also an occasion in which the congregation corporately expresses its faith and gives God praise and thanksgiving for the redemption in Christ. For a careful discussion of Zwingli's eucharistic theology in the context of its historical setting and development, see W. P. Stephens, *The Theology of Huldrych Zwingli* (Oxford: Clarendon, 1986), pp. 248-59.

[38]Zwingli, *Commentary on True and False Religion*, p. 250.

[39]For an extensive account of the Marburg Colloquy, based on scholarly reconstructions of later accounts by the participants, see Sasse, *This Is My Body*, pp. 187-294.

[40]Luther, "Confession Concerning Christ's Supper," p. 217: "The words, 'This is my body' ought to be believed as they read. For it is contrary to no article of faith, and moreover it is scriptural."

[41]Ibid., p. 214 ("God has and knows various ways to be present at a certain place, not only the single one of which the fanatics prattle, which the philosophers call 'local,'" p. 217).

128 WORSHIP AND THE REALITY OF GOD

ating position between Luther and Zwingli, being somewhat more
"symbolic" than the former but more "realistic" than the latter. Calvin's view might be termed a "real spiritual presence" view. At the
Lord's table, through the action of the Holy Spirit, the believer, in
faith, is made "one in body, spirit, and soul" with Christ; the Spirit of
Christ is "like a channel through which all that Christ himself is and
has is conveyed to us."[42] In Communion the believer is mystically
united with Christ in both his human and divine natures, and receives not only the *benefits* of the life, death and resurrection of Christ,
but Christ *himself.* The Holy Spirit "causes us to possess Christ completely and have him dwelling in us."[43]

If it is asked how it is possible for the believer to have such comprehensive and intimate communion with Christ in the fullness of his person, when Christ's body is in heaven and not on earth, Calvin points to
the mysterious action of the Spirit, whose reality and actions transcend
human reason and the physical senses. Let us remember, says the Genevan Reformer, "how far the secret power of the Holy Spirit towers
above all our senses, and how foolish it is to measure his immeasurableness by our measure. What, then, our mind does not comprehend, let
faith conceive: that the Spirit truly unites things separated in space."[44]
If Luther, in effect, believed that the omnipotent power of God "brought
down" from heaven the body of Christ to the believer, Calvin believed
that in faith, by the action of the Spirit, the believer was "lifted up" to
heaven to have communion with the risen Christ in his glorified
humanity.[45]

---

[42]Calvin *Institutes* 4.17.12.

[43]Ibid.

[44]*Institutes* 4.17.10. Calvin's views as expressed in the 1559 edition of the *Institutes* are remarkably consistent with his earlier views as expressed in the "Confession of Faith Concerning the
Eucharist" (1537) and the "Treatise on the Lord's Supper" (1541); there is very little development here: see *Calvin: Theological Treatises,* ed. J. K. S. Reid, Library of Christian Classics 22
(Philadelphia: Westminster Press, 1954), pp. 142-66 and 168-69.

[45]On this point, see Christopher B. Kaiser, "Climbing Jacob's Ladder: John Calvin and the
Early Church on Our Eucharistic Ascent to Heaven," *Scottish Journal of Theology* 56, no. 3
(2003): 247-67. In a writing of 1554 Calvin stated that "Christ is absent from us in respect of
his body, but, dwelling in us by His Spirit, he raises us up to heaven to himself, transfusing into
us the vivifying vigor of his flesh, just as the rays of the sun invigorate us by his vital warmth."
(*Tracts of John Calvin,* 2:240; cited in Kaiser, "Climbing Jacob's Ladder," p. 255). Hughes Old
has concluded that for Calvin, "Christ's presence at the Lord's Table is not so much a local

It is clear that for Calvin, the Lord's Supper is no bare memorial where the church (only) remembers the death of Christ, though it is at least that. Calvin clearly wants to teach that, through faith and by the action of the Spirit, Christ and the believer are actually present to one another and commune with one another in body, soul and spirit. While for Calvin the bread remains bread and the wine remains wine, in the context of the whole action of the Eucharist, they become the divinely ordained means and instruments through which this personal union is actually experienced. The elements are not symbols in the modern sense of symbol—that is, a pointer to or reminder of that which is really absent—but rather are symbols in the patristic sense of signs that actually convey and manifest that which is really present.[46]

Calvin makes clear his realistic view of *symbol* in the following passage of the *Institutes:* "I indeed admit that the breaking of bread is a symbol. . . . But, having admitted this, we shall nevertheless duly infer that by the showing of the symbol the thing itself is also shown. . . . there ought not to be the least doubt that he truly presents and shows his body. . . . the godly ought by all means to keep this rule: whenever they see the symbols appointed by the Lord, to think and be persuaded that the truth of the thing signified is surely present there."[47]

Like Luther, Calvin wanted to restore frequent Communion to the church, and he urged the Geneva town council in 1537 to authorize its celebration "at least once every Sunday when the congregation is assembled, in view of the great comfort which the faithful receive . . .

---

presence as it is a personal presence. Again, it is not so much that Christ is present on the table as that he is present at the table" (*Worship that Is Reformed According to Scripture* [Louisville: Westminster John Knox, 1984], p. 134).

[46]This distinction is made helpfully in Alexander Schmemann, *The Eucharist* (Crestwood, N.Y.: St. Vladimir's Seminary Press, 1987), p. 38; cited by Laurence C. Sibley Jr., "The Church as Eucharistic Community: Observations on John Calvin's Early Eucharistic Theology (1536-1545)," *Worship* 81, no. 3 (2007): 249-67 at p. 252. This distinction could be illustrated as follows: The symbol "H_2O" written on a chalk board *points* to the reality of water but does not convey it; the *dove* that descended on Jesus at his baptism (Mt 3) was a "symbol" or image of the Holy Spirit that actually *conveyed* the Spirit to Jesus.

[47]*Institutes* 4.17.10. For an insightful discussion of the critical differences between Zwingli and Calvin on the meaning of *symbol*, see B. A. Gerrish, "The Lord's Supper in the Reformed Confessions," *Theology Today* 23, no. 2 (1966): 224-43 at pp. 230-31; the article presents a careful survey of Reformed eucharistic understandings in the sixteenth and seventeenth centuries.

[and] the fruit of all sorts which it produces."[48] In the *Institutes* Calvin made the same plea for the restoration of weekly Communion, arguing that this was the practice of the New Testament church, and that such frequent recollection of Christ's passion had the following benefits: (1) the sustaining and strengthening of Christian faith; (2) encouragement in the singing of thanksgiving to God and the proclamation of his goodness; (3) the nourishing of mutual love among believers; (4) the public witness to this mutual love; and (5) the discerning of the bond of unity in the body of Christ.[49] Unfortunately, Calvin was not able to persuade the Geneva town council to restore frequent Communion, and many churches in the Reformed tradition in subsequent centuries have celebrated the Supper only four times a year.

At the Council of Trent (1545-1563) the Roman Catholic bishops met to respond to the criticisms of the Protestant Reformers. Issues of eucharistic theology and practice were addressed at session seven in 1547 and session thirteen in 1551. The Council adopted an essentially defensive stance, initiating some reform but largely rejecting the central Protestant criticisms of the Mass. There was no restoration of the cup to the laity; transubstantiation was reaffirmed; private masses were to continue; the liturgy of the Mass was not to be translated into the language of the people; the Mass was defended as a propitiatory sacrifice efficacious for the sins of the living and the dead.[50] Substantive changes such as translation of the Mass into the vernacular languages and the practice of frequent Communion were only to become realities some four hundred years later, as a result of the actions of the Second Vatican Council (1963-1965).

The English Puritans of the seventeenth and eighteenth centuries adhered in large measure to the reformed theology of Calvin, and like him, had high views of the Lord's Supper. Matthew Henry, in *The Communicant's Companion*, which appeared in 1704, stated that at the

[48]Howard G. Hageman, *Pulpit and Table: Some Chapters in the History of Worship in the Reformed Churches* (Richmond: John Knox Press, 1962), p. 25.
[49]*Institutes* 4.17.44.
[50]James F. White, *A Brief History of Christian Worship* (Nashville: Abingdon, 1993), p. 121. See also Joseph Jungmann, *The Mass of the Roman Rite* (New York: Benziger Bros., 1951), pp. 96-106, "The Close of the Middle Ages and the Tridentine Reform."

Communion table God "not only assures us of the Truth of the Promise, but, according to our present Case and Capacity, *conveys* to us [emphasis original], by his Spirit, the good things promised; *Receive Christ Jesus the Lord,* Christ and a pardon, Christ and peace, Christ and grace, Christ and heaven."[51] Horton Davies notes that for Henry the sacrament is not mere "memorialism"; "It seals to believers the benefits of the Redeemer's Sacrifice."[52] Similarly, the *Savoy Declaration* of 1658, the confession of the English Independents (Congregationalists), reflected the Reformed and Puritan theology of the time and stated that, at the table, "worthy receivers outwardly partaking of the visible elements in this Sacrament do then inwardly by faith, really and indeed, yet not carnally and corporally, but spiritually, receive and feed upon Christ crucified, and all the benefits of his death."[53] In the Westminster Directory of Worship, prepared by the Westminster divines to accompany the Westminster Confession of Faith, the prayer of consecration thanks God "for this Sacrament in particular, by which Christ and all his benefits are applied and sealed unto us."[54] These expressions of Reformed and Puritan understandings of the Lord's Supper have in common a conviction that the elements not merely point to, but actually convey both the benefits of the atonement and Christ himself as well. Such an understanding, while not explicitly invoking the language of the believer's mystical union with Christ ("in Christ"; branch and vine, Jn 15), in fact presupposes it.

According to Horton Davies, a leading scholar of the history of Protestant worship, New England Puritanism in the seventeenth and eighteenth centuries exhibited a variety of eucharistic views, ranging from Zwinglian to more Calvinistic understandings. New England Puritans tended to focus on the sacrament as a "seal of the Covenant of Grace; for Calvin, however, it was a seal of the promised presence of Christ himself."[55] Davies concluded that New Eng-

---

[51]Cited in Horton Davies, *The Worship of the English Puritans* (Westminster: Dacre Press, 1948), p. 212.

[52]Ibid., p. 213.

[53]Ibid.

[54]Ibid.

[55]Horton Davies, *The Worship of the American Puritans* (New York: Peter Lang, 1990), p. 168.

land Puritan sacramental theology was prone to weaknesses in the
following respects: difficulty in accepting the notion that material
elements could convey spiritual grace; introspective concentration
on benefits to the individual, rather than the objective presence of
Christ at the table; and a growing emphasis on giving a public tes-
timony of dramatic conversion as a condition for admission to Communion, which tended to overshadow the objective reality of the
Supper as a means of grace.[56] The New England Puritans' emphasis
on the "introspective conscience" recalls the observations of Krister
Stendahl concerning the "introspective conscience" of Western piety from Augustine to Luther.[57] The focus on dramatic conversion
testimonies was to be given even greater prominence in the nineteenth-
century frontier revivals. This latter development, as will be further
noted below, was to have the unintended effect of shifting the spiritual center of gravity in Protestant evangelical piety from the altar
to the altar call as the primary "means of grace."

In the nineteenth century John W. Nevin, a theologian at the Ger-
man Reformed seminary in Mercersburg, Pennsylvania, and colleague
of the noted church historian Philip Schaff, made a significant contribution to sacramental theology with the publication of his treatise *The
Mystical Presence* (1846). This work could, arguably, be seen as one of
the most significant works of eucharistic theology by any American
theologian. Nevin, a former student of Charles Hodge at Princeton
Theological Seminary, argued that many of Calvin's spiritual descendants in America (including Hodge) had drifted away from Calvin's
high view of the real spiritual presence of Christ in the sacrament to
lower, Zwinglian memorial views.[58] He argued that American churches
needed to recover such a richer and higher view of the sacrament, one
in which the believer not merely remembered the death of Christ or

---

[56]Ibid.

[57]See note 13 above.

[58]Nevin cites as examples statements by Timothy Dwight, John Dick, Albert Barnes and others.
  According to Barnes, for example, the "whole design of the sacramental bread . . . is to call to
  remembrance, in a vivid manner, the dying sufferings of our Lord" (John W. Nevin, *The Mystical Presence and Other Writings on the Eucharist*, ed. Bard Thompson and George H. Bricker
  [Philadelphia: United Church Press, 1966], p. 104).

had pious feelings strengthened, but actually enjoyed spiritual communion with the whole, living Christ with whom he or she was mystically united. Such an understanding of the Lord's Supper did not have great appeal to Nevin's more pragmatically minded contemporaries, but in recent years his view has attracted renewed interest and respect from American Presbyterians and others.[59]

The Enlightenment of the eighteenth century was to have a profound impact on the theology and practice of the church in the West. The confidence in the powers of human reason led to a diminished appreciation of ritual[60] and mystery in Christian worship and theology. A scientific and empirically oriented worldview and deistic notions of God's relation to the world made it increasingly difficult for Christians influenced by such a mindset to view the Eucharist as an occasion in which the actual presence of divine realities could be experienced at the Communion table.

A notable expression of such a rationalistic mindset can be seen in Immanuel Kant's *Religion Within the Limits of Reason Alone* (1793). Kant spoke somewhat dismissively of three kinds of "illusory" faith: "faith in miracles . . . faith in mysteries . . . faith in means of grace."[61] Such a belief in "means of grace" was "illusory" for Kant, insofar as it was based on a belief that "through the use of merely natural means" the "influence of God *upon our morality*" could be brought about. The Christian "formality of a common partaking at the same table" can be justified insofar as it expands the "narrow, selfish, and unsociable cast of mind among men, especially in matters of religion" and enlivens the community to the "moral disposition of brotherly love."[62] The philosopher

---

[59]See, for example, Daryl G. Hart, *John Williamson Nevin: High Church Calvinist* (Phillipsburg, N.J.: Presbyterian & Reformed, 2005); Keith Mathison, *Given for You: Reclaiming Calvin's Doctrine of the Lord's Supper* (Phillipsburg, N.J.: Presbyterian & Reformed, 2002); Richard E. Wentz, *John Williamson Nevin: American Theologian* (New York: Oxford University Press, 1997).

[60]For insights into the recent renewal of interest in ritual and symbolism as means of renewal in worship, see Paul Bradshaw and John Melloh, eds., *Foundations in Ritual Studies* (Grand Rapids: Baker Academic, 2007), and Bernard Cooke and Gary Macy, *Christian Symbol and Ritual: An Introduction* (New York: Oxford University Press, 2005).

[61]Cited in White, *A Brief History of Christian Worship*, p. 144.

[62]Kant, *Religion Within the Limits of Reason Alone* (emphasis added), cited in James F. White, ed., *Documents of Christian Worship* (Louisville: Westminster John Knox, 1992), pp. 140-41.

of Konigsberg had no patience for a sense of mystery or the supernatural in matters of religion; Christianity was a system of morality, and religious practices were justified to the extent that they produced virtue. The consequence of such Enlightenment rationalism was to see the human being not so much as the recipient of the sacrament but its performer. The Lord's Supper is a way we remember what God did in times past, not a way of experiencing a personal encounter with the Holy One in the present. As James F. White has observed, the Enlightenment Christian kept the sacraments "as biblical commands, and therefore obligatory, but celebrated them infrequently and with little enthusiasm."[63]

As American churches moved into the nineteenth century, it would be difficult to underestimate the impact of the frontier revivals and the "new measures" of Charles Finney on subsequent worship practices and eucharistic piety. Finney introduced a strong pragmatic element into evangelical worship that has continued down to the present—from Finney to Willow Creek, so to speak. In his widely read and influential *Lectures on Revivals* (1835) the evangelist asserted that "God has established, in no church, any particular *form*, or manner of worship, for promoting the interests of religion. . . . the church is left to exercise her own discretion in relation to all such matters." All things should be done "decently and in order," but by "order," argued Finney, we are not to understand "any particular mode, in which any church may have been accustomed to perform their service."[64] Church practices were not to be prescribed by tradition, but by pragmatic considerations of what worked—what presumably would work in bringing lost souls to a decision for Christ. According to James F. White, "Finney and his associates represent a liturgical revolution based on pure pragmatism. . . . Pragmatism has triumphed over biblicism. The meaning of freedom has shifted from being free to follow scripture to being free to do what works."[65]

---

[63]White, *A Brief History of Christian Worship*, pp. 144-45; and James F. White, *Protestant Worship: Traditions in Transition* (Louisville: Westminster John Knox, 1989), p. 53.
[64]Charles Finney, *Lectures on Revivals of Religion*, ed. W. G. McLoughlin (Cambridge: Harvard University Press, 1960), p. 276; see esp. chap. 14, "Measures to Promote Revivals," pp. 250-76.
[65]White, *Protestant Worship*, p. 177. In fairness to Finney, it should not be suggested that Finney

According to Finney, the church had to recognize the changing conditions of American culture in order to be effective in reaching the lost. Without innovative new methods in evangelism (such as his own) it would be difficult or impossible for the church to gain "the attention of the world to religion." The church cannot, thought Finney, "command attention, without *very exciting* preaching, and sufficient *novelty* in measures, to get the public ear. . . . we must have more *exciting preaching,* to meet the character and wants of the age."[66] Finney had evidently concluded that historical precedents such as that of a Jonathan Edwards delivering in very undramatic fashion a doctrinally weighty sermon such as "Justification by Faith Alone" (1734)—and in so doing helping to ignite the Great Awakening—could no longer answer to the needs of the modern age. This focus on "excitement" as a point of contact in evangelism was the beginning of a trajectory in American evangelicalism that culminated in an entertainment mode of worship in some seeker-driven services of the present.

This desire for exciting preaching had the important consequences of elevating the position of the charismatic personality of the preacher in the evangelical tradition of frontier worship, of making the sermon central and other elements secondary, and of diminishing the role of the Lord's Supper. This latter development represented a significant shift in evangelical piety, for since the seventeenth century and well into the 1840s, "communion seasons" had been integral parts, and indeed the culminating climaxes, of Presbyterian revivals in Scotland and in America.[67] The excitement of frontier revival preaching tended

---

proposed in his "new measures" to be *contrary* to Scripture; White's point is that a discernable shift in a pragmatic direction was encouraged in American Protestantism by Finney's innovations.

[66]Finney, *Lectures on Revivals of Religion,* pp. 272-73, emphasis added.

[67]This important history has been retrieved in the important scholarly work of Leigh Eric Schmidt, *Holy Fairs: Scotland and the Making of American Revivalism,* 2nd ed. (Grand Rapids: Eerdmans, 2001). I wish to thank my colleague Garth Rosell for drawing my attention to this work. Schmidt demonstrates that prior to the "Finney revolution," Scottish and American revivalism was characterized by both fervent evangelistic preaching *and* high sacramental practice. Schmidt provides dramatic firsthand accounts of such "communion seasons" during the Kentucky and Cane Ridge revivals of 1803 in which an at times overpowering sense of the presence of Christ was experienced at Communion: The Presbyterian evangelist James McGready marveled at "God's power and presence" at the Red River camp meeting of 1803; "So many souls happy in the love of God, I never saw on earth before. . . . The exercise at the

to replace the Lord's Supper as the focus of revivalism as the nineteenth century wore on, and the Communion table was displaced by the anxious bench and the altar call as the places where the sinner could find a gracious God.[68]

It was not only the Presbyterians whose practices were accommodated to the new pressures of the American frontier and its pragmatic and individualistic spirit. It had been John Wesley's hope that Methodists in America would use his worship services largely adapted from the Anglican Book of Common Prayer, in which both sermon and the Lord's Supper would be present. Francis Asbury, however, facing the conditions of the frontier and the lack of ordained Methodist clergy, authorized in the 1789 *Doctrine and Discipline* a simplified preaching service, with Communion optional, that became the standard for subsequent Methodist worship.[69]

All the historical influences briefly surveyed have contributed to a diminished role for the Lord's Supper in the worship of many evangelical churches. These historical influences are compounded by other currents and influences in modern and postmodern American life. Postmodern philosophers and literary critics such as Jacques Derrida and others have argued for the deconstruction of texts and ordinary meanings in language, asserting that words are arbitrary signs or signifiers that point only to other arbitrary signs, and not beyond themselves to any transcendent realities.[70] In such a philosophical atmosphere a

---

tables was indeed a heaven upon earth. Christians at the tables, almost universally, from first to last, were so filled with joy unspeakable, and full of glory, that they might, with propriety, be compared to bottles filled with new wine"; the occasions were so glorious as to resemble for McGready the "descent of the New Jerusalem" depicted in the book of Revelation (pp. 63-64).

[68]See, further, John D. Witvliet, "Theological Issues in the Frontier Worship Tradition in Nineteenth Century America," in *Worship Seeking Understanding* (Grand Rapids: Baker Academic, 2003), pp. 179-200, on the influence of Finney and the diminishing role of the Lord's Supper. Witvliet notes that the Disciples of Christ, in practicing weekly Communion, were an exception to the general tendencies of much of nineteenth-century American evangelicalism.

[69]Doug Adams, *Meeting House to Camp Meeting: Toward a History of American Free Church Worship from 1620 to 1835* (Saratoga, Calif.: Modern Liturgy Resource Publications, 1981), p. 104.

[70]On Derrida, for example, see Christopher Norris, *Derrida* (Cambridge, Mass.: Harvard University Press, 1987), pp. 85-86: "From the moment that there is meaning there are nothing but signs. . . . To think logocentrically is to dream of a 'transcendental signified,' of a meaning outside and beyond the differential play of language that would finally put a stop to this un-

more biblical understanding of symbol as that which both points to and conveys a spiritual reality beyond the senses is not likely to flourish.

The hurried and fragmented conditions of modern American life also compound these problems; in our fast-food nation family meals are the exception, not the rule. Hurried moms and dads can be driving their children from one school or athletic activity to another and go for days without a leisured family meal or significant conversation. One Roman Catholic religious educator has raised the pointed question, "How do we teach the nature of the Eucharist as a *meal* to families who never eat together?"[71] In the workplace, lunchtime can be swallowed up by other business meetings or by isolated meals in a cubicle. The Eucharist began as a Passover meal celebrated by Jesus with his disciples,[72] and in the early church (cf. 1 Cor 11:20-22) the celebration was in the context of an *agape* or fellowship meal; only in later centuries was the agape meal abandoned. This loss of the sense and sensibility of the Eucharist as a meal has been theologically and spiritually damaging since it implies the loss of the sense of intimate fellowship and friendship that shared meals connoted in Old Testament and New Testament biblical cultures.

THE ROAD TO EUCHARISTIC RECOVERY: INSIGHTS FROM THE NEW TESTAMENT AND THE EARLY CHURCH

If many circumstances in church history have contributed to a sense of a real absence of the living, risen Christ at the table in many Protestant evangelical observances of the Lord's Supper, various aspects of the eucharistic celebrations in the New Testament and early church can contribute to a recovery of this reality and to a richer eucharistic experience. These insights include, for example, a more biblical understanding of the term "remembrance" *(anamnesis)* in the words of institution,

---

nerving predicament."

[71] Andrew D. Ciferni, "The Rituals of Dinner," *Assembly* 18, no. 3 (May 1992) <http://liturgy .nd.edu/assembly18-3aciferni.shtml>.

[72] Some New Testament scholars have argued that the Last Supper was not a Passover meal; for a defense of the historic understanding that the Last Supper was indeed a Passover meal, see Joachim Jeremias, *The Eucharistic Words of Jesus* (New York: Charles Scribner's Sons, 1966), chap. 1; and I. Howard Marshall, *Last Supper and Lord's Supper* (Grand Rapids: Eerdmans, 1980).

"do this in remembrance of me" (1 Cor 11:24); a recovery of the vivid sense of the presence of the risen Christ in his post-Easter table fellowship with the disciples in Luke/Acts; a recovery of the spiritual and theological reality of the believer's *mystical union* with Christ in the Communion of the Holy Spirit as the context within which every true Lord's Supper takes place; and a fresh appreciation of the spiritual power of the atonement as the basis for intimate fellowship of the believer with Christ at the table. We will reflect briefly on each of these considerations in turn.

When Jesus commanded the disciples to "do this in remembrance of me," it should be noted in the first instance that our English words "remember" or "remembrance" do not capture the spiritual depth and significance of the Greek word *anamnesis* that the apostle Paul uses in 1 Corinthians 11:24. Modern New Testament and liturgical scholarship has pointed out that this term in its original biblical context meant a "re-presenting" of a thing or event regarded not as being absent and only in the past, but rather being presently operative by its effects.[73] Jerome Kodell points out that "remembrance" in the Passover and Lord's Supper for the participants was "not simply in their subjective memory. In Hebrew thought, the thing remembered comes alive to the person as a present and effective reality."[74] Kodell cites the passage from the Mishnah in which the participant in the Passover meal is instructed as follows: "a man must regard himself as if he came forth himself out of Egypt" (Pesahim 10:4).[75] This statement in the Mishnah itself reflects the understanding of Deuteronomy 5:2-4, in which Moses tells the current generation of Israelites, poised on the plains of Moab and about to enter the promised land, "The LORD our God made a covenant with us at Horeb. It was not [only] with our fathers that the LORD made this covenant, but *with us*, with all of us who are alive here today. The

---

[73]Dix, *Shape of the Liturgy*, p. 245.

[74]Jerome Kodell, *The Eucharist in the New Testament* (Wilmington, Del.: Michael Glazier, 1988), p. 80. Similarly, H. Ringgren notes that in the Passover the "remembrance" involved a reenactment in symbolic form "of some basic event, the abiding results of which are made visibly present, and even reinforced, by the rites. . . . commemoration or 'memorial day' implies *re-experiencing* the results of the basic event as something that is present and real now" (*Sacrifice in the Bible* [London: Lutterworth, 1962], pp. 48, 50, emphasis added).

[75]Kodell, *Eucharist in the New Testament*, p. 80.

LORD spoke to *you* face to face out of the fire on the mountain" (emphasis added). Even though the generation of Israelites to whom Moses was speaking was not literally at Mount Sinai when God instituted the covenant, they are regarded by Moses as having been spiritually present; this re-presenting of the spiritual reality of Sinai is reenacted during each Passover meal for subsequent generations of Israelites. And so it is at the Lord's table: in a spiritual but very real sense, all later generations of Christians were there at the first Lord's Supper and continue to enter into communion with the living Christ and into the spiritual benefits of his death and resurrection conveyed by the new and better covenant.

These considerations show that the ordinary English sense of "remembrance" and a Zwinglian view of the sacrament are too weak to adequately translate the words of institution, "do this in remembrance of me." In a town's Memorial Day parade, there may be ceremonies and speeches that honor those who fought and died in foreign wars, but in remembering these people and events in the past, there is no expectation of an actual living presence of the dead among the living. At the Lord's table, on the other hand, while we indeed remember the death of Christ as a defining event in the past, we also celebrate his resurrection and living presence as a present reality, and look forward to his coming again in the future (1 Cor 11:26, "you proclaim the Lord's death until he comes"). As Kodell has pointed out, for Paul, "Lord" is Paul's favorite title for the risen Jesus (Rom 10:9; 1 Cor 12:3; Phil 2:11);[76] this Lord's table is not, so to speak, in a funeral parlor, but in a banquet room that experiences joyful fellowship with the Living One.

This understanding of remembrance can be reinforced by reflection on the meaning of the term "participation" *(koinonia)* in the body and blood of Christ in 1 Corinthians 10:16-20. This crucial text can be seen as the apostle Paul's own commentary—in fact, the earliest Christian commentary—on the meaning of the words of institution that he later quotes in 1 Corinthians 11:23-24. In admonishing the Corinthians to avoid idolatry and ritual meals in pagan temples he asks:

---

[76]Ibid., p. 77.

Is not the cup of thanksgiving for which we give thanks a participation
[koinonia] in the blood of Christ? And is not the bread that we break a
participation *[koinonia]* in the body of Christ? . . . Consider the people
of Israel: Do not those who eat the sacrifices participate *[koinonoi]* in the
altar? . . . the sacrifices of pagans are offered to demons, . . . and I do not
want you to be participants *[koinonous]* with demons.

It is clear from this text that to participate in the body and blood of
Christ means much more than simply to remember his death as a past
event; participation implies living communion and actual personal contact. Anthony Thiselton translates the word as "communal participation"; it denotes "having an active *common share* in the life, death,
resurrection *and presence* of Jesus Christ as the Lord."[77] Similarly,
J. Schattenmann renders *koinonia* in 1 Corinthians 10:16 as "participation" in the body and blood of Christ in the sense of "union with the
exalted Christ" and "incorporation into Jesus' death, burial, resurrection, and glory."[78] Ernst Kasemann notes that in this text Paul is expounding the word "is" *(estin)* in the words of institution in the sense of
"participation," *koinonia;* the cup and the bread are not bare symbols in
some Zwinglian sense; they "actually bring about the presence of what
is represented and therefore mediate participation in it." Kasemann
further observes, "whatever objections may be raised against the term
'Real Presence,' it expresses . . . what Paul wants to say."[79]

These realistic readings of participation are consistent with the parallels that the apostle cites in 1 Corinthians 10:18-19. In the Old Testament sacrifices, the fellowship offerings were understood as a fellowship meal between the Israelites and Yahweh who was present at the
meal. In Deuteronomy 12, for example, the Israelites are instructed to

[77]Anthony C. Thiselton, *The First Epistle to the Corinthians: A Commentary on the Greek Text*
(Grand Rapids: Eerdmans, 2000), p. 761, emphasis added. George Panikulam, in his compre-
hensive study, *Koinonia in the New Testament: A Dynamic Expression of Christian Life* (Rome:
Biblical Institute Press, 1979), p. 30, concludes that for Paul, *koinonia* "is at the same time
Christocentric and communitarian," i.e., that in Communion there is a real fellowship of the
believer with the risen Christ and with other believers in the church, the body of Christ.
[78]J. Schattenmann, "*koinonia*" [fellowship], in *New International Dictionary of New Testament
Theology*, ed. Colin Brown (Grand Rapids: Zondervan, 1975), 1:639-44 at 642-43.
[79]Ernst Kasemann, *Essays on New Testament Themes* (London: SCM Press, 1964), "The Pauline
Doctrine of the Lord's Supper," p. 28.

make their sacrifices in the place that the Lord will choose, and there "*in the presence of the* LORD *your God,* you and your families shall eat and shall rejoice" (Deut 12:7, emphasis added); bring "your burnt offerings and sacrifices. . . . And there rejoice before the LORD your God. . . . [E]at them in the presence of the LORD your God" (Deut 12:11-12, 18).[80] Yahweh was not thought of as absent when the priest and people shared in some of the meat offered on the altar.

As Larry Hurtado has pointed out, in the Greco-Roman world of the New Testament numerous texts from pagan sources show that "the god in whose honor the meal was held was understood to be present at the table participating in some spiritual way in the meal . . . as its host or guest of honor."[81] When in 1 Corinthians 10:20 the apostle warns the Corinthians to avoid having "participation" with demons, he could, for example, be thinking of a cultic meal celebrated in a function room of the temple of Apollo or another god, to which their pagan neighbors might have invited them. To participate in such a cultic meal would open the Corinthians to the real influence of the demon who is actually present in the pagan idols and at the meal/sacrifice. For Paul, pagan worship is not merely a matter of thinking about a pagan deity. The rituals open one up to real spiritual powers.[82] Being a participant in a meal dedicated to Apollo would open the participant to the (malig-

---

[80]As Alfred Cave has observed, in the Old Testament fellowship offerings, the feast "was a call, as every Oriental mind would especially realize, to fellowship and friendship . . . the way for joyous reunion. . . . It is Jehovah taking the sinner to His house, preparing him a feast, and eating and drinking with him at His table" (*The Scriptural Doctrine of Sacrifice* [Edinburgh: T & T Clark, 1877], p. 127).

[81]Larry Hurtado, *At the Origins of Christian Worship* (Grand Rapids: Eerdmans, 2000), p. 27 n. 37; citing, among other examples, a text from Oxyrhynchos that reads, "The god calls you to a banquet being held in the Thoereion tomorrow from the ninth hour," and other texts cited in G. H. R. Horsley, "Invitations to the *kline* [meal] of Sarapis," in *New Documents Illustrating Early Christianity,* ed. G. H. R. Horsley (North Ryde, N.S.W.: The Ancient History Documentary Research Centre, Macquarie University, 1981), pp. 5-9.

[82]Modern parallels to these pagan concepts, in which the image or idol of the god or goddess is thought of as the actual location in which the spirit of the deity dwells and is mediated to the worshiper can be found, for example, in Hinduism. Diana Eck, a specialist in comparative religions, points out that "the image is the real embodiment of the deity. It is not just a device for focusing of human vision, but is charged with the presence of the god . . . [popular *bhakti* or devotional piety] sees the image "as one of the many ways in which the Lord becomes accessible to men and women, evoking their affections" (*Darśan: Seeing the Divine Image in India* [Chambersburg, Penn.: Anima Books, 1985], p. 45).

nant) spiritual presence of the demon inhabiting the image of Apollo;
conversely, the believer, in coming to the meal of the risen Lord Christ,
is being opened to the spiritual presence and power of the one who is
the true host and celebrant of the meal. To participate in the body and
blood of Christ involves, then, real-time, person-to-person, spirit-to-
spirit contact with Christ. It is as different, so to speak, as merely thinking about a blood transfusion and actually receiving one, or perhaps
more personally, merely thinking about kissing your wife and actually
kissing and embracing her.

In recent years New Testament and liturgical scholars have increasingly realized that the theology of Luke-Acts can make a vital contribution to traditional understandings of the Lord's Supper that have
tended to focus almost exclusively on the words of institution recorded
in 1 Corinthians 11:17-34. As I. Howard Marshall has pointed out,
"Luke's contribution is to stress that the Lord's Supper is the joyous
celebration of salvation in the presence of the risen Lord."[83] Three elements of Marshall's observation are worthy of careful attention: the
joyous ethos of the Lord's Supper in Lukan theology, the sense of the
presence of Christ in the post-Easter table fellowship and the grounding
of these latter two elements in the fundamental reality of the *resurrection* of Jesus. All three elements are found in the relevant texts in Luke-
Acts.

In Luke 24:13-35 the risen Jesus appears to two disciples on the road
to Emmaus, opens the Scriptures (Luke 24:25-27) and then enjoys table fellowship with them: "When he was at the table with them, he
took bread, gave thanks, broke it and began to give it to them. Then
their eyes were opened and they recognized him, and he disappeared
from their sight" (Luke 24:30-31). The disciples returned to Jerusalem
and told the others "how Jesus was recognized by them when he broke
the bread" (Luke 24:35). I. Howard Marshall observes concerning this
Lukan passage that Jesus is preparing the disciples for "further occasions when his presence would still be with them but not in a visible or
tangible manner. . . . it is becoming evident that the exposition of the

---

[83]Marshall, *Last Supper and Lord's Supper*, p. 133.

Scriptures and the breaking of bread are the modes by which the presence of the risen Jesus is known."[84]

In Luke 24:30 the sequence of words "took . . . gave thanks . . . broke . . . gave" unmistakably recalls both the eucharistic actions of Jesus at the Last Supper (cf. Lk 22:19, "he took bread, gave thanks and broke it, and gave it to them, saying, 'This is my body given for you; do this in remembrance of me'"), and the actions of the feeding of the five thousand: "Taking the five loaves . . . he gave thanks and broke them. . . . Then he gave them to the disciples to set before the people. They all ate and were satisfied" (Lk 9:16-17).

Luke makes it clear that the joyful table fellowship that Jesus enjoyed with his disciples before his death and crucifixion now continues after the resurrection.[85] Perhaps more clearly than the other evangelists, Luke shows that the table fellowship of Jesus with sinners, so prominent in his Galilean and Judean ministries, now continues in the post-Easter period, demonstrating that this open table fellowship is, as Jerome Kodell has suggested, a "parable of God's offer of life and salvation to all. Jesus does not turn away from the outcast, the sinner, the betrayer. . . . The meals portray Jesus as teacher and healer, the one who is willing to forgive and to reconcile."[86]

---

[84]Ibid., p. 126. It is notable that in the Emmaus events recorded in Lk 24:13-35, two elements of Christian worship—the exposition of the Scriptures and the celebration of the Supper—that in later Protestant practice have been separated are here held together. The modern evangelical churches might well be reminded that, in effect, "What God has joined together, let no man separate."

[85]This insight has become incorporated into the eucharistic understanding of the modern ecumenical and liturgical renewal movements, as evidenced, for example, in the influential text, *Baptism, Eucharist and Ministry* (Geneva: World Council of Churches, 1982), p. 8: "After his resurrection, the Lord made his presence known to his disciples in the breaking of bread. Thus the Eucharist continues these meals of Jesus during his earthly life and after his resurrection, always as a sign of the Kingdom. . . . Christ commanded his disciples thus to remember and *encounter him* in this sacramental meal, as the continuing people of God, until his return" (emphasis added).

[86]Kodell, *Eucharist in the New Testament*, p. 117. This sense of continuing table fellowship with the risen Christ is not limited to Luke-Acts, however; in Rev 3:20, Christ, after the resurrection *and* the ascension, says to the church at Laodicea: "Here I am! I stand at the door and knock. If anyone hears my voice and opens the door, I will come in and eat with him, and he with me." Alan Culpepper has shown that while the Gospel of John does not contain the narrative of institution, nonetheless, in the Johannine communities, "Participation in the community's sacred meal was a vital element in sustaining the life of the resurrection. . . . [In John] those who do participate in the sacred meal have both eternal life and the promise of future

Meals and table fellowship in the book of Acts are important occasions during which the risen Lord is present with his disciples, both visibly and bodily before the ascension, and invisibly and spiritually after the ascension. On one occasion, "while he was eating with them" he gave them the command to wait in Jerusalem for the promised gift of the Holy Spirit (Acts 1:4).[87] Luke describes the worship of the early Jerusalem church as characterized by devotion to the "apostles' teaching and to the fellowship, to the breaking of bread and to prayer. . . . They broke bread in their homes and ate together with glad and sincere hearts, praising God and enjoying the favor of all the people" (Acts 2:42, 46-47). New Testament scholars generally see the term "breaking of bread" in Acts as a technical term for the Eucharist; in this Lukan text, which has inspired so many renewal movements in church history, the Eucharist of the early Jerusalem community is depicted as both a joyous and frequent practice. The joyous nature of the eucharistic fellowship in the Jerusalem church reflected both the presence of the Holy Spirit given at Pentecost, and the sense of the continuing presence of the risen Christ among the believers.

In Acts 10 Peter addresses Cornelius and his household, giving witness to Jesus' death and resurrection. The risen Christ did not appear to all the people, but to chosen witnesses, to "us who ate and drank with him after he rose from the dead" (Acts 10:41). Peter summarizes various occasions during which the disciples enjoyed table fellowship with their risen Lord. In Acts 20:7 the apostle Paul and his companions are in Troas, and Luke tells us that "on the first day of the week [Sunday] we came together to break bread." Paul prolongs his discourse until midnight, and then subsequently restores Eutychus to life (Acts 20:8-12). In this account we see combined the three elements of the celebration of the Sunday Eucharist, the exposition of the Word, and

---

resurrection" (Jn 6:53-57) (Alan Culpepper, "Realized Eschatology in the Experience of the Johannine Community," in *The Resurrection of Jesus in the Gospel of John,* ed. Craig Koester and Reimund Bieringer [Tübingen: Mohr Siebeck, 2008], pp. 270-71).

[87]The "promise" may be connected with Old Testament prophetic passages such as Joel 2:28-32 and Is 44:3 ("I will pour water on the thirsty land, and streams on the dry ground; I will pour out my Spirit on your offspring, and my blessing on your descendants") that looked forward to a great outpouring of the Spirit in the last days.

the presence of the power of the risen Lord to heal and restore (cf. 1 Cor 11:18, 20; 12:27-28).[88]

In the early church the *"certainty of the Resurrection* was the essential religious motive of the primitive Lord's Supper," as Oscar Cullmann has argued,[89] and this is notably the case in Lukan theology. This latter point has been argued forcefully by Hans-Josef Klauck, and his conclusions merit extensive citation at this point:

> Without the resurrection of Jesus and the experience of Easter on the part of the disciples, there would never have been a regular practice of the Lord's Supper, because it would have lacked the central theological presupposition . . . the communal Lord's Supper was the place at which the believer who was temporally removed from the first Easter, could gain the assurance of the presence of the risen Lord. Seen as a whole, the resurrection of Jesus is the real foundation for the shaping of the practice of the Lord's Supper and the conceptual development of sacramental categories. . . . The determinative theological impulse for the development of a new Christian meal, which is a kind of recapitulation of the communal Eating with Jesus, comes first of all, from the Easter event.[90]

This critical observation—that the very existence and continuance of the practice of the Lord's Supper in the early church presupposed and was energized by the reality of the ongoing experience of the presence of the resurrected Lord—needs to be recovered by the contemporary church. If Jesus had only died on the cross and not risen from the dead, there would have been no Christian church, and no "doing this" in remembrance of him, no sense of his continuing presence with them at the table.

As Yngve Brilioth has observed, just as the risen Lord was present to the disciples at Emmaus, so it is today that "he is present 'in the midst'

---

[88]Klauck ("Lord's Supper," p. 366) sees clear allusions in this account of Paul's ministry in Troas to the accounts of the Last Supper in the upper room; the upper room in Troas is likewise a place of fellowship (Acts 20:7, "we came together to break bread"), a place of light (Acts 20:8, "there were many lamps in the upstairs room"), and a place of life (Acts 20:12, "the people took the young man [Eutychus] home alive and were greatly comforted").

[89]Cullmann and Leenhardt, *Essays on the Lord's Supper,* p. 12.

[90]Klauck, "Lord's Supper," pp. 366, 370.

at every Eucharist as the true celebrant; present, according to this point
of view, rather 'at' than 'on' the Holy Table, personally feeding his own
with the sacred gifts, and imparting his own great gift, the forgiveness
of sins and communion with God through him."[91]

This sense that the risen Christ was the true celebrant at the table
was also expressed by Bishop Handley Moule of Durham, an evangelical bishop of the Church of England, at a conference at which he spoke
in 1900:

> I believe that if our eyes . . . were opened to the unseen, we should in-
> deed behold our Lord present at our Communions. There and then,
> assuredly, if anywhere and at any time, He remembers His promise,
> "Where two or three are gathered together in My Name, there am I in
> the midst of them" [Mt 18:20; cf. 28:20, "surely I am with you to the
> end of the age"]. Such special presence, the promised congregational
> presence, is perfectly mysterious in mode, but absolutely true in fact; no
> creation of our imagination or emotion, but an object for our faith. I
> believe that our Lord, so present, not *on* the Holy Table, but *at* it, would
> be seen Himself in our presence to bless the Bread and the Wine for a
> holy use, and to distribute them to his disciples. . . . I believe that we
> should worship Him thus present in the midst of us in His living grace,
> with unspeakable reverence, thanksgiving, joy and love.[92]

In this remarkable statement Moule anticipated some of the key insights of modern Lukan New Testament scholarship as noted above,
and captured the joyous sense of the experience of table fellowship with
the risen Christ that was so evident in the early church.

It should be abundantly clear, then, that the church was never meant
to merely "remember" a *dead Jesus* at the Communion table. Believers
indeed remember with profound reverence and gratitude the atoning
death of Christ, as a core conviction of the faith, but in the New Testament, the death of Christ is integrally tied to the resurrection, apart
from which it would not have spiritual power and meaning. "He was

---

[91]Yngve Brilioth, *Eucharistic Faith and Practice: Evangelical and Catholic* (London: SPCK, 1930),
p. 286. Brilioth was a bishop in the Swedish Lutheran Church and an important contributor
to the liturgical renewal movement in his day.
[92]Cited in ibid., p. 219, emphasis added.

delivered over to death for our sins *and was raised to life for our justification*" (Rom 4:25). Cross and resurrection are distinguished but should never be separated in the faith and life of the church. Unfortunately, in the history of the Western church, and typically in modern evangelical churches, at the table the death of Christ is remembered, but with only a muted recollection of Christ's victory over death, and a largely absent sense of his actual, continuing spiritual presence with the church.

The symbolism of the crucifix in many Roman Catholic churches—a dead Jesus on the cross—has focused Western piety on the death of Christ in the past rather than on the joy of fellowship with the living Lord in the present. Consequently, for many in the modern church, the experience of the Lord's Supper can, emotionally, feel more like a funeral or a wake, when it could rather be more like that of a joyful wedding feast. The rediscovery and reintroduction of this more joyous note into many modern eucharistic liturgies ("Christ has died, *Christ has risen,* Christ will come again") is a welcome contribution of the modern liturgical movement that deserves even more attention and emphasis than it has yet received.[93]

I have reflected on the concepts of "remembrance" *(anamnesis)* and "participation" *(koinonia)* in the Pauline texts on the Lord's Supper and on the Lukan witness to the post-resurrection table fellowship of Jesus and the disciples. I'll now remark briefly on three other aspects of biblical theology that are germane to a robust eucharistic understanding: the believer's mystical union with Christ, the benefits of the atonement and the "transparency" of the material creation to spirit. I have already noted how, in the history of the church, eucharistic reflection since the Middle Ages has been preoccupied with the question of how Christ was to be understood as being present in the physical elements. This narrowing of focus has had the effect of obscuring the broader scope of Christian doctrine as the proper framework for understanding the fullness of the eucharistic reality. These remarks, then, suggest some systematic connections that may contribute to such a fuller understanding.

---

[93]It could be acknowledged that in general, the Orthodox churches historically appear to have succeeded more than those of the West in preserving a healthy balance between the cross and the resurrection in eucharistic piety and liturgical practice.

In the first instance we note the reality of the believer's mystical union with Christ.[94] Jesus teaches the disciples that he is the true vine, and they are the branches; apart from him they can do nothing (Jn 15:1-8). Abiding in him is the source of all life and true fruitfulness. This vivid image is one of an ongoing, intimate, living and organic union over time, with the life of Christ flowing into the believer. The image teaches that the relationship of Christ to the disciple is not mechanical, distant, atomistic or only "voluntary," in the sense of a human organization organized according to some social contract theory. Rather, life is bonded to life, and the life of Christ is flowing into the life of the believer.

Such an intimate, organic understanding of the believer's relationship to Christ finds expression in Pauline theology in both the concepts of the body of Christ and the church as the bride of Christ. For Paul, at conversion the believer is baptized by the Holy Spirit into the body of Christ: "For we were all baptized by one Spirit into one body—whether Jews or Greeks, slave or free—and we were all given the one Spirit to drink" (1 Cor 12:13). There is a common experience of the Spirit shared by all who are truly converted, irrespective of their ethnic origin or social or economic class. This initial experience and gift of the Spirit is not merely an initial experience: the body into which the believer is baptized remains an abiding metaphysical reality—whether or not the believer is conscious of it at any given time. The reality of the body of believers and their unity with Christ is in fact the basis for the apostle's distress in the face of their disunity when the Corinthians celebrated the supper (1 Cor 11:17-22). Their disunity and selfish individualism contradicted their actual unity of being the body that the one loaf (1

---

[94]This theme is expounded in relation to the Eucharist in Nevin, *The Mystical Presence*, especially pp. 151-256. For biblical and theological studies of the mystical union, see, for example, John Ashton, *The Religion of Paul the Apostle* (New Haven, Conn.: Yale University Press, 2000), esp. chap. 4; Richard B. Gaffin, "Union with Christ: Some Biblical and Theological Reflections," in *Always Reforming: Explorations in Systematic Theology*, ed. A. T. B. McGowan (Downers Grove, Ill.: IVP Academic, 2006), pp. 271-88; Paul Brooks Leath, "The 'In Christ' Phrase of Paul: A Genetic and Interpretive Study of the Interrelationship of the Pauline Mysticism and Concept of Salvation," Th.D. thesis, New Orleans Baptist Theological Seminary, 1946; and R. Tudor Jones, "Union with Christ: The Existential Nerve of Puritan Piety," *Tyndale Bulletin* 41, no. 2 (1990): 186-208.

Cor 10:17) was intended to exemplify and strengthen.

J. J. von Allmen has noted that for Paul, Christ's intention in the Eucharist was "to incorporate believers into *Christ himself,* gift and Giver being received together."[95] Similarly, Ernst Kasemann observes that the Lord's Supper takes place within the context of "the Body of Christ, in the presence of the Exalted One who, having passed through death, now reigns."[96] The risen Christ, present to the church, as head of the living body, exists not as an isolated individual in heaven, unto himself, "but in relationship to us and on our behalf. . . . He exists for us 'in the body,' he gives us 'bodily' participation in himself . . . he who is now exalted can, in the Lord's Supper, continually give us that which in his death he gave us once and for all."[97]

John A. T. Robinson, in his influential study *The Body: A Study in Pauline Theology,* has argued that the concept of the body of Christ forms the keystone of Paul's theology. He claims that the analogy of the human body holds because Christians "are in literal fact the risen organism of Christ's person in all its concrete reality." Each believer is not merely "like" the body; "each of them *is* [a member of] the body of Christ, in that each is the physical complement and extension of the one and same Person and Life."[98] Robinson is thus forcefully emphasizing the ontological and not merely metaphorical nature of this Pauline concept.

To recognize this crucial aspect of Pauline theology is not to endorse some notion of the church as a "continuing incarnation" that erases in a pantheistic sense the distinction between Creator and creature. It is, rather, a recognition of the real, continuing communion of the saints, and of the actual bond created between believers by the Holy Spirit in the body of Christ.

The believer's intimate mystical union with Christ is expressed in

---

[95]J. J. von Allmen, *The Lord's Supper* (London: Lutterworth, 1969), p. 56, emphasis added.

[96]Kasemann, *Essays on New Testament Themes,* p. 132.

[97]Ibid., p. 133.

[98]John A. T. Robinson, *The Body* (Philadelphia: Westminster Press, 1952), p. 51. It may be observed that the basic insights from biblical theology drawn from the New Testament by the bishop at this time (1952) were much sounder and more orthodox than his later controversial and heterodox writings such as *Honest to God.*

Paul not only in the image of the body, but also through that of the *bride* of Christ, notably in the well-known passage in Ephesians 5:22-33. Husbands are instructed to love their wives as Christ loved the church (Eph 5:25), his bride. Just as a man feeds and cares for his own body, so Christ does the church—for we are members of his body (Eph 5:29-30). Here the images of body and bride coalesce, and both are images of a mysterious (Eph 5:32, "a profound mystery") and intimate union. As Allmen has noted, this marital imagery of Christ's relationship to his people is not limited to the fifth chapter of Ephesians: elsewhere in the New Testament Jesus is described as the bridegroom (Mk 2:20) and he has his bride (Jn 3:29); the coming kingdom is described as a marriage feast (Mt 22:2-14); and Jesus' first miracle in the Gospel of John is performed at a village wedding (Jn 2:1-11).[99]

At this point the reader may be more inclined to take seriously— indeed, "ontologically"—the reality of the believer's mystical union with Christ, expressed in the images of vine, body and bride. Yet the question may remain, So what? What difference does the mystical union as an "ontological" reality make when I come to the Communion table?

An answer could be suggested along the following lines. When I come to church on a Sunday that Communion is being celebrated, I can approach the table with a consciousness that I am already a member of the living body of Christ, his bride and a branch in the vine. I have been redeemed for the specific purpose of enjoying an intimate, loving relationship with my Savior. This spiritual reality is a fact (ontologically) whether I am aware of it or not (epistemically) when I walk through the front door of the church. However, to the extent that I am aware of this spiritual-ontological reality of my mystical union with Christ, this can enhance my experience of communion with Christ at the table. The context in which an event takes place and the self-understandings and expectations of the participants can have a substantial effect on the quality and nature of the participants' experience.

As an example, consider the invited guests at a wedding and wed-

---

[99]Allmen, *The Lord's Supper*, p. 57.

ding reception and the bride and bridegroom themselves. The guests presumably enjoy the wedding and the reception, but their context of experience—"outside" the wedding vows and the actuality of the marriage relationship entered into by the bride and groom—affect their expectations; they do not expect the same type of experience (at least during the wedding and reception) that the bride and groom expect and hope for on their honeymoon! Conscious awareness and appreciation of the reality of my mystical union with Christ can then enhance my experience at the Communion table, insofar as my own sense of Christian identity is that of one redeemed for the purpose of enjoying intimate, loving communion with the Savior. Awareness of the actual fact of the mystical union can affect positively my expectations and experience. I come to the table not as a stranger or spectator or even just as a guest, but as a *beloved bride* of the bridegroom. Perhaps too many Christians do not experience a richer sense of communion with Christ at the table because their expectations are too low—and their low expectations reflect a low consciousness of who they are in union with Christ.

This expectation of a more intimate communion with Christ at the table can also be enhanced by a stronger sense of the connection between the atonement and the Eucharist. It is, of course, commonly well understood that the central point of the death of Christ is the forgiveness of sins, and that in his institution of the supper, Christ explicitly connected his atoning death and his shed blood with the forgiveness of sins: "This [cup] is my blood of the covenant, which is poured out for many for the forgiveness of sins" (Mt 26:28). It is also commonly understood that the elements, received in faith, either "signify" (Zwingli) or actually convey (Luther, Calvin) the forgiveness of sins. What needs to be added to this common understanding, which is true as far as it goes, is the recognition that enjoying the benefit of having one's sins forgiven—and this is indeed a monumentally important aspect of the divine-human relationship—does not necessarily translate, in practice and experience, into the reality of an *intimate relationship* and sense of communion with Christ. To clarify: consider the case of parents and a daughter who was brutally abused and raped by a criminal; the daugh-

ter and parents, in an extraordinary act of Christian grace may forgive
the rapist, and yet have no desire for a continuing, much less intimate
relationship of friendship with the forgiven criminal; all parties may
choose to go their separate ways. The extraordinary character of the
gospel, the truly astounding good news, is not merely that my sins are
forgiven, but further, that on this basis, Christ wants to draw me as his
bride into loving, intimate communion with himself, and through himself, into the unending love within the inner life of the Trinity.

The writer of Hebrews makes this crucial point clear, that the blood
of Christ cleanses us from all sin; consequently intimacy with God, and
closeness of relationship to him, is now possible (not just after death)
for a believer in a way that was not possible in the Old Covenant: "since
we have confidence to enter the Most Holy Place by the blood of Jesus,
. . . and since we have a great priest over the house of God, let us *draw
near* to God with a sincere heart *in full assurance of faith*" (Heb 10:19,
21-22, emphasis added). To the objective aspects of the atonement (forgiveness of sins) we need to add a stronger sense of and appropriation of
the subjective benefits and experience (intimate relationship), for indeed the fundamental purpose and design of the atonement—indeed,
of the incarnation, resurrection and entire plan of redemption—was to
draw believer and God together in the enjoyment of intimate relationship. The forensic and penal imagery of the cross and the courtroom
needs to be completed by the marital image of the bride and bridegroom. The verdict of "not guilty" has been pronounced not merely so
that the accused can go free to walk the city streets alone, but in order
to be invited to experience the joyous experience of the wedding feast
and the bridal chamber, a foretaste of which is experienced as Christ
the bridegroom awaits to meet us at his table. "He has taken me to the
banquet hall, and his banner over me is love" (Song 2:4).

In addition to the doctrines of the mystical union and the atonement, the biblical theology of creation calls for fresh reflection in relation to the theology of the Eucharist and understandings of real spiritual presence. A dualistic separation between mind and matter
exacerbated by the impact of the modern scientific worldview since the
seventeenth century has made it more difficult for many modern Chris-

tians to see the material elements of bread and wine as meaningful conveyances of spiritual realities and grace.

As the early church struggled to formulate its theology of creation, it faced challenges on two fronts: the Aristotelian doctrine of the eternity of matter, and Gnostic denials of the goodness of matter and the human body.[100] In the confession of faith that was later to be known as the Apostles' Creed, the opening statement, "I believe in God the Father Almighty, Maker of heaven and earth," addressed both challenges. Matter was not eternal, nor was it evil; the God who made heaven and earth, and who pronounced them "good," was the God and Father of Jesus Christ, not an inferior God who made an evil, material world from which a spiritual elite should flee, as the Gnostics thought. The material world was an expression of the goodness and wisdom of a beneficent God; the human body could in fact be the subject of divine incarnation and redemption, and material elements such as bread and wine could be suffused with the gracious presence of the divine.

In the modern period, however, it has not been gnosticism but rather scientific materialism that has impeded "sacramental"[101] perceptions of nature and material objects. In what has been called the "mechanization of the world picture," images of a clockwork universe replaced the earlier, premodern organic and sacramental images of the natural world.[102] The new scientific outlook exemplified in Galileo, Newton and Descartes had the effect of devaluing secondary qualities of material objects such as color and taste in favor of the presumably more real primary qualities of particles in motion, as described by impersonal mathematical equations. Descartes's sharp dualism of mind and matter, of "extended substances" and "thinking substances" promoted a mechanistic understanding of the world, and had the effect of removing God from immediate involvement in the world. In the judgment of Colin

---

[100]On the Gnostic sense of alienation from the material world see Hans Jonas, *The Gnostic Religion: The Message of the Alien God and the Beginnings of Christianity* (Boston: Beacon Press, 1963).

[101]It should be noted here that the term "sacramental" sense of nature is not intended in a pantheistic sense, but rather in a biblical sense that the creation can be seen, through the eyes of faith, as suffused with the "glory of God."

[102]See E. J. Dijksterhuis, *The Mechanization of the World Picture* (London: Oxford University Press, 1961), esp. pp. 431-33, "The Mechanization of Qualities."

Gunton, "Descartes' philosophy, along with Galileo's, contained the seeds of deism."[103] A deistic view of God's relation to the world emphasizes God's transcendence to the detriment of divine immanence. If God is thought to be essentially transcendent to the world, then there will be little expectation that the Spirit of God might operate directly through and with the material elements in the Eucharist.[104]

In light of this scientific "disenchantment" of the natural world,[105] Christian theology needs to retrieve those elements of the biblical tradition that can help the Christian imagination see the created world and material objects not as opaque, so to speak, but rather as transparent or translucent to the divine glory, grace and Spirit. The Scriptures teach that the material world is "very good" (Gen 1:31) and has intrinsic value in the sight of God, not merely instrumental value for human use. The preincarnate Son, involved in the acts of creation (Jn 1:3, "through him all things were made"; Heb 1:2; Col 1:16), as the Wisdom of God "was filled with delight day after day . . . rejoicing in his whole world, and delighting in mankind" (Prov 8:30-31). Ephesians 1:4, in teaching that God the Father "chose us in him [Christ] *before the creation of the world*," implies that the fitness of the universe for life is no accident, but rather that God created the world with a spiritual purpose—the redemption of humans—already in view. The fine-tuning of the basic laws and constants of nature[106] can be seen, from a biblical perspective, to show how matter is inherently friendly to spirit and spiritual purposes, since it was envisioned as such before time began.

---

[103]Colin E. Gunton, *The Triune Creator: A Historical and Systematic Study* (Grand Rapids: Eerdmans, 1998), pp. 126-27.

[104]Biblical theism balances both the transcendence of God over creation and the immanence of God within creation, e.g., Ps 139:7-10, "Where can I go from your Spirit? . . . if I make my bed in the depths, you are there." The Spirit of God is present within the material world and material objects without being limited or circumscribed by them.

[105]In the nineteenth century the romantic and transcendentalist movements were important reactions to this "disenchantment" of nature. In the current modern and postmodern climates, movements such as New Age spiritualities, the Wiccan and neo-Pagan revivals, interest in Eastern and Native American religions, various expressions of the "Green" environmental movement such as "deep ecology" and the "Gaia" philosophy, and the *Harry Potter* phenomenon point, in their different ways, to a longing for the "re-enchantment" of nature.

[106]On the fine-tuning of the basic laws and constants of nature, without which carbon-based human life would not be possible, see Martin Rees, *Just Six Numbers: The Deep Forces that Shape the Universe* (New York: Basic Books, 2000).

The incarnation of Jesus Christ, which could rightly be considered the fundamental miracle of the entire Christian faith, in which the eternal, purely spiritual Son joins himself forever to humanity in the form of a real material body, is the most emphatic repudiation imaginable of any gnostic devaluation of matter. Matter is not opaque to the divine presence, purpose or glory. Furthermore, at the transfiguration, the uncreated divine glory of God shines forth in the face of Jesus Christ, anticipating the final resurrection and glorification of believers, indeed the glorification of the cosmos in a luminous new creation (Rev 21–22). The goodness of the material creation and human embodiment is also powerfully affirmed in the bodily resurrection of Christ, his glorified body being itself a pointer to the glorious new creation. It is along these lines that biblical theology can help restore a Christian eucharistic imagination that can perceive, by faith, the presence, grace and glory of God in the sacramental event, without repudiating the penultimate truths of a scientific understanding of the world.

INSIGHTS FROM ECUMENICAL THEOLOGY, RECENT PHILOSOPHY AND CYBERSPACE

Since the 1960s there have been ecumenical dialogues involving Anglican, Roman Catholic, Lutheran, Methodist and Presbyterian churches in a search for greater degrees of visible unity, ecclesiastical cooperation and liturgical renewal.[107] There has been significant convergence—but not unanimity—in eucharistic theology and in discussions of real spiritual presence. As the Lutheran liturgical scholar Frank Senn has noted, a very significant element in these eucharistic discussions was the attempt of some Roman Catholic theologians to advance beyond the exclusive identification of Christ's presence with the physical elements of bread and wine, and to frame this understanding in terms of the actual experience of persons enjoying a communal meal rather than in terms of substances and Aristotelian metaphysics. "What one encounters in a

---

[107]For a survey of these trends, see John Reumann, *The Supper of the Lord: The New Testament, Ecumenical Dialogues, and Faith and Order on Eucharist* (Philadelphia: Fortress, 1985), pp. 78-201, and Frank Senn, *Christian Liturgy: Catholic and Evangelical* (Minneapolis: Augsburg, 1997), pp. 651-57, "Ecumenical Convergence on Eucharistic Theology."

shared meal," notes Senn, "is the presence of other persons and not just the food elements that are consumed."[108]

Roman Catholic theologians such as Eduard Schillebeeckx proposed, as alternatives to transubstantiation, notions of "transignification" (changed meaning) and "transfinalization" (changed purpose), in which the elements of bread and wine took on new meaning, purpose and indeed spiritual reality in the divinely ordained context of the Eucharist and the words of institution.[109] In a very significant historical observation, Schillebeeckx drew attention to the fact that in Roman Catholic theology the identification (and effectively, limitation) of Christ's real presence to the physical elements of the sacrament dates only from the time of Duns Scotus in the thirteenth century.[110] While it is true that attention began to shift toward the physical elements at least by the ninth century with Paschasius Radbertus, it is nevertheless the case that in the early church there was a more holistic sense of the Eucharist as event and action within which the meaning of the celebration was understood.

Schlillebeeckx argued for a shift of emphasis from objects to events, and to a more personal sense of Christ's presence not only in the Eucharist but also "in the service of the Word and in the liturgical assembly of the faithful. He is also really present in anyone who is in a state of grace. . . . he is also really present in the Eucharist."[111] While such new views of "transignification" were not to be officially endorsed by the Vatican, they were fruitful points of ecumenical dialogue and can in fact be incorporated in the understanding of real spiritual presence that is being advanced in the present essay.

Some of these new insights concerning real presence were to be in-

---

[108]Senn, *Christian Liturgy*, pp. 651-52.
[109]See Eduard Schillebeeckx, *The Eucharist* (New York: Sheed and Ward, 1968), chap. 2, "A New Approach Towards the Formulation of Faith"; for an overview and analysis of these developments by a Roman Catholic scholar, see Powers, *Eucharistic Theology*, chap. 4, "The Real Presence and 'Transignification.'"
[110]Schillebeeckx, *The Eucharist*, p. 103.
[111]Ibid. He argues that in such an understanding "an attempt is made above all to situate this presence within the sphere of Christ's real presence *in the believer* and *in the whole believing community* . . . the eucharistic presence is thus no longer isolated. We no longer say, 'Christ is there' without asking for whom he is present," p. 104, emphasis added.

corporated into Roman Catholic liturgical understanding at the Second Vatican Council. In the important *Constitution on the Sacred Liturgy*, it was significantly noted that the personal presence of Christ during gatherings for worship was to be encountered throughout the liturgy, not only in the eucharistic elements:

> To accomplish so great a work [salvation], Christ is always present in His Church, especially in her liturgical celebrations. . . . By His power He is present in the sacraments, so that when a man baptizes it is really Christ himself who baptizes. He is present in His word, since it is He himself who speaks when the Holy Scriptures are read in the church. He is present, finally, when the church prays and sings, for He promised: "Where two or three are gathered together for my sake, there am I in the midst of them" (Mt 18:20).[112]

According to Joseph Powers, the Council thus situated the presence of Christ throughout the worship service, in the wider context of all the actions in which the Church celebrates Christ's redemptive work.[113]

Certain trends in modern philosophy may be mentioned for the help they might provide for a renewal of the evangelical eucharistic experience. These remarks are not intended to provide a comprehensive discussion, but only to draw attention to developments that merit further investigation. Mention has already been made of a renewed interest in liturgical circles in the role of ritual and symbol in Christian worship.[114] In the 1940s Susanne Langer argued in her influential *Philosophy in a New Key* that symbols were crucial conveyers of meaning not only in the arts and literature and religion but in all aspects of human experience. Reacting to a scientific and historical positivism that would reduce all meaningful language to the discourse of science, mathematics,

---

[112]*The Documents of Vatican II*, ed. Walter Abbott, S.J. (New York: Corpus Books, 1966), pp. 140-41.

[113]Powers, *Eucharistic Theology*, pp. 131-32.

[114]E.g., Bradshaw and Melloh, *Foundations of Ritual Studies;* and Cooke and Macy, *Christian Symbol and Ritual.* See also Catherine Bell, *Ritual Theory, Ritual Practice* (New York: Oxford University Press, 1992), and idem, *Ritual: Perspectives and Dimensions* (New York: Oxford University Press, 1997); cf. Evelyn Underhill, *Worship* (New York: Harper & Bros., 1937), the "Value of Ritual," p. 37: "Ritual weaves speech, gesture, rhythm and agreed ceremonial into the worshipping action of man; and thus at its best can unite his physical, mental, and emotional being in a single response to the Unseen."

logic and empirical "fact," she argued that the human brain was constantly carrying on a process of the symbolic transformation of human experience, not as a poor substitute for action, but as a basic human need for integration and meaning.[115] Symbols are not poor substitutes for more literal uses of language, but are the means by which the human spirit can access realities that are not apparent to empirical observation. The saturation of the modern and postmodern consciousness with the barrage of images provided by television, movies, the Internet and other digital media, and a growing interest in icons and the visual arts in some evangelical circles, point to a shift in sensibility in which numbers of worshipers desire not only to hear the gospel story in words, but to see it portrayed and enacted in the visual symbols of the eucharistic liturgy as well.

Philosophers of language such as George Lakoff and Mark Johnson have challenged prevailing views of metaphor that have tended to see all metaphors as replaceable by more literal descriptions of states of affairs. According to Lakoff and Johnson, metaphors are not merely embellishments of more literal and descriptive linguistic forms, but are deeply connected to the human brain and the body's experience of the world, are shared widely across all cultures, and provide an essential function in mapping and integrating one domain of human experience with another. Symbols and metaphors are grounded in our basic human experiences (e.g., eating, bread) and provide essential means of comprehending religious and cultural concepts (e.g., spiritual life, communion with Christ).[116] Seen from the perspective suggested by Lakoff and Johnson, symbols such as bread and wine and metaphorical language ("This is my body") are not secondary to more literal understandings; metaphors are in fact more basic, more primary and closer to actual lived human experience than the abstractions of scientific language, mathematical formulas or the generalized statements of systematic theology.[117]

---

[115]Susanne K. Langer, *Philosophy in a New Key: A Study in the Symbolism of Reason, Rite, and Art* (New York: Mentor, 1948); see esp. chap. 2, "Symbolic Transformation," and chap. 6, "Life-Symbols: The Roots of Sacrament."

[116]George Lakoff and Mark Johnson, *Metaphors We Live By* (Chicago: University of Chicago Press, 1980), p. 40.

[117]George A. Lindbeck's contention that religious language (including eucharistic language)

In his *Personal Knowledge: Towards a Post-Critical Philosophy* (1958), Michael Polanyi attempted to outline a theory of knowledge that moved beyond the confines of the Enlightenment and scientific positivism, in a way that could build bridges between the ways of knowing in the scientific and religious communities.[118] The broader implications of Polanyi's epistemology will not be addressed here;[119] we will only mention a helpful distinction that has implications for eucharistic understanding, namely, Polanyi's distinction between *focal* and *subsidiary* awareness in a given human action.[120]

When, for example, a skilled pianist sits down at the piano bench and begins to play Beethoven's *Moonlight Sonata,* the pianist is focally aware of the music itself written in the score, and only subsidiarily aware of the keys on the piano and his own fingers that are touching the keys. If the pianist shifts his focal awareness to the keys or his fingers, he or she can no longer focus on the music, and confusion may result. Likewise, it could be observed that in the history of eucharistic practice and theology the focal awareness has been shifted to the physical elements themselves, with the result that the risen Christ as indeed personally (though invisibly) present with the community during the Eucharist has been lost in subsidiary awareness. The present essay is arguing, in effect, for a "reversal of the reversal": the believers meeting Christ at (not on) the table are subsidiarily aware of the elements, but focally aware of the risen, living Christ who meets them there in the power of the Word and Spirit. The eyes of faith are not so much looking primarily at the elements as through and past the elements to see, in a focal sense, the risen Christ who is present at the table by virtue of his "Holy Spirit avatar" or "Spirit-hologram."

In addition to these new dimensions for eucharistic understanding

---

has a "cultural-linguistic" function that constitutes a religious world inhabited by a religious community, and not a merely descriptive function, can be acknowledged without giving up the descriptive and realistic understanding of language. See Lindbeck, *The Nature of Doctrine* (Philadelphia: Westminster Press, 1984).

[118]Michael Polanyi, *Personal Knowledge: Towards a Post-Critical Philosophy* (New York: Harper Torchbooks, 1964).

[119]See Jerry H. Gill, *The Possibility of Religious Knowledge* (Grand Rapids: Eerdmans, 1971) as one example of the appropriation of Polanyian insights in the philosophy of religion.

[120]Polanyi, *Personal Knowledge*, p. 55.

suggested by linguistics and the philosophy of language, it may also be
noted that the emergence of the Internet, digital media and cyberspace
suggest new perspectives and analogies for understanding the vexed
question of the nature of the presence of the risen Christ, and especially
of his human nature, in the event of the Lord's Supper. It may be recalled how, in the debate between Zwingli and Luther, the relationship
of the body of Christ in heaven to the elements on earth at the table was
at the heart of the controversy. Zwingli insisted that since the resurrected and ascended body of Christ was in heaven at the right hand of
God, it could not at the same time be on earth, in the elements or on
the table, without losing its very nature as a real physical body with a
definite, circumscribed location. Consequently, concluded Zwingli, the
word *is* in the words of institution, "this is my body" had to mean "rep-
resents" my body, for Christ's body was literally and actually present in
heaven, not on earth. Luther, on the other hand, argued that the "right
hand of God" meant the place of God's power and authority—and in
this sense, the "right hand of God" was everywhere, including the
Communion table.

David C. Steinmetz has pointed out how the controversy between
Luther and Zwingli reflected fundamentally different understandings
of the nature of Christ's ascension. For Zwingli, the ascension means
that the physical body of Christ, his humanity, is no longer accessible to
the believer in earthly space and time; the glorified body of Christ remains in heaven until the second coming. For Luther, on the other
hand, what changes with the ascension is not the fact of Christ's presence with the believer, but rather the mode of that presence. Christ's
words, "I am with you always, to the very end of the age" (Mt 28:20)
are as true after the ascension as before. For Luther, before the ascension, Christ was accessible to believers physically by sight; after the
resurrection and ascension, Christ is still present with the church on
earth, but invisibly (though truly), by faith, in the preached word and
sacraments.[121] Luther also drew attention to the facts that after the
resurrection the body of Jesus was evidently not subject to some of the

[121]David C. Steinmetz, "Scripture and the Lord's Supper in Luther's Theology," *Interpretation*
37 (1983): 253-65 at p. 262.

limitations of a normal human body and could appear to the disciples in a room with locked doors (Jn 20:26).

For Luther, the immanence and transcendence of God and Christ in relation to space was not essentially a matter of "up" and "down," but rather a matter of accessibility and inaccessibility. The transcendence of Christ after the ascension is his inaccessibility by human power and sight. His immanence is his accessibility to the believing church by God's promise and ordained sacraments.[122]

Just as a one-sided Zwinglian view of the Lord's Supper can contribute to a sense of the real absence of the risen Christ on Sunday morning, so can a one-sided understanding of the ascension of Jesus Christ contribute to such a sense of absence.[123] While it is perfectly true that Christ, after the ascension, is at the right hand of God until his return, and as such is bodily and visibly *absent* from the church, this is not the whole story. He is still present with the church (Mt 18:20; 28:20; 1 Cor 5:4; cf. 1 Cor 14:25) in an invisible and spiritual and very real sense. The basic ontological axiom of New Testament theology applies here: The heavenly is as real or more real than the earthly; the spiritual and invisible is just as real or more enduringly real than the material and the visible. We need to see the full reality through the eyes of faith, not merely by the senses.

Jesus promised the church, "I will not leave you as orphans; I will come to you" (Jn 14:18; cf. Rev 3:20, "I stand at the door . . ."), and Jesus has not revoked his promise. Jesus also said, quite remarkably, that it was to the disciples' advantage that he leave them bodily (but not spiritually) and ascend to the Father (Jn 16:7), for otherwise the Holy Spirit would not come to empower an even deeper and more intimate union with Jesus than was possible during the days of his physical presence.

The key theological point to be noticed here—and it has a great impact on how we conceptualize the presence of Christ with the church

---

[122]Ibid., p. 274.

[123]In the same way—as has been repeatedly mentioned in this essay—a one-sided emphasis on the resurrection of Jesus as a fact of history in the *past* can be to the detriment of the existential reality of the risen Christ's presence in the Spirit to the church *in the present*. Many church services in practice have an "underrealized" eschatology of the resurrection: Jesus is "already" and really though "not yet" finally present to the church.

in worship—is that the *ascension changes not the fact and the reality of Christ's presence with the church, but its mode—and this change is for the better.* The believing church needs to re-vision and re-cognize the ascension: the risen Lord is not absent from us, we are not orphans![124]

This historic controversy between Luther and Zwingli, involving different understandings of how a body can be present in space, can now be viewed from the perspective of some modern analogies drawn from the Internet and digital technology: real-virtual presence and holographic projection. First, with respect to the concept of real-virtual presence (as a possible analogy for "real spiritual presence"), consider the question, Where is the homepage for Google located? The answer to this question is not as obvious as it may seem. It is true to say that the homepage of Google is located now, even as we speak, on the screen of the laptop computer on my desk. It would also be equally true that the Google homepage is located simultaneously on the screen of every computer in the world that is currently connected to that address; the Google screen is in a real sense ubiquitous. On the other hand, it might be argued that the homepage really is located inside a computer server of the Google corporation in Mountain View, California; this is the location of the "original" Google screen. Could not all three answers be plausibly true?

This question suggests that the emergence of cyberspace raises new questions about how the location of an entity in space is conceptualized, inasmuch as the relationship of cyberspace to our ordinary physical spaces raises metaphysical questions that philosophers (and a few theologians) have only begun to explore. What, ontologically, is cyber-

---

[124]Cf. Thomas F. Torrance, *Space, Time and Resurrection* (Edinburgh: T & T Clark, 1976), p. 132: "The ascension of Christ is thus an ascension to fill all things with himself [Eph 1:20, 22; 4:10], so that in a real sense he comes again in the Ascension. He had to go away in one mode of presence that he might come again in this mode of presence, leaving us in the mode of man's [physical] presence to man, and returning to us in the [spiritual, real] mode of God's presence to man." Christ is present to us in the Spirit on earth; we are *present to Christ* in heaven in the Spirit, seated with him in the heavenlies (Eph 2:6); in a real sense, the Christian *after the resurrection and ascension* is "closer" to Christ than were the disciples on the night of the Last Supper! For a survey of views in modern theology on the ascension and the question Where Is Jesus (now)? see Douglas Farrow, *Ascension and Ecclesia: On the Significance of the Doctrine of the Ascension for Ecclesiology and Christian Theology* (Grand Rapids: Eerdmans, 1999), pp. 165-254.

space? Where does it exist, and how is it related to physical space and material objects as we customarily conceive of them?[125]

To pursue this Internet/cyberspace analogy further, if I have a digital picture of myself in my camera, it seems clear that the picture is "in" the camera; if I upload it to my laptop, the picture is then located on my hard drive, and accessible on my screen; if I chose to upload my photograph or video to an Internet site such as Facebook or YouTube, then the images are both on my computer, on the social network's central server—and through it, my image becomes ubiquitous in the sense of being present and accessible to anyone with Internet access. To complete this proposed analogy between cyberspace and the eucharistic presence of Christ, we can imagine that in the ascension Christ uploads himself into the "heavenly server"; he is then virtually/spiritually/really present on earth—hyperphysically present, as it were—to anyone with access to the divinely ordained terminals: faith, word, Spirit, sacrament. The Lord's table is an earthly server for the church where Christ meets his people in a hyperphysical yet real manner.

The second analogy is drawn from the newly emerging technology of holographic projection. It is now possible to project lifelike, three-dimensional human images and computer animations, with voice and sound effects, of a given person or object from an originating projection studio to a live stage at a remote location. This technology is already being used for conferences, trade shows, industrial demonstrations of new products, and concerts and artistic performances.[126] In one recent

[125]For very tentative explorations of such questions, see William J. Rapaport and David R. Koepsell, "The Ontology of Cyberspace: Questions and Comments" (SUNY Buffalo Department of Computer Science Technical Report 95-25 and SUNY Buffalo Center for Cognitive Science Technical Report 95-09; two papers originally presented at the Tri-State Philosophical Association Meeting, St. Bonaventure University, April 22, 1995) <http://citeseer.ist.psu.edu/31641.html>; and Julie Van Camp, "How Ontology Saved Free Speech in Cyberspace," The Paideia Project On-line: Twentieth World Congress of Philosophy, Boston, Mass., August 10-15, 1998 <www.Bu.edu/wcp/Papers/LawVanC.htm>. In the latter paper the author outlines the attempts of Supreme Court justices in the case of *Reno v. ACLU* (1997) to extend traditional (physical) notions of "zoning" to cyberspace in cases of access to Internet pornography and free speech rights.

[126]The British firm Musion Systems Ltd. describes its product as follows: "The Musion Eyeliner is a high definition holographic video projection system allowing spectacular 3-dimensional moving images to appear within a live stage setting using Peppers Ghost technology"; see "About Musion Eyeliner Holograms" <www.musion.co.uk>.

application Prince Charles of England had himself projected onto the stage of the World Future Energy Summit in Abu Dhabi, in the United Arab Emirates. "His Royal Hologram, as he was dubbed by the press, delivered a powerful speech on the environment to the world's leaders before vanishing into thin air." By addressing the conference holographically rather than flying to Abu Dhabi in person, it was estimated that he reduced his carbon footprint by some twenty tons of carbon waste that otherwise would have been produced.[127]

To complete this holographic projection analogy, we could imagine that at the Lord's table Christ projects himself "holographically" into the midst of the believing church gathered around the table. He is not on the table but at the table; the Holy Spirit, the Spirit of Christ, is the "hologram" or "avatar" of the presence of Christ.[128] Christ is simultaneously in heaven at the right hand of God, and with his people in the worshiping church on earth. We see him by the "night vision goggles of the eyes of faith," truly, though he is invisible to the eyes apart from faith.

The reader may find these suggested analogies from cyberspace more or less plausible; the point, however, is not to attempt to remove the inherent mystery involved in the real spiritual presence of Christ at the Eucharist, but only to suggest ways in which the evangelical imagination could be renewed in certain ways by these new developments in the world of digital media. We are no longer limited just to the categories of physically present or physically absent. Digital media provide a third way that persons can be present to one another, and they suggest, by way of analogy and metaphor, new ways of understanding the spiritual presence of Christ to his people.

CONCLUDING REFLECTIONS:
ADVANTAGES OF MORE FREQUENT COMMUNION

Having surveyed some of the historical and theological factors that have contributed to a diminished place for the Lord's Supper in the

---

[127]Ibid.

[128]Recall at this point the illustration of Bishop Handley Moule, of having one's eyes of faith being opened to the invisible presence of Christ at the table, p. 146 above.

worship of many evangelical churches, and having considered some aspects of New Testament theology that could contribute to a recovery in this area, it now remains in this concluding section to briefly indicate some of the advantages and benefits of a richer eucharistic theology and more frequent celebration of the supper.

First of all, it can be argued that the Lord's Supper, as one of the two sacraments directly instituted by Christ, was intended by the Lord to be a basic and substantial means of spiritual formation and discipleship in the church. Christ said and commanded, "do this in remembrance of me" (Lk 22:19). Christ's memory is to be perpetuated and strengthened not only by good sermons but also by the Lord's Supper as a core practice in Christian worship. Its right use would contribute to the spiritual growth of individual believers and to the corporate body as a whole, while its neglect or misuse would produce the contrary effects.

It can be plausibly argued that the larger patterns of church history support this thesis. The Protestant Reformers, in calling the church back to its biblical foundations, were concerned to restore to the church both the "right preaching of the Word" and the "right administration of the sacraments." As noted earlier, John Calvin reminded his followers that the Lord's Supper was ordained "to be frequently used among all Christians in order that they might frequently return in memory to Christ's passion, by such remembrance to sustain and strengthen their faith, and . . . by it to nourish mutual love."[129] In the context of the problems of the late medieval Roman Catholic Church, the Reformers rightly called for a revitalization and recovery of biblical preaching, and this call was heard and practiced in later Protestantism; the call for more frequent Communion, was, however, for the most part, not consistently followed.

One basic reason why frequent Communion, rightly administered, can be a powerful means of spiritual formation is that it focuses the church's attention on the core realities of the Christian faith: the incarnation, the cross, the resurrection and the return of Jesus Christ. No Christian doctrines are more fundamental than these for Christian

---

[129]Calvin *Institutes* 4.17.44.

faith. Week by week the church is reminded in the Eucharist that
"Christ has died. Christ has risen. Christ will come again." Like following a doctor's orders to take prescription medicine,[130] or eating a
steady diet of wholesome food, or building bodily strength through
regular exercise, so it is in the spiritual life that the steady observance
of good practices such as the Eucharist over long periods of time con-
tributes to health and well-being. Topical preaching, so popular in
many evangelical churches, has a place in the life of the church, but the
danger here is that issues that are secondary matters can displace a primary focus on the essentials and the "whole counsel of God." The practice of frequent Communion refocuses the attention of the church,
week by week, on the core foundations of the faith, and on the basis of
those foundations, it reinforces the sense of basic Christian identity.

Second, it can be argued that frequent Communion, rightly practiced, can strengthen the distinctiveness of the church in relation to the
world as the holy people of God. The Lord's Supper is a Christ-
ordained boundary marker between believers and unbelievers that reminds the church that in order to transform the world, the body of
Christ must first be different from the world. As Gregory Dix noted
long ago, in the early church, the totality of the worship service was
never intended to be public (or "seeker sensitive") in the modern sense.
Unbelievers were welcome during the liturgy of the word, but dismissed
at the time of the Eucharist. The Lord's Supper was a private celebration, a domestic gathering in a house setting for the family of God; it
was a highly exclusive and not inclusive rite in the early church.[131]

The early church historian Robert Louis Wilken, in an interview in
Christian History, stated forcefully that this sense of distinctiveness
from the surrounding culture, exemplified and celebrated in the Eucharist, was in fact one secret of its spiritual strength. Rather than having as its primary focus impact on the culture, the early church, he said,

---

[130]In the patristic period the fathers could speak of the Eucharist as the "medicine of immor-
tality" or as the "food and drink of everlasting life"; Luther could say that when we come to
the table, "the food is so strong that it changes us into itself and out of carnal, sinful, mortal
men makes us spiritual, holy, immortal men" (cited in Ewald M. Plass, *What Luther Says* [St.
Louis: Concordia, 1959], p. 818).
[131]Dix, *Shape of the Liturgy*, p. 16.

"was itself a culture and created a new Christian culture." In answer to the question, "Did the church strive to be 'user-friendly'?" Wilken responded as follows:

> Not at all—in fact, just the opposite. One thing that made early Christian community strong was its stress on ritual. There was something unique about Christian liturgy, especially the Eucharist. . . . Pagans entered a wholly different world than they were used to. Furthermore, it was difficult to join the early church. . . . I think seeker-sensitive churches use a completely wrong strategy. A person who comes into a Christian church for the first time *should* feel out of place. He should feel this community engages in practices so important they take time to learn. The best thing we can do for "seekers" is to create an environment where newcomers feel they are missing something vital, that one has to be inculcated into this. . . . Few people grasp this today. But the early church grasped it very well.[132]

Some readers may think that Wilken has overstated his case, but nonetheless concede that his point is well taken, that is, that the church must be truly distinctive to have a lasting spiritual impact on the world.

One specific way that frequent Communion, rightly practiced, can contribute to the church's spiritual health and distinctiveness from the world is by providing a counterweight to the rampant individualism and narcissism of contemporary American culture. Communion was ordained to both signify and contribute to a unity in the body of Christ that overcomes the individualism and egocentricity of the natural person: "Because there is one loaf, we, who are many, are one body, for we all partake of the one loaf" (1 Cor 10:17).[133] The Corinthians were denying this body-building and unifying dimension of the Lord's Supper by their divisiveness and selfish disregard for some of the members

---

[132]Robert Louis Wilken, "The Link Interview," *Christian History* 57 (1998): 44.

[133]Fritz Chenderlin has noted the causative sense of this language: *"Because [hoti]* there is one loaf . . . *for [gar]* we all partake of the one loaf"; partaking of the one loaf not only signifies a unity to be realized, but actually and causally may contribute to it. "These forceful expressions seem to show that Paul saw the Eucharist as an essential element of Christian living" (*Do This as My Memorial: The Semantic and Conceptual Background and Value of Anamnesis in I Corinthians 11:24-25* [Rome: Biblical Institute Press, 1982], p. 176).

of the church (1 Cor 11:18-22). Their practices were undermining the "one new man" (Eph 2:15), the new, distinctively Christian way of being human, that the death and resurrection of Christ and incorporation into his living body were designed to produce. Today, in our own American setting, where historic cultural proclivities toward individualism are exacerbated by niche-marketing strategies of church growth that further divide Christians into lifestyle enclaves by age, education and music preferences, it is all the more urgent to recover the unifying and body-building dimensions of the Eucharist as the sign of unity in Christ.

Third, a more frequent celebration of Communion enhances worship by presenting the gospel in a holistic way. The Word is not only preached but also enacted and displayed. As James F. White has noted, the Eucharist "supplies movement and action," elements that tend to be lacking in traditional Protestant services dominated by preaching. "Modern man," observes White, "who participates so much in the communications revolution also needs to be shown what God has done, to be drawn into acting out the drama of salvation himself."[134] The modern church is located in a visual culture dominated by the ubiquitous images of digital media, and the Eucharist connects with the visual imagination as well as with the ear and the mind. Children and teenagers, and those whose learning styles may be more visual or kinesthetic, can appreciate a gospel message encoded in tangible, visual elements and physical movements.

As Thomas Aquinas pointed out, there is an intrinsic fitness between the elements of the Eucharist and the human person who is both body and soul, since the "sacramental medicine" is so proportioned that through a visible thing the body is touched and through the audible word grace is conveyed to the soul. Just as in the incarnation the Son of God assumed body and soul, in the Eucharist Christ enters deeply into our humanity, so that eucharistic worship is consonant with the mystery of the Word made flesh and with the human being's embodied existence.[135]

---

[134]White, "The Order of Worship," p. 28.
[135]Aquinas *Summa Theologica* 3.60.6, cited in Senn, *Christian Liturgy*, p. 32.

Finally, to conclude this section, the evangelical churches of the present may be called back to a rediscovery of the joy that characterized the frequently celebrated Eucharists in the New Testament and early church. As we have noted earlier, in the words of Norman Perrin, it was that "remarkable sense of fellowship between the early Christians and the risen Lord" that characterized the table fellowship of primitive Christianity. This eucharistic fellowship, in which the risen Christ was encountered at the table, was a table-fellowship "of such joy and gladness that it survived the crucifixion and provided the focal point for the community life of the earliest Christians."[136] As Martin Heinecken has stated, Communion in the New Testament period was a "joyful looking forward to the final consummation of God's work as well as a joyful celebration of the Lord's immediate presence." If the modern church has lost this sense of joy in the celebration of the Supper, then "so much worse for the church."[137]

The early Christians knew, through their worship experiences of the real presence of the risen Lord in the power of the Spirit, that the Communion table was not placed in a funeral parlor, but, so to speak, by the empty tomb, or on the road to Emmaus, or at a wedding feast. This note of joy has been reflected in the traditional liturgical elements such as the *Sursum corda* ("Lift up your hearts") and "Hosanna in the highest! Blessed is he who comes in the name of the Lord." This reappropriation of the central reality of the resurrection of Jesus as a fundamental reality of every Sunday's worship, to be experienced by faith at the Communion table, would "cast out fear" and replace it with joy and thanksgiving as the dominant emotions of weekly worship.

Today's church can again rediscover the New Testament truth that the bodily resurrection of Jesus Christ is not just a fact of history to be defended, but a spiritual power and reality in the present to be experienced at the Communion table. Such a faith-experience around the table can be an answer to the apostle Paul's prayer that the post-Easter church may know and experience the power that raised Christ from the dead (Eph 1:19, "his incomparably great power for us who believe"),

---

[136]Perrin, *Rediscovering the Teaching of Jesus*, p. 107.
[137]Heinecken, "An Orientation Toward the Lord's Supper Today," pp. 182-83.

that same power of the Lord Jesus that is present and available when
the church assembles as a church (1 Cor 5:4, "When you are assembled
in the name of our Lord Jesus . . . and the power of our Lord Jesus is
present").

Approaching the table by faith, believing that the risen Christ comes
to fellowship with his people (Rev 3:20, "I stand at the door and
knock"), means that the church is not so much concerned with an ontological argument for the existence of God, but rather looks for the
doxological manifestation of the reality and presence of God—a reality
so manifest that even an unbeliever would "fall down and worship God,
exclaiming, 'God is really among you'" (1 Cor 14:25).

The resurrection of Jesus Christ as reality-available-now is the
church's ace in the hole, and it is now time to lay this winning card on
the table. This resurrection-reality manifestation can empower the
church not only to resist the world's alien ontologies that would squeeze
the church into its mold (Rom 12:2), but also to be transformed by the
compelling presence of the Resurrected One, and consequently to then
be in a position to transform the culture around it—as did the early
church.

"The Spirit and the bride say 'Come!' *Maranatha.* Come, Lord Jesus.
Lord Jesus, come now to be our guest, and come once again and be
present with us in thy great glory! Amen" (Rev 22:17, my paraphrase).

5

From Ontology to Doxology

FROM THEORY TO PRACTICE
IN WORSHIP RENEWAL

I t is now time to turn from ontology to doxology and to consider some concrete ways in which this proposal for a new way of understanding worship can be implemented at the congregational level. These suggestions will be presented in two parts: first, some ideas on the teaching of the new ontological way of understanding biblical worship; second, some specific recommendations on how the new paradigm can be implemented in terms of an order of service, liturgy, music, spiritual gifts, visual arts and the celebration of the Eucharist. In some ways, the first element—the teaching of the new paradigm for worship to the congregation—is the really critical piece from which the specific steps of implementation can flow. At the heart of the application I suggest that some form of an ancient-modern blended worship style be implemented to embody the new paradigm of the real, dynamic, personal presence of God in Christian worship.

TEACHING THE NEW FRAMEWORK

It is essential that the pastor teach the congregation the new theological understanding of worship before moving ahead with changes in the existing worship services. The teaching program can begin with the theology of worship; then move to a consideration of ecclesiology, the ontology of the church (and of the self); and then take up some teaching on ontology in general, that is, some instruction on how scientific naturalism (and commonsense naturalism) and postmodern virtualism challenge a Christian mindset for worship.

In teaching the new theological understanding of worship, the main content could be drawn from chapter three, "The Ontology of Worship." This chapter (or the entire book) could be the basis for an adult Sunday school class on the nature of worship. This material could be communicated from the pulpit, but the church school setting would have the advantage of allowing for discussion and the engagement of the people with the new ideas being presented.

In teaching the ontology of worship, the pastor could begin by noting how worship in the church tends to be taken for granted, in that it is a customary, habitual activity that we do week after week, usually not reflecting intentionally on what we are doing, unless problems or controversies arise, for example, "worship wars" over what style of music we should use in the proposed new service. It would be helpful to provide some historical observations on how worship practices in the evangelical churches up to the present have been shaped by the controversies (especially concerning the Eucharist) between Roman Catholics and Protestants, by the practices of revivalism in the nineteenth century and by church growth methodologies in the twentieth century.

In the present context, the church is reflecting biblically and theologically on a fundamental aspect of its common life not just out of controversy, but in order to grow deeper in its life with God. Like other important human activities—parenting or good communication with one's spouse, for example—worship does not just happen but is a learned behavior. To be done successfully, it must be done knowledgeably, intentionally and skillfully. This series of discussions on a new biblical understanding of worship can help the members of the congregation to have a common mind and a shared understanding of what is really happening on Sunday morning. Without a shared understanding of *who we really are* and *what we are really doing,* all sorts of secondary purposes and agendas can operate during Sunday morning and diminish the richness and coherence of the fundamental purpose for being there: experiencing communion with the living God. If one were to ask typical attendees in an American "Bible believing" church what were their real expectations in going to church on Sunday, one might get an answer along the following lines: "I hope to hear an interesting and relevant sermon, and I look forward to seeing my friends." These are reasonable expectations, of course, and can be part of authentic worship; however, we are working toward a new mindset that says, in effect, "I know that the living God is really here to meet with us, and as one of his redeemed children, I am here to glorify him, and to enjoy being in his presence."

The central point to be made, then, is the real presence of God as the central reality of every worship service. This divine presence is the fundamental reality of all true worship "in Spirit and in truth," and all true worship should be conscious of and organized around this central truth.

This divine presence is threefold in nature: God above us, God among us and God within us. All three aspects are important and reflect both the transcendence ("above," "in heaven") and immanence ("among," "within") of God in his gracious presence with his covenant people. But it is the truth of God among us that calls for special emphasis in the renewal of worship in our time.

In teaching this truth, the pastor could expound the outlines of biblical history, focusing on the presence of God in the world and with his people, beginning with the presence of the Spirit hovering over the primeval waters of creation; humankind driven from the presence of God in the Garden; God coming in search of humanity in the covenant with Abraham; God coming to his people in Egypt and leading them through the waters of the Red Sea and through the wilderness wanderings with his Shekinah Glory cloud; God revealing himself in power and glory at Sinai, leading the new generation into the promised land, and filling Solomon's temple with his glory; the glory leaving the temple at the time of judgment and exile, and then the return of the glory to the temple in the person of his incarnate Son; the descent of the Spirit on the people of God, the new temple, on the day of Pentecost; the promise of Christ's abiding presence where two or three are gathered in his name, to the very end of the age; and the consummation of life in God's presence in the heavenly Zion, the new Jerusalem in the new creation.

The entire sweep of biblical history is an illustration of God's purpose to be with his redeemed people: *I will be your God, and you will be my people; I will dwell among you, and you will behold my glory.* This is a summary of the good news of the gospel. God is actively seeking those who will enjoy worshiping him "in spirit and truth" (Jn 4:23); God himself is more eager to "enjoy worship" than we are!

The fundamental purpose for which God created the universe and for which humans have been redeemed is that God might be glorified and that we might *enjoy* communion with God. This communion is enjoyed now in worship and is consummated in union with God in eternity.

Two portions of Scripture that are especially pertinent for teaching these truths are Exodus 19–24, where God calls the people into his covenant and presence at Mount Sinai, and Hebrews 12:18-29, which presents the new covenant as the fulfillment of the Sinai revelation. Both texts could be preached in a sermon or series of sermons on the biblical theology of worship. Exodus 19–24 illustrates some of the key elements of worship: the call to assemble; God's coming to be present with his people; God speaking his words; the people responding with promises of obedience; the covenant formed with sacrifice; the covenant celebrated with a fellowship meal in God's presence. Hebrews 12:22-29 illustrates both the supernatural environment (heaven, the angels) and the emotional ethos (joy, reverence and awe) of early Christian and New Testament worship.

In preaching these texts, the pastor can point to the basic revelation-and-response pattern (God speaks; we respond) of biblical worship, and can emphasize the truth that in biblical worship, the primary actor and active agent is God, not human beings. It is God who is present and sovereignly manifesting himself to us through the elements of the service. It is God himself who calls us to assemble in his presence through the words of the human worship leader; God speaks through the biblical texts as they are read; God himself is speaking through the human words of the preacher. It is God himself, in the person of the risen

Lord, who meets with his people in fellowship at the Communion table; it is God himself who is pronouncing his favor upon his people as the benediction is pronounced at the end of the service. Meeting the risen Lord at the Communion table is not an occasional "extra" in New Testament worship, but the normal and natural expression of communion with the living God, of enjoying a happy and joyous family meal in our loving Father's house.

The people must be taught to listen with the "ears of faith" and to look heavenward with the eyes of faith during the service, and to look past and beyond the human leaders to the invisible God truly present among them. Believers need to come to church with a transformed mindset (Rom 12:1-2), a set of spiritual eyes and ears that are tuned in to and focused on the invisible realities of faith.

The next critical teaching point is the ontology of the church. Here the pastor can challenge the congregation not to think of church primarily in terms of buildings or the activities that take place in these buildings on Sundays, but rather in terms of the unique being or fundamental nature of the church as captured in the three foundational images of the church in the New Testament: the family of God the Father, the body and bride of Christ the Son, and the temple of God the Holy Spirit. The trinitarian reality to which these images point is unmistakable, and it reminds us that the church is a "communion of communities," in which the original community—the triune God, Father, Son and Holy Spirit—graciously invites us as the adopted children of God into an ever-deepening and joyous experience of friendship and fellowship with Father, Son and Holy Spirit. In worship the people of God are drawn into the Son's joyous adoration of the Father, in the communion of the Holy Spirit, being caught up into the joyous inner life of the Trinity, a glorious, dynamic communion that has existed since before the beginning of time.

The preacher can find much helpful material for sermons in studies like Paul Minear's *Images of the Church in the New Testament* and, on the trinitarian nature of the church, in John Zizioulas's *Being and Communion* (both mentioned in chap. 2 and listed in the bibliography). The three images of the church as family of God, body/bride of Christ and

temple of the Holy Spirit are so crucial that they merit a series of sermons or adult education classes or Bible studies. The term *images* of the
church itself is pedagogically significant, in that effective teaching and
preaching connect biblical images with biblical concepts and implant
them in the mind of the listener—as Jesus himself did so effectively in
his parables: "The kingdom of God is like a mustard seed . . ." The
vividness of the biblical images of the church can help the believer
withstand the never-ending barrage of images from the surrounding
digital culture that are competing for shelf space in the mind and that
distract attention from the unseen realities of the Spirit in the church.

In teaching a biblical ontology of the church, the pastor might em-
ploy the term *theanthropic* or "divine-human," in order to highlight the
sui generis or unique reality of the church. The church of Jesus Christ,
assembled in the presence of the real and living God, in the name and
authority of Jesus, for the explicit, shared and intentional purpose of
giving glory to God and enjoying him now and forever, is an entity unlike any other in the universe—unlike a shopping mall, unlike a place
of entertainment like Hollywood, unlike a rock concert, unlike a factory, unlike a business like Microsoft, unlike a school like Harvard,
unlike a financial world like Wall Street, unlike a place of political
power like Washington—and in God's sight, more valuable and significant than them all. All these humanly constructed institutions have
limited shelf lives; the church, as God's divinely constructed project,
has a future that will endure into eternity.

The church is unique because it is, at the core of its being, in its fundamental reality, the only theanthropic ("God-bonded-to-man") reality
in the universe, the likes of which never has been before and never will
be again, a reality in which the members are bonded forever to the triune God—the gold standard of reality—in the communion of the Holy
Spirit. Because of our theanthropic union with God the Father, through
Jesus Christ, in the communion of the Holy Spirit, and since the ascension of Jesus to the right hand of the Father, where we are already seated
with him in the heavenly places (Eph 2:6), we as the people of God are
closer to God, in the act of true worship in spirit and truth, than the
cherubim and seraphim, the holy angels themselves. True worship on

earth is the beginning of a never-ending journey into the very heart of the Trinity.

In connection with the unique, theanthropic nature of the biblical church, the pastor can also make the point that the church as the body and bride of Christ is not just a means to certain important ends such as missions, evangelism and discipleship; rather, the church is an end in itself in God's eternal plan. The church, in fact, is the purpose for which God created the world (cf. Eph 1:4: the church "chosen in him [Christ] before the creation of the world"); God created the universe to provide the raw materials for humanity and his church. Had God not wanted to form a bride for his eternal, beloved Son, the Father would never have bothered to create the universe in the first place. In light of the fact of sin, what pain, what suffering, what agony of soul could the Father have spared himself by not creating a world at all!

Discipleship and mission are, of course important, necessary and biblical aspects of the threefold purpose of the church, but worship should be recognized as having primacy, for worship is the eternal duty and joy of the people of God. In the new creation, in the eternal state, the Great Commission will have been completed and God's people will have been brought to maturity in Christ (Eph 4:13), but God's people will continue to sing God's praises and to enjoy him forever, in ever deepening measure (Eph 3:19, "filled to the measure of all the fullness of God"), unto the eternity of eternities, forever, world without end.

In connection with this point concerning the theanthropic reality of the church, it would also be helpful for the pastor to emphasize the charismatic nature of the church in the New Testament. The existence and being of the church is integrally related to its permanent bonding with all three persons of the Trinity: Father, Son *and Holy Spirit*. Popular evangelical piety and worship typically focus on only one of the three persons—Jesus—to the neglect of the Father and the Spirit. The New Testament makes it abundantly clear that there is no true Christian or Christianity apart from the Holy Spirit: "if anyone does not have the Spirit of Christ, he does not belong to Christ" (Rom 8:9). Biblical Christianity is "charismatic" to the core; it is the Holy Spirit at the beginning of the Christian life (regeneration, justification), in the continuation of the Christian life (sanctification) and in the consummation of the Christian life (final resurrection, glorification) into eternity. The Christian life—and true worship—is supernatural from start to finish, and this supernatural reality is imparted by the Holy Spirit who comes to indwell the believer's spirit and the church.

John Zizioulas, whose work has contributed so much to the renewal of trinitarian theology in recent times, has rightly emphasized this intrinsically charismatic nature of the church. The Holy Spirit is not an add-on or option for the New Testament church; the Holy Spirit is essential to its very being:

> The Spirit is not something that "animates" a Church which already somehow exists. The Spirit makes the Church *be*. Pneumatology does not refer to the well-being but to the very being of the Church. It is not about a dynamism which is added to the essence of the Church. It is the very essence of the Church. . . . Pneumatology is an ontological category in ecclesiology.[1]

It is commonly and correctly said that Acts 2 describes the birthday of the New Testament church at Pentecost. The church was born when the Spirit was poured out by the ascended Lord from on high. The Holy Spirit did not disappear from the church when the day of Pentecost was over; Jesus can be trusted to have told the truth when he promised us that he would send the Counselor, the Holy Spirit, to be with his disciples forever (Jn 14:16). There has never been a minute since the day of Pentecost that the Holy Spirit has not been at the core of the church's being.

Likewise, the Holy Spirit is not incidental to true worship, but intrinsic to it. It is in fact impossible to worship God "in spirit and in truth" without the Holy Spirit. And as Andrew Lincoln has pointed out in his fine commentary on Ephesians 5:18-20 ("keep on being filled with the Spirit" cjb), the fullness of the divine presence is not primarily about private ecstatic or mystical experiences; being "filled with the Spirit" in this passage involves *corporate worship and relationships. . . .*

---

[1]John Zizioulas, *Being as Communion: Studies in Personhood and the Church* (Crestwood, N.Y.: St. Vladimir's Seminary Press, 1993), p. 132.

the passage links Spirit-led worship with the wisdom required for living in this present evil age. . . . being filled with the Spirit gives believers understanding of their Lord's will, and it is the spiritual songs that are a means of promoting the knowledge of that will. . . . the community's worship can be seen to make a vital contribution to its wise living in the world."[2]

At this point readers who are from conservative Reformed or dispensationalist theological traditions may be feeling somewhat nervous about this "charismatic" emphasis in the ontology of the church. This nervousness and concern is certainly understandable in light of the theological shallowness and at times bizarre and aberrant practices that surface in the current charismatic and "prophetic" wings of the American church. These prophetic enthusiasts are correctly pointing to supernatural dimensions of New Testament Christianity (tongues, prophecy, miracles) that are neglected or denied in Reformed churches. Conservative churches can run the risk of quenching the Spirit and ignoring what may be genuine manifestations of the power of God. The prophetic enthusiasts, on the other hand, may run the risk of marginalizing sound doctrine, neglecting expository preaching and drifting into the vagaries of subjective experience.

As pastor Roberto Miranda of Boston's Lion of Judah Church has observed, today's American evangelical church scene is in danger of being polarized between charismatic churches that are like a "fire without a fireplace" and noncharismatic churches that are like a "fireplace without a fire." There needs to be a happier balance somewhere in between. Biblically, we need not be forced to choose between a strong emphasis on the sovereignty of God and *sola scriptura* on the one hand, and, on the other hand, the power of the Spirit and the reality of the supernatural.

Both sides can agree on the basic biblical teaching that every true Christian—man or woman, Builder, Boomer, Millennial or Xer—has been given one or more spiritual gifts, and both can agree that the identification, promotion and use of these gifts in the ministry

---

[2]Andrew T. Lincoln, *Ephesians*, Word Biblical Commentary (Dallas: Word, 1990), pp. 348-49, emphasis added.

and worship of the church can be encouraged by the leadership. This emphasis on spiritual gifts, which was quite popular in the 1970s and 1980s with "body life" concerns, but is now somewhat less prominent, deserves a fresh look and rediscovery in evangelical churches today.

FROM NICHE-MARKET CHURCH TO DEEP, THICK, DIFFERENT

Finally, in this matter of the ontology of the church, I would like to challenge pastors to lead their churches to a consciously multigenerational vision of the church. Many churches are de facto multigenerational to some extent, while others, either by design (niche-market churches) or circumstances have attracted a narrower, generationally defined demographic. This multigenerational model of the church, if owned by the congregation, can provide the basis for implementing the proposed ancient-modern blended style of worship to be presented below.

The multigenerational model of the church being advocated here is also timely in that American society is increasingly being divided into lifestyle enclaves that are divided and segmented along generational lines. The culture desperately needs models of human communities that reach out and include people of all ages in their community life. The evangelical church has a real cultural opening here, if it is bold and discerning enough to see it.[3]

What I am calling for here is an intentional abandonment and disavowal of niche-marketing strategies that have animated seeker-driven models of the church since the adoption of Donald Mc-Gavran's church growth theories in the 1970s. I am arguing, on the contrary, that this model has run its course, and that it is time for the American evangelical church to return to the biblical model of a multigenerational church that ministers to all ages, from the cradle to the grave, across the whole life cycle. The apostle Paul, when his letters were read to the churches, assumed that children would

---

[3]The need for multigenerational congregations is perceptively argued in Jackson Carroll and Wade Clark Roof, *Bridging Divided Worlds: Generational Cultures in Congregations* (San Francisco: Jossey-Bass, 2002).

be present (cf. Eph 6:1-3); he had a vision of a church that was not defined by ethnic demographics ("our kind of people"), but reflected the "one new man" (Eph 2:15), the new way of being human and building human community that was not simply a reflection of the world's way of being human or of the world's voluntary associations or affinity groups or lifestyle enclaves. Niche marketing the church is and has been a capitulation of the evangelical churches to the worldly values of business and marketing. It is time to acknowledge this theological and strategic error, and to move forward with a new vision of what Christ intended the church to be. "His purpose [Christ dying on the cross] was to create in himself one *new* man out of the two" (Eph 2:15), not to imitate the world's humanity.

Advocates of the niche-marketed, seeker-driven church may say, "But your proposal for a multigenerational, 'biblical' church condemns the church to be small; it inhibits church growth." If so, then so be it: the vision here for a multigenerational church values depth over numerical growth (while not repudiating healthy numerical growth as such). The vision of a multigenerational church being proposed here is not that of the megachurch model, but rather that of a mesochurch (mid-sized) community, for which the key descriptors are *deep, thick* and *different. Deep* is the opposite of shallow. The vision here is that of a church that has a deep understanding of the holiness and weightiness of God in its theology, and a deep experience of the reality and presence of God in its weekly worship. It is a *thick* church in that the people have thick relationships and commitments to one another rather than the thin relationships of the surrounding culture. It is a *different* church that is unashamedly distinct from the consumerist, sexually saturated and narcissistic culture around it. The pastor of such a mesochurch is more concerned about being a shepherd to the flock, about providing pastoral care to the people, than concerned about being (or becoming) the CEO of a numerically growing religious corporation. The deep, thick and different church is, in fact, a vision much like that of the pre-Constantinian church, a fellowship that was more concerned about the depth of its worship and loving one another well than it was about transforming the culture (though this did occur). These "resident aliens"[4] instinctively realized that before the church could transform the culture, the church first needed to be deeply transformed itself, and realized that at the heart of this transforming process was the depth of its encounter with the risen Christ in its weekly Sunday gatherings.

Finally, to complete this project of teaching a new framework for worship, the pastor can give instruction on ontology in general, with special reference to the influences of Enlightenment scientific natural-ism and the postmodern world of digital media. In addressing the mindset of scientific naturalism and everyday common sense, it can be pointed out that while modern science and common sense reinforce the mindset that "seeing is believing" and that what is evident to the senses is "really" real, the New Testament focuses the believer's mind on the unseen world of the Spirit and on heavenly realities. For some back-ground reading on the pervasive influences of the scientific naturalism of the Enlightenment on the day-to-day mindset of the modern Chris-tian, the pastor could profitably study Charles Kraft's book mentioned earlier, *Christianity with Power: Your Worldview and Your Experience of the Supernatural*, especially chapter three, "How Do Westerners Pic-ture the World?" and chapter four, "Enlightenment Christianity Is Powerless."

A good sermon text to make this latter point is 2 Corinthians 4:18, "We fix our eyes not on what is seen, but on what is unseen. For what is seen is temporary, but what is unseen is eternal." The unseen God is more lastingly real and eternal than Mount Everest; when God invades space and time at the end of history, Mount Everest will "melt like wax" (Ps 97:5) in the presence of the burning reality of the great *I AM* Creator of the universe. When God even looks at the earth it trembles; when he touches the mountains, they smoke (Ps 104:32). The point here is that from the perspective of a biblical ontology, a biblical way of un-derstanding reality, spirit is more powerfully real than matter. The triune God is more enduringly real than Mount Everest because the

---

[4]The allusion here is to Stanley Hauerwas and William Willimon, *Resident Aliens* (Nashville: Abingdon, 1989), which has suggested to the present author a "deep, thick and different" vi-sion of the church, for a time in history that is post-Constantinian, post-Christendom and postcolonial.

triune God is eternal and self-existent, and these other entities are not. The mindset that the invisible, spiritual realities of the Bible and heaven are just as real—in fact, more lastingly real—than the physical objects around me that I can see and touch and measure, is the mindset that the people of God need to bring to the church on Sunday mornings, in order to focus their attention during the worship service on the unseen God who is *really present* in the midst of his people, who speaks through the Word and the sacraments, who wants to enjoy communion with his people, and who wants their minds focused on himself and not on the human preacher or members of the praise band.

Another good sermon text to make these points is found in Colossians 3:1-4:

> Since, then, you have been raised with Christ, set your hearts on things above, where Christ is seated at the right hand of God. Set your minds on things above, not on earthy things. For you died, and your life is now hidden with Christ in God. When Christ, who is your life, appears, then you also will appear with him in glory.

This text implicitly contains the new ontology of God, the church and the self that was presented in chapter two. It makes sense, from the apostle's point of view, for the Christian to focus attention on the heavenly things above because Christ, the Son of God, reigns in heaven above, and his kingdom is now the center of the dominant reality in all the universe. We are not the center of the universe, Christ is. We may not see him with the physical eyes, but he is most truly real, and is seen by the eyes of faith. The apostle also assumes an ecclesiology at the heart of which is the believer's mystical union with Christ: we have been spiritually resurrected with him in our conversion and regeneration; we are now, by virtue of that mystical union, spiritually seated with him in the heavenly places (Eph 2:6); at his return at the end of time, again by virtue of our union with him, we will be resurrected in new-creation bodies that will be like his own glorious resurrection body ("you also will appear with him in glory," Col 3:4).

The pastor may have to deal with an objection at this point, namely, that such an "otherworldly" orientation is impractical and idealistic. It might be said, "Christians can be so heavenly minded that they are no earthly good." The point here, however, is not to neglect the world or escape from it, but rather to gain some critical distance from it by adopting a more fully biblical perspective on this world and its spiritual dangers. The lives of great Christians in church history such as those of William Wilberforce and Mother Teresa demonstrate that being deeply rooted in a relationship with the unseen God can have a profoundly energizing influence on service to the world.

There is also in this text a reference to the new Christian self: "You died, and your life is now hidden with Christ in God" (Col 3:3). When the apostle says, "you died," he is teaching that our conversion and baptism marks the end of the old personal identity based on nationality, ethnicity, gender, or social class; the Christian has a new identity, a new self based on his or her union with Christ, the head of the body, and communion with other believers. This is the new *trinitarian-ecclesial self* that was presented in chapter two. The believer can say when walking through the door of the church, "This is who I really am in Christ; I will not let myself be defined by Hollywood, by the media, by modern science, or by the marketplace and shopping malls."

It seems easy enough for the apostle Paul—or the pastor—to speak about a "new self," but in practice, it is extremely difficult for any Christian to truly and consistently think of himself or herself in this way since the force of lifelong habits and the unremitting pressure of the world keeps "squeezing us into its mold" (cf. Rom 12:1-2 LB), unless we make conscious and intentional efforts to see ourselves in the light of these New Testament truths.

In teaching on the challenges of postmodern virtualism to the formation of a Christian mindset for worship, the pastor might use the concept of digital distraction to focus the discussion. Almost everyone living in our modern world today, including the people in our churches, are acutely aware of the never-ending bombardment of digital images, commercial messages, advertisements, phone calls, emails, text messages, Internet websites, talk radio voices and 24/7 news channels that constantly call for our attention and distract our overstimulated minds from the still small voice of the living God. Key teaching points could include the abiding reality of God, in contrast with the simulated and humanly constructed virtual realities of the Internet and digital entertainment; the power of the digital media to distract the Christian from the truly important world of the Spirit; the connection of the digital media and the entertainment industries with the consumerist values of modern capitalism; and the need to develop new cognitive skills, a new mindset that is more contemplative and collected, to protect the Christian mind and imagination from being colonized[5] by the seductive influences of the Enlightenment and postmodernity.

For the pastor who wishes to do some further background study on the influences of postmodernity and digital media, the following books are recommended: Stanley Grenz's *A Primer on Postmodernism*, Neil Postman's *Amusing Ourselves to Death*, Thomas de Zengotita's *Mediated* (mentioned previously) and Shane Hipps's *The Hidden Power of Electronic Culture: How Media Shapes Faith, the Gospel, and Church*. Any of these books could be used as the basis for a discussion class in the church's adult education program or for discussions with the church's staff and leadership.

APPLYING THE FRAMEWORK: ANCIENT-MODERN BLENDED WORSHIP

The new ontological framework can best be implemented with some form of ancient-modern blended worship, which can bring together biblical foundations, historic elements from the liturgical tradition, the visual arts, and traditional and contemporary Christian music in a way that connects with the contemporary culture, in a congregational setting that bridges the generations.

The pastors who wish to lead their churches in this direction or to consolidate efforts already achieved in such a direction can find much practical help in Martin Thielen's *Ancient-Modern Worship* (Abingdon, 2000), including sample orders of worship, in Robert Webber's *Plan-*

---

[5]I borrow this metaphor of a "colonized imagination" from a sermon preached by the Rev. Beth Maynard at Christ Church of Hamilton and Wenham, Mass., on July 6, 2008. "Colonization" suggests the cultural takeover of a native population by a foreign power and the replacement of its values and traditions by those of the colonizing power. Here the point is to recognize how the modern Christian imagination has been colonized by the scientific naturalism of the Enlightenment and by the digital media of the postmodern world.

ning Blended Worship (Abingdon, 1998),[6] and in a classic liturgical resource such as the Book of Common Prayer. A wealth of helpful worship and liturgical resources is available at the website maintained by
the Calvin Institute of Christian Worship (www.calvin.edu/worship/).

In making this case for an ancient-modern style of worship, five elements will be considered: the value of liturgy, tradition and ritual; the
celebration of the visual arts and the right use of electronic media; the
promotion of spiritual gifts; the use of an ancient-modern musical
canon; and a weekly Eucharist as the climax of the church's worship.

If the pastor is currently leading a church that comes from a nonliturgical denominational tradition, some resistance to a worship style
informed by liturgy, tradition and ritual is to be expected. There are at
least seven historical elements that have contributed to an anti- or nonliturgical sensibility in evangelical churches, together with a suspicion
of tradition and ritual: the Protestant Reformers' strong reactions
against the practices of the late medieval Roman Catholic Church; the
reaction of Puritan pastors in England in the seventeenth century to
the forced imposition of the Book of Common Prayer by the bishops of
the Church of England; the Enlightenment's rationalism and suspicion
of religious ritual as "superstition"; the frontier revivalism of Charles
Finney that stripped away many of the historic elements of Protestant
worship; the American pragmatic temperament and orientation toward
the future rather than the past; the modern fascination with technology
in which "the newest is the best"; and the ephemeral nature of pop
culture and digital media which focuses attention on the "now." Simply
drawing attention to these historical influences can give a congregation
some healthy critical distance from its current worship practices.

Fortunately, there has in recent years been a renewal of appreciation
for the positive value of liturgy and tradition in a growing number of
quarters in the evangelical community. The book by Simon Chan, a
Pentecostal scholar, *Liturgical Theology: The Church as Worshiping Community* (InterVarsity Press, 2006), is a notable contribution in this re-

---

[6]Webber, an influential leader in the modern revival of liturgical worship in American evangelicalism, has further developed his theological rationale for ancient-modern blended worship in
Ancient-Future Faith (Grand Rapids: Baker, 1999).

gard.[7] More evangelicals are now willing to distinguish between a positive sense of tradition and the negative connotations of "traditionalism," recognizing the truth of Jaroslav Pelikan's now-famous aphorism, "Tradition is the living faith of the dead, traditionalism is the dead faith of the living."[8] Tradition in the good sense is simply a recognition of the *communion of the saints,* a recognition of the fact that the current generation of Christians and our practices of the faith are not the first or necessarily the best ones, and that we may have something to learn from the history of what the Holy Spirit has taught to the generations of believers that have preceded us.

Carl Anderson, the senior pastor of Trinity Fellowship Church in Richardson, Texas, had come to the conclusion about eight years ago that "there was a sense of disconnectedness and loneliness in our church life." He sensed that the entrepreneurial models of seeker-friendly services and programs were not helping to build the congregation. Anderson led the congregation to adopt a more liturgical style of worship, with a weekly Eucharist, saying the Nicene Creed every two or three weeks, and following the church calendar. The liturgy, he said, helped the church to grow beyond a "celebrity-status" pastor model; liturgy is "not just about this church but the connection with other Christians."[9]

As the Lutheran liturgical scholar Frank Senn has noted, the "church may be the only institution left in Western society that maintains continuity with tradition. That continuity is embodied in the church's historic liturgy."[10] This renewed appreciation for tradition has also been accompanied, as we have noted earlier, by a new perspective on the positive functions of ritual. The new discipline of ritual studies has shown that all cultures, not only in the religious areas of life, but

---

[7]Simon Chan, *Liturgical Theology: The Church as Worshiping Community* (Downers Grove, Ill.: InterVarsity Press, 2006). I have received much inspiration for the present book from Chan's work, especially chapter 1, "The Ontology of the Church."

[8]Jaroslav Pelikan, *The Vindication of Tradition* (New Haven, Conn.: Yale University Press, 1984), p. 65.

[9]Jay Tolson, "A Return to Tradition," *U.S. News & World Report*, December 24, 2007, p. 47.

[10]Frank Senn, *Christian Liturgy: Catholic and Evangelical* (Minneapolis: Augsburg, 1997), p. 699. The concluding section of the book from which this citation is taken, "Epilogue: Postmodern Liturgy," pp. 693-705, contains valuable observations on worship in a postmodern cultural setting.

throughout the society as a whole, use various ritual behaviors to build a sense of solidarity in the community, to foster group identity and to pass along core values to the next generation. The singing of the national anthem at the beginning of a major league baseball game is an obvious example of a secular ritual in American society.

Ritual studies have also pointed to these stylized behaviors as valuable learning tools that can communicate to the participants at many different levels simultaneously, appealing, as it were, to many different learning styles in a holistic way. As Evelyn Underhill pointed out over a generation ago in her classic study *Worship*, "Ritual weaves speech, gesture, rhythm and agreed ceremonial into the worshipping action of man; and thus at its best can unite his physical, mental, and emotional being in a single response to the Unseen. . . . It is only by recourse to our image-making faculty, or by some reference . . . to the things that are seen [e.g., sacraments], that we can ever give concrete form to our intuition of that which is unseen."[11]

In short, a renewed appreciation for tradition, liturgy and ritual in the worship of the evangelical church can have at least the following six advantages: (1) affirming the catholic nature of the church across the generations since the first century (intergenerational church across the centuries); (2) providing a firewall and spiritual spam filter, so to speak, that can help filter out the forces of secular and pagan culture that continually try to infiltrate the church and to colonize the Christian's imagination; (3) helping to build a "thick" Christian identity and sense of corporate solidarity in the fellowship of the congregation by building a common yet distinctive language and practice of worship; (4) providing theological and liturgical accountability for the worship leaders; (5) providing access to the rich spiritual and liturgical resources from the past; and (6) providing a hermeneutical context or framework (liturgy, creed) for the reading and preaching of the Bible that is driven not by the culture but by the Bible's own big story or metanarrative.

---

[11]Evelyn Underhill, *Worship* (New York: Harper & Bros., 1937), p. 37. Other ritual scholars have suggested that ritual promotes holistic learning by engaging both sides of the brain, both the (right brain) imaginative and the (left brain) analytic functions (Charles D. Laughlin, "Ritual and the Symbolic Function: A Summary of Biogenetic Structural Theory," *Journal of Ritual Studies* 4 [1990]: 15-40 at 29).

In relation to this last point, media and communications theorists have noted how people hear and understand messages differently depending on whether they bring to the communication event the background of a low-context culture or a high-context culture.[12] In a low-context culture people have relatively little shared experience, and consequently the mass media and pop culture will provide the background of shared stories, symbols and heroes that occupy peoples' minds as they listen to a message. Modern American culture, with its individualist tendencies and weakened family and neighborhood structures, is low context in this sense; many Americans may be more familiar with the characters in *Sex in the City* than with David and Bathsheba and the stories of the Bible. In such a context, it is easier for the Bible to be hijacked by the alien metanarrative of a "health and wealth" or "feel good" gospel.[13] A liturgical structure of worship—including, ideally, use of the lectionary readings and following the great events of the liturgical year—has the advantage of providing a biblical framework and context within which the Bible's own voice may be heard with integrity.

A second element in the implementation of an ancient-modern blended style of worship is the encouragement of the visual arts and a critical and appropriate use of electronic media. For a variety of historical and theological reasons, the evangelical Protestant tradition in America has not been known for its excellence in the visual arts or in the aesthetic dimensions of life generally. The invention of the printing press in the latter part of the fifteenth century and, in the sixteenth-century, the Protestant Reformers' emphasis on the Bible and its preaching in the language of the people very understandably had the effect of shifting the center of attention in the churches from images and sacraments to the expounding of texts. As James White has noted, the impact of the invention of the printing press on worship "was tremendous. For many people, much ceremonial in worship simply became redun-

---

[12]Raymond Gozzi Jr., "Mass Media Effects in High-and-Low-Context Cultures," in *Mass Media Effects Across Cultures*, ed. Felipe Korzenny and Stella Ting-Toomey (London: Sage, 1992), pp. 55-66 at p. 62.

[13]The preaching of a popular megachurch pastor such as Joel Osteen may be seen as a case in point.

dant because they now could experience the same realities serially through the spoken or read word."[14] Protestantism has remained a largely word-oriented tradition ever since.

The English Puritans who migrated to the American colonies brought with them a sensibility from the mother country that did not place a high value on the visual arts. Forerunners of the Protestant Reformers, such as John Wycliffe and the Lollards, focused on Scripture, preaching and a somewhat moralistic version of the Christian life. Paintings in pre-Reformation England were largely confined to the manors of the nobility and the upper classes, and middle-class Englishmen might not be exposed to a single painting in the course of a year. The destruction of the monasteries under Henry VIII, and later by the followers of Oliver Cromwell, left a vacuum of the visual arts in the English churches.[15] The iconoclastic zeal of Cromwell's followers led to the smashing of many stained-glass windows and the "stripping of the altars"[16] throughout the land.

Today, of course, the evangelical churches in America stand in a quite different historical and cultural situation. Centuries have passed since Martin Luther nailed his ninety-five theses on the church door in Wittenberg to trigger the Reformation, and we have enough critical and historical distance to recognize that in some areas the Reformers may have overreacted to features of late medieval Catholicism that were seen as barriers to the clarity of the gospel and the centrality of Scripture in the life of the church. The pendulum swung a bit too far in an iconoclastic direction, and it is now time to bring it back to a more centrist position where the visual arts have an appropriate and honored place in the worship of the church. We now live in a culture dominated by visual images. The Christian's spiritual imagination needs to be nourished by images that provide better alternatives to the images of the secular culture, which all too often are ugly,

---

[14]James F. White, *A Brief History of Christian Worship* (Nashville: Abingdon, 1993), p. 106.

[15]John Dillenberger, *The Visual Arts and Christianity in America: The Colonial Period through the Nineteenth Century* (Chico, Calif.: Scholars Press, 1984), pp. 9, 12.

[16]As noted earlier in the previously cited history by Eamon Duffy, *The Stripping of the Altars: Traditional Religion in England, c. 1400-1580* (1992; reprint, New Haven, Conn.: Yale University Press, 2005).

violent, sexually explicit or commercially driven.[17]

Biblically oriented Protestants have compelling theological reasons to recognize beauty as a Christian value that should be reflected in church architecture, church interiors, liturgical art, vestments, banners and music. God as a God of *glory* is beautiful and majestic in the core of his being; his creation reflects the beauty of his character and purposes. The God of Israel was worshiped in a tabernacle and in a temple that displayed notable outward beauty. Well could the inspired psalmist exclaim, "How lovely is your dwelling place, O LORD Almighty!" (Ps 84:1). In Exodus 35:30-35 the skilled craftsmen Bezalel and Oholiab are recognized as exercising a spiritual gift in their work of decorating the wilderness tabernacle. In the New Testament churches of our day, those who have been gifted with artistic talent can be encouraged to use their gifts in the enhancement of the church's worship.

It is, of course, easier to speak in general terms of the value of the visual arts in the life of the church than it is to implement forward motion in these areas in a way that maintains unity in the church. As is the case with church music, personal tastes in the congregation may vary widely, reflecting generational and other differences, and evangelical Protestants have no longstanding historical traditions to guide them in such areas. However, this being said, sufficient consensus in the church is not an impossible ideal. Most would probably agree with the sentiments of Tanja Butler, a Christian artist and professor of the arts, who has stated that liturgical art "exists to enhance worship, to deflect attention from itself to that of the community's relationship with its transcendent Creator."[18] Butler suggests that church art should be guided by the criteria of authenticity, appropriateness and accessibility in judging its fitness for use in worship.

---

[17]Anthony Ugolnik, writing from the perspective of a Greek Orthodox Christian in America, has noted that in America, beauty tends to be a private matter, with no communal consensus on standards; beauty tends to be peripheral in (Protestant) faith and worship (*The Illuminating Icon* [Grand Rapids: Eerdmans, 1989], p. 185). It is no accident that in recent years many evangelicals—not just those in "emerging" churches—are showing increased interest in icons.

[18]Tanja Butler, "A Transfigured Vision: Art and Worship in Community," *Stillpoint*, Fall 2007, pp. 4-5. Butler is associate professor of arts at Gordon College in Wenham, Mass., and author of the CD, *Icon: Visual Images for Every Sunday* (Minneapolis: Augsburg Fortress, 2000).

"Authenticity" refers to artwork that reflects the artist's individual giftedness and high standards of artistic merit, while at the same time being rooted in the Christian context of the church. "Appropriateness" signifies artwork that fits the theological and regional identity of a particular congregation and its particular history. Beautiful interiors in a traditional Episcopal church in Connecticut and a Southern Baptist church in Texas could look quite different, but both be fitting for their particular contexts. "Accessibility" means that the artwork should both be understandable to the congregation and integrated into the other elements of the life of the church, such as Christian education and outreach. Liturgical art is more likely to be perceived as "accessible to the congregation if the people of the church or key committees have been able to participate in its planning, selection, and production."[19]

Some special comments are in order concerning the at-times controversial matter of the use of electronic media and projection equipment in the worship service. Here is an area in the life of the church where the technology continues to change quite rapidly, and the danger is that the adoption of new technologies will run ahead of careful theological reflection about possibly unintended consequences. The church's biblical theology of worship should drive the use of technology and not vice versa.

I would recommend that the pastor and the church leadership read a book such as Shane Hipps's *The Hidden Power of Electronic Culture*[20] and have frank discussions before deciding to invest a lot of the church's money in the latest digital technologies. Hipps makes the point that technology is not value-neutral and should be critically scrutinized for any "subtexts" that are being communicated. For example, PowerPoint slides may have a place in the life of the church, but the business context for which PowerPoint was developed should be remembered; a series of bullet points and graphs that are designed to close the deal in a sales presentation is quite different in its purpose than visual media

[19]Ibid.
[20]Shane Hipps, *The Hidden Power of Electronic Culture: How Media Shapes Faith, the Gospel, and Church* (Grand Rapids: Zondervan, 2005).

whose purpose is to enhance worship and to point the viewer to the invisible God.[21]

The pastoral staff could well discuss the questions, How is what we are trying to do in worship different from a concert; different from a trip to the mall; different from a classroom lecture; different from a visit to a movie theater? And what difference does our answer make in how we use electronic media in our services? The position that I am suggesting here is not an anti-media stance, but one that is intentionally understated, one of understimulation in an already overstimulated society. People coming to church on Sunday do not need just another set of PowerPoint slides or another barrage of loud, high-intensity images. If anything, they need less—a more focused and contemplative visual environment that enhances their awareness of the presence of the unseen God, rather than distracting them from it.

Is this to say that one should never use, for example, video clips from current films to illustrate the sermon? Not necessarily; but it should be asked, Will the viewers remember the illustration better than the point the preacher is trying to make? Will the video clip take the viewer's mind and imagination away from the church, rather than closer to the world of the spiritual, and simply reinforce Hollywood's colonization of the Christian mind? What is being argued for here is a critical use of visual media that is consistent with an intentional and carefully thought out understanding of the ontology and purpose of worship.

THE REALITY OF THE SPIRIT IN THE LIFE OF THE CHURCH

A third important dimension for implementing ancient-modern worship is the encouragement of the discovery and use of each member's spiritual gifts.[22] This is true whether or not the church happens to be part of a denominational tradition that is considered "charismatic,"

---

[21]More specifically, the choice of type fonts in PowerPoint slides should reflect awareness of the different contexts of business, school and worship in the church.

[22]At the level of congregational study and practical implementation, resources such as Peter Wagner, *Discover Your Spiritual Gifts* (Ventura, Calif.: Regal, 2002) and *Your Spiritual Gifts Can Help Your Church Grow* (Ventura: Regal, 2005) can be helpful; for the identification of spiritual gifts, many churches have used the "Wagner-Modified Houts Questionnaire," available from the Charles E. Fuller Institute of Church Growth, P.O. Box 91990, Pasadena, CA 91109.

since from the perspective of a New Testament doctrine of the church, every true church is "charismatic" in that its very birth, growth and continuing life is marked by the real, personal presence of God the Holy Spirit.[23]

Evangelical churches in the United States gave significant attention to spiritual gifts in the 1970s and 1980s, but this emphasis is much less evident now. There are a number of reasons why a rediscovery of this dimension of New Testament ecclesiology and pneumatology seems timely, not the least of which is the dramatic growth of the Pentecostal movement in the churches of the Global South, which has now become the demographic center of the world Christian movement. The world Christian movement as a whole is becoming more charismatic and more open to the reality of the supernatural than has been the case with many of the older churches in the West.[24] The Hispanic population in the United States is a rapidly growing segment, and many of these Hispanic Christians practice Pentecostal forms of spirituality and worship.

A fresh encouragement of the use of spiritual gifts also seems timely in light of the growing interactivity promoted by the cultures of the Internet and digital technology. People are increasingly expecting to be interacting and networking with one another through cell phones, text messaging, Internet blogs, and audience polling at educational, business and entertainment events. People today see themselves not merely as passive consumers of information and experiences, but as active participants in the dynamic group interactions made possible by digital technology. The body life in the church could see the Holy Spirit as the wireless network of the body, so to speak, with each person having a

---

[23]One very important manifestation and gift of the Spirit, the gift of healing (1 Cor 12:9), will only be mentioned here, though it is worthy of book-length treatment in and of itself. It is notable that the apostle mentions this gift in the context of manifestations of the Spirit for the common good (1 Cor 12:7), implying that the exercise of the gift of healing was *a* normal part of the worship meetings of the church in Corinth. Churches today should be much encouraged to rediscover the spiritual gift of healing and integrate it into a normal part of Christian worship, in prayers for the sick, either with or without the laying on of hands, either in the service itself or after the service by a ministry team. For a starter resource in this area, see Peter Wagner, *How to Have a Healing Ministry in Any Church* (Ventura, Calif.: Regal, 1992).

[24]This remarkable change in the demographics of the world Christian movement has been documented in Philip Jenkins, *The Next Christendom: The Coming of Global Christianity* (New York: Oxford University Press, 2002).

spiritual gift that like a Blackberry or handheld device enables them to give and to receive. Such a body-life mindset has resonance with the new dimensions of contemporary culture and is consistent with a New Testament view of the church in which the clergy lead and equip the people but are not seen as doing all the ministry.

As noted earlier, the reality and presence of the Holy Spirit is not incidental to the life of the church but constitutive of its very existence: the church is the temple of the Holy Spirit, whether or not we are consciously aware of that reality at any given moment. The New Testament understanding of the church presents a doctrine of the triplex presence of the Spirit in the church: The church is triply charismatic or "three-dimensionally charismatic," so to speak, because the Spirit, in an essential and continuing sense, is (1) present *within* each believer; (2) present *among* the believers as a church; and (3) present *above* the assembly as the Shekinah Glory of God. Each believer, upon conversion, is baptized by the Spirit into the body of Christ (1 Cor 12:13), receives the gift of the Holy Spirit (Acts 2:38), has the Holy Spirit dwelling in the heart (Jn 14:16-17), and from that time forward is a temple of the Holy Spirit (1 Cor 6:19), who indwells his or her physical body.

The Holy Spirit is, secondly, continually among the believers as they assemble as a church. The Spirit is the "bond of peace," the Connector (Eph 4:3) that connects the members of the body to one another just as really as the supporting ligaments of a physical body (cf. Eph 4:16) connect all the bones and bodily parts together. The Holy Spirit is the invisible but real high-speed, broadband network connection that connects the body in the worship-event just as surely as a wireless network connects all the members of a family speaking on their cell phones in a family conference call. The Holy Spirit is more enduringly real than Verizon Wireless or AT&T. When the believers assemble as a church in the name of Jesus, for the intentional and specific purpose of communing with him in worship, then "the power of our Lord Jesus is present" (1 Cor 5:4) because the risen Christ and the Spirit are really present. When the whole church comes together in the name of Jesus, the reality and power of the Spirit's presence is so real that even unbelievers are impelled to exclaim, "God is really among you!" (1 Cor 14:25).

The third dimension of this triplex presence of the Spirit is the presence of the Shekinah Glory with and upon the church. Moses entered the Shekinah Glory cloud of God on Mount Sinai and came down from the mountain glowing with the glory of God (Ex 34). After the Sinai covenant was ratified, seventy of the elders ascended Mount Sinai, saw the glory, and ate and drank in the presence of God (Ex 24). The glory cloud filled the wilderness tabernacle at its dedication, and led the people through their journeys toward the Promised Land (Ex 40). The glory filled the temple of Solomon at its dedication (1 Kings 8), but later left the temple (Ezek 10) when God sent the people into exile in Babylon. The good news of the new covenant, as foretold by the prophets, when the kingdom of God draws near, is that the exiles will return, God will return to Zion and dwell with his people in Jerusalem (Zech 8:3), and the house of the Lord will again be filled with his glory (Hag 2:7, "the desired of all nations [Messiah] will come, and I will fill this house with glory"). These promises were fulfilled through the incarnation, death, resurrection and ascension of Christ, who is the incarnate glory of God (Jn 1:14, "the Word became flesh and made his dwelling among us. We have seen his glory, the glory of the One and Only, who came from the Father, full of grace and truth").

On the day of Pentecost the glory cloud returned to the new covenant temple, descending on the whole church (Acts 2) in flaming tongues conveying the presence, power, purity and love of God. Before the cross, resurrection and ascension the glory cloud enveloped Peter, James and John on the Mount of Transfiguration for a brief time (Mt 17:5); after Pentecost, all God's people, not just a few selected apostles, are dwelling under the Shekinah Glory continuously in true worship, beholding the glory of God in the face of Christ and being transformed by that glory, as was Moses on the holy mountain (2 Cor 3:18).

Isaiah looked forward to a time when the Shekinah Glory would cover Mount Zion and all God's people continually:

> In that day the Branch of the LORD will be beautiful and glorious. . . .
> Those who are left in Zion, who remain in Jerusalem, will be called
> holy. . . . Then the LORD will create over *all* of Mount Zion and over

those who assemble there a cloud of smoke by day and a glow of flaming fire by night; over all the glory will be a canopy. It will be a shelter and shade from the heat of the day, and a refuge and hiding place from the storm and the rain. (Is 4:2-6)

Isaiah foresees the time when the Shekinah Glory cloud, which the people could only see from a distance in the wilderness, would cover and envelop all Mount Zion and all the true remnant. That vision was fulfilled on the day of Pentecost, and now God's people, who have come to the true and heavenly Zion (Heb 12:22, "you have come to Mount Zion, to the heavenly Jerusalem" in worship), have the glorious privilege of dwelling under the glory now.

Acts 2 and the descent of the Glory-Spirit is commonly seen as a one-time event in the church's past. In fact, Pentecost is a continuing reality because the Spirit, the Shekinah Glory, has not deserted the church. Jesus Christ has promised his people that he would send the Spirit to be with them forever (Jn 14:16). Even at the present moment, the risen and ascended Christ, who is still alive and who still really exists, is at the right hand of God as Lord of the universe, continually filling the church with all the fullness of God (Eph 1:22-23). God's Word-Promise is constitutive of reality; God's promise makes things so and is received by faith.

We may not see this Shekinah Glory with the physical eyes, but it is a spiritual and ontological fact of the life of the church and real New Testament worship in Spirit and truth. God can open the spiritual eyes of his children during the act of worship, in answer to their prayers,[25] to see the glory that is truly there. God is always sovereign in the ways and times that he chooses to manifest the divine presence that is truly present; we pray for these manifestations, but can never control them.

At this point, readers who come from cessationist theological traditions may be feeling uneasy. I would encourage such readers to reexam-

---

[25]A number of years ago my wife and I attended a worship service at Bethlehem Baptist Church in Minneapolis, led by John Piper. The service—music, preaching, singing—was "glorious"; the sense of the presence of God was evident. We later learned that during the service, a group of people in the church were gathered in the basement for the express purpose of praying that the Holy Spirit would "anoint" the entire service to the glory of God. A fine practice indeed for any worship service!

ine some of these cessationist assumptions in the light of Scripture and global realities. It is quite possible to maintain—as they should be maintained—the vital Reformation principles of the primacy of biblical authority in the church (test all things by Scripture) and of the sufficiency of Scripture for all doctrines essential to salvation (2 Tim 3:16), and yet at the same time to be more open to the reality of the supernatural and the freedom and sovereignty of God the Holy Spirit to manifest himself among his people as he wills (cf. 1 Cor 12:11: "the Spirit . . . gives . . . as he determines"). Cessationist churches might ask themselves if their beliefs and practices can amount to a quenching of the Spirit and treating prophetic utterances with contempt (1 Thess 5:19-20).

On the other hand, the charismatic and "prophetic" wings of the church, who have no problems acknowledging the supernatural, do need to reexamine some of their beliefs and practices in the light of Scripture. In some popular expressions of charismatic worship, it seems that the "Spirit" is more a spirit of financial prosperity than a Spirit of holiness. The prophetic movement needs to remember that the Holy Spirit, not the prophet, is sovereign in how, when or if the power of God is manifested supernaturally. In many prophetic gatherings the clear commands of Scripture to "test the spirits to see whether they are from God" (1 Jn 4:1) are routinely ignored or violated, as are the apostle's admonition that in a meeting, when two or three prophets speak, "the others should weigh carefully [test, discern] what is said" (1 Cor 14:29). Also frequently ignored is the Pauline injunction that any public utterance in a tongue should be interpreted (1 Cor 14:13) in order that the whole assembly can be edified. The practices of some charismatic and "prophetic" ministries today are not in practice as "Bible believing" as they profess to be.

O COME LET US MAKE MUSIC TOGETHER

Any pastor who has led the congregation in a transition from a traditional to a contemporary worship style will probably tell you that music was the most difficult and contentious issue to be addressed. The diversity of musical tastes, genres and choices represented in a typical congregation has increased dramatically in the last several generations and shows no signs of abating. Music, like any other consumer product in our modern, globalized world, has experienced a choice explosion that makes achieving consensus in any given group very difficult indeed. In an op-ed piece in the *New York Times* columnist David Brooks wrote about the "Segmented Society" and the increasing segmentation in popular music; the iPod culture gives us all our own private playlists, but no common shared musical heritage. Brooks pointed to the need in America for a "musical canon" for greater cultural cohesion,[26] and his observations apply to the church as well.

Researchers in musicology have found that most people tend to bond to a particular musical style, whether secular or religious, between the ages of sixteen and twenty-four; the type of music you liked then, you will probably still like now. For example, many people born prior to 1927 prefer old gospel hymns written between 1870 and 1935; those born from 1927 to 1945 tend to gravitate toward the older, classic hymns such as "The Church's One Foundation" and the hymns of Charles Wesley; about 75 percent of those born from 1946 to 1964 ("boomers") will prefer praise hymns and praise songs (composed 1960-1980); those born since 1964 tend to prefer contemporary praise songs composed since 1980 and that have even faster tempos.[27]

This wildfire growth in musical diversity is fueled by the social mobility of the culture. Songs and hymns sung in one church may not be known in another church in a different part of town or of the country. Modern popular music is performer and performance oriented, for the most part, designed for being listened to, not for purposes of singing along. According to Brian Wren, a scholar in the area of church music, this cultural trend has tended to discourage the practice of Americans singing together in public groups, including in the church.[28] Fewer

---

[26]David Brooks, "The Segmented Society," *New York Times*, November 20, 2007 <www.ny times.com/2007/11/20/opinion/20brooks/>.

[27]Herb Miller and Lyle Schaller, "Transitioning Through Worship Transitions," *The Parish Paper: A Resource for Congregational Leaders* 12, no. 1 (July 2004): 2.

[28]Brian Wren, *Praying Twice: Music and Words of Congregational Song* (Louisville: Westminster John Knox, 2000). This is one of the best books available on church music and congregational singing. The summary of Wren's guidelines for encouraging congregational singing is found on pp. 123-25. Other recommended resources in the area of church music are found in the sec-

public schools offer music education, adding to the loss of a tradition of public singing.

Then what is the pastor to do in the face of this seemingly insurmountable musical diversity? The effort, though difficult, is well worth making, because music in the worship of the church can express a unity in the church that crosses generational lines—indeed a unity of generations across the centuries of the church. It can teach foundational biblical and theological truths, embedding them on both sides of the brain, and can help to communicate the Christian faith to outsiders.[29]

The most important thing that the pastor can do in moving toward an ancient-modern blended musical style of worship is to communicate a biblically based vision of an intentionally multigenerational church: "This is who we are and who we are trying to be; we are not a niche-market church targeted at just one generation. We are trying to be a body of Christ for many generations." This is a vision of the church that is consciously different from the market-driven organizations that operate on the principles of the world. If the members of the congregation can own a vision of becoming a people that are building "one new man," a new humanity (Eph 2:15) that reflects the fundamental purpose for which Christ died on the cross, then individual members will be less tempted to *expect* that their generation's musical preferences should predominate.

The generations can consciously defer and "cut some slack" to one another out of concern for the unity of the Spirit and the bond of peace (Eph 4:3). It may take a supernatural act of the Spirit to achieve such a working unity, but miracles are still possible! In practice, this decision to implement a musically blended service could involve a conscious policy of trying to include all four musical types each week: gospel, classic, early contemporary and recent contemporary. Members of each of the four generations would find at least one selection that connected with their primary preferences. One guideline for musical selections could be copyright dates for the music in question: traditional (1520-1870), gospel (1871-1935), early contemporary

tion "Church Music" of the appendix, "Theology and Practice of Worship" (annotated).
[29]Ibid., pp. 84-97.

(1961-1980), late contemporary (1981-present).[30]

Part of the challenge of achieving musical harmony and consensus in the church stems from the fact that while the Bible gives clear, normative teaching in the areas of doctrine and ethics, the Bible does not contain a systematic theology of music. Musical practices are presupposed and sometimes described, but there are few explicit prescriptions. There are, however, several passages from which helpful principles can be derived, and to these we now turn: 1 Chronicles 25 and Ephesians 5:18-21.

In 1 Chronicles 25 the writer describes King David's efforts to organize the music and musicians for the temple worship. From this text we can infer that (1) musicians ("the sons of Asaph, Heman and Jeduthun") were set apart for full-time ministry (1 Chron 25:1) and were considered worthy of support (cf. 1 Chron 23:5, "four thousand"). (2) Those who sang ("prophesied," 1 Chron 25:1) were accompanied by instruments; the instruments supported and did not displace the human voice in the praise of God. (3) These musicians were "under supervision" (1 Chron 25:2); in current parlance, it could be said that the "praise band is accountable to the pastoral leadership." And (4) the musicians were "trained and skilled" (1 Chron 25:7): musical excellence and skill was expected in the praise of God.[31]

In Ephesians 5:18-21 the apostle Paul gives some instructions for Spirit-filled worship, and from these instructions we can glean some principles for music in the church. The members of the assembly are to be (1) "filled with the Spirit" (Eph 5:18), consciously dependent on the Spirit rather than on their human strength to offer God praise and worship (you cannot worship God "in Spirit and in truth" apart from the Holy Spirit). (2) They are, as they sing and praise, to speak to one another (Eph 5:19), which implies that the human voice is not drowned out by loud instrumentation. (3) They are to speak to one another in "psalms, hymns, and spiritual songs," which suggests a variety of musical genres. (4) They are to make music (Eph 5:19; lit., "psalming"),

---

[30]Miller and Schaller, "Transitioning Through Worship Transitions," p. 2.

[31]On the musical life of ancient Israel, see Alfred Sendrey, *Music in the Social and Religious Life of Antiquity* (Madison, N.J.: Farleigh Dickenson University, 1974), pp. 77-267.

which implies that words and melody are not overwhelmed by the beat of percussive instruments. (5) They are to give thanks (Eph 5:20), which implies words that recall God's character and saving acts, and not just human emotions.[32]

The pastoral team and musicians, in planning and evaluating music, can profitably ask the following three questions: Does the electronic amplification and instrumentation overshadow the human voice?[33] Does the beat overshadow the words and melody?[34] Do the visible performers and personalities overshadow the invisible presence of God?[35] Too many contemporary worship services run afoul in one or more of these areas.

Other commonsense criteria for musical selection include quality, substance and singability. Does the quality of the piece and its execution reflect musical excellence? Do the words communicate theological and biblical substance, reminding worshipers of the character and mighty acts of God? Is the selection in question singable by the average member of the congregation, or is it more suited to display the skill of the performer? The criteria for "singability" in church music suggested by Lowell Mason in the nineteenth century are still helpful: "Simplicity of intervals and rhythm [e.g., "Holy, Holy, Holy" vs. "The Star-Spangled Banner"]; range not exceeding an octave; 'D' (or perhaps 'E')

---

[32]Lincoln, *Ephesians*, pp. 343-49.

[33]Brian Wren has offered the following rule of thumb to the musicians on the stage: If you can't hear the congregation, you are probably too loud (*Praying Twice*, p. 122). Most contemporary Christian musicians would be surprised to learn that it was not until the middle of the Middle Ages that musical instruments were introduced into the Western church (Joseph Gelineau, *Voices and Instruments in Christian Worship* [London: Burns & Oates, 1964], p. 152). From the perspective of the New Testament, the human voice is the only "instrument" that is essential for Christian worship.

[34]Musicologists who have studied music crossculturally have found that throughout the world melody is the basic unit of musical experience: "most people remember a piece of music by associating a melody with words" (Robert Jourdain, *Music, the Brain, and Ecstasy: How Music Captures Our Imagination* [New York: William Morrow, 1997], p. 256). The problem with many recent praise choruses is that neither their melodies nor their words are very memorable; consequently, their value for teaching biblical truths in a lasting way is limited.

[35]One Wednesday evening my wife and I attended the "believers' service" at a megachurch. The expository message that night was excellent, but we were struck that, during the "worship time," when the focus was supposedly on God, our attention was dominated by the twenty-something musicians whose faces were magnified on the huge Jumbotron video screens—with the words on the screen (not very memorable) placed in a small font below. The unintended message was, in effect, "Look at us—not God."

as the high note or upper limit."[36] Guidelines such as these will not solve all our musical challenges but will certainly help in building congregational consensus and a blended worship that honors God and edifies the people.

THE MARRIAGE SUPPER OF THE LAMB

The natural culmination of a congregation's move to an ancient-modern blended worship service would be the practice of weekly Communion. If the previous practice of the church was quarterly Communion, then as an interim step, monthly observance might be a good way to begin the transition.

As with the other aspects of ancient-modern blended worship, preparing the congregation with good teaching from the pulpit would be essential for a successful change in eucharistic practice, especially in light of the theological and logistical challenges involved. Much of the material presented in chapter four, "The Eucharist," could be used as the basis for this teaching. It would be helpful to give the congregation some historical perspective on the role of Communion in the history of the church, noting especially how the Protestant Reformers' reaction against the Roman Catholic Mass affected later Protestant practices and how frontier revivalism in the nineteenth century shifted the attention away from the Communion table to the evangelistic preacher and the "altar call."

The central biblical and theological concept to be emphasized in the preparatory teaching would be the concept of the real spiritual presence of the risen Christ, who is meeting his people not *on* but rather *at* the table, in the power of the Holy Spirit. The pastor can show how the Christian church's celebration of Communion in the New Testament and early centuries was based on the fundamental conviction and awareness that Jesus was alive and now present to the church in the Spirit. His crucifixion, achieving salvation from sin, was not the end of the story; God raised him from the dead; Jesus is still alive now, and we as his people can now celebrate Jesus'

---

[36]Cited in Senn, *Christian Liturgy,* p. 599.

victory over sin and death as we meet him at worship around the Communion table.

In explaining the familiar words of institution in 1 Corinthians 11:23-26, the pastor can explain how the word "remembrance" in biblical usage means much more than merely calling to mind a past event, but rather implies the continuing presence of and personal participation in a crucial redemptive event of the past such as the exodus from Egypt, or the death and resurrection of Jesus Christ. It can be shown that the apostle Paul himself, in the earliest New Testament commentary on the words of institution, in his use of the term "participation" in 1 Corinthians 10:16 ("is not the bread we break a *participation* in the body of Christ?") points to the fact that the believing Christian in communion has personal, living, "soul-to-soul" contact and fellowship with a Christ who died but who is now alive and present in the Spirit with his church. The view being presented here is not a Zwinglian, bare memorial view, but rather that of the real, dynamic, personal presence of the risen Christ at the table with his people, in the power of the Holy Spirit.

A crucial move in this transition to a new understanding and practice of Communion involves a change in the fundamental emotional tone of the service: from mourning to joy. The fundamental emotional tone of eucharistic services in the early church was one of celebration, because the reality of the resurrection of Jesus Christ was known, appreciated and felt at a very visceral level. The later church, and most of Protestantism, lost this sense of joy and replaced it with a predominantly penitential mood.

Reverence and awe (cf. Heb 12:28) are indeed needed and appropriate in worship, but the fundamental reality of New Testament worship is that of a joyful assembly (Heb 12:22), and Christians have the best of all reasons to rejoice: because Christ has risen from the dead, sin and death have been defeated, and victory is assured! The Communion table is not in a funeral parlor, so to speak, but in the banquet hall of the King of Kings.

In teaching on the words of institution in 1 Corinthians 11, it would be good to place this text in the larger context of other important passages in the New Testament, especially texts such as Matthew 18:20

("where two or three come together in my name, there am I with them"), and Matthew 28:20 ("surely I am with you always, to the very end of the age"), which point to the crucial fact of the real spiritual presence of Christ with his people as the heart of any Christian worship assembly. It would also be helpful to surround 1 Corinthians 11 with passages such as Luke 24:13-35 (Jesus meets the disciples on the road to Emmaus) and Acts 2:42-47 (fellowship of the early Jerusalem church), both of which testify to the strong sense in the early church that the table fellowship the disciples enjoyed with Jesus before the passion was now continuing after his resurrection from the dead.

The danger in the traditional focus on the words of institution from 1 Corinthians 11 alone, apart from these other New Testament teachings, is that the unintended consequence is to focus the church's attention on the problems in Corinth—not discerning the body, and so forth—rather than on the good news and very positive message of resurrection, forgiveness, new life and joy in Christ. "Fencing the table" should not overwhelm the truth of the resurrection. All too often, in typical evangelical Communion services, there is more of a spirit of fear—if the truth would be known ("I hope I don't drop the elements")—than a spirit of joy and celebration.

Finally, a few suggestions are in order concerning the logistics and administration of the Communion service. A Communion table that looks like a table and that is placed on the same level as the people would certainly be appropriate, in order to communicate the New Testament sense of Communion as a fellowship meal. The meal character of the Eucharist has been lost in later Christian history, the meal becoming a token meal and cultic act. Consistent with the words of 1 Corinthians 10:16-17, it would be desirable to have a real cup or cups (not just the small plastic cups commonly used in many churches) on the table, to recall the first Lord's Supper, and from which Communion could be served. Having one or more real loaves of bread visible on the table to represent the unity of the body (1 Cor 10:17) would also help to recall the meal character of the celebration. These details will need to be adjusted, of course, in light of local needs and circumstances.

The essential point is to teach, recognize, expect and celebrate the real personal presence of the risen Lord who comes in the Spirit to enjoy fellowship with his people. "I stand at the door and knock. If anyone hears my voice and opens the door, I will come in and eat with him, and he with me" (Rev 3:20). Christ's promise is true yesterday, today, and forever.

> Hallelujah!
> For our Lord God Almighty reigns.
> Let us rejoice and be glad
> and give him glory!
> For the wedding of the Lamb has come,
>   and his bride has made herself ready. . . .
> Blessed are those who are invited to the wedding supper of the
>   Lamb! (Rev 19:7, 9)

Come, Lord Jesus, and be our host, and meet us in joyous communion around your table. *Maranatha!* Amen!

Appendix

THEOLOGY AND PRACTICE OF WORSHIP

Asterisks denote books that are particularly recommended.

Selected Readings

Adams, Doug. *Meeting House to Camp Meeting: Toward a History of American Free Church Worship from 1620 to 1835.* Saratoga, Calif.: Modern Liturgy Resource Publications, 1981. Shows how, in some free church traditions, Communion became less frequent and worship more pulpit and clergy dominated in the nineteenth century than was the case in the seventeenth.

*Allmen, J. J. von. *Worship: Its Theology and Practice.* New York: Oxford University Press, 1965. Theology of worship; Reformed perspective.

Barth, Karl. *The Knowledge of God and the Service of God According to the Teaching of the Reformation.* New York: Charles Scribner's Sons, 1939. Given as the Gifford Lectures for 1937 and 1938; see chapter 17, "The Church Service as Divine Action," and chapter 18, "The Church Service as Human Action," on the theology of worship. "The church service (of worship) is in the first instance and primarily . . . divine action, and is then only human action secondarily. . . . The primary ground for the church service lies outside ourselves. It lies in the presence and action of Jesus Christ" (pp. 192-93).

Brilioth, Yngve. *Eucharistic Faith and Practice: Evangelical and Catholic.* London: SPCK, 1953. Note the summary on pp. 276-89, on the fivefold significance of the Eucharist in New Testament and patristic tradition: thanksgiving; communion with God and the church; commemoration of the death of Christ; the sacrifice on the cross; the mystery of the real presence of Christ *among* his people—not only "in their hearts."

Bradshaw, Paul F. *The Search for the Origins of Christian Worship.* New York: Oxford University Press, 2002. Technical, state-of-the-discipline study of how liturgics as a field has developed over time.

Bradshaw, Paul, and John Melloh, eds. *Foundations in Ritual Studies.* Grand Rapids: Baker, 2007. Significant articles by scholars in the newly emerging area of "ritual studies"; important resource for new insights on value of ritual, liturgy and sacraments.

Brunner, Peter. *Worship in the Name of Jesus.* St. Louis: Concordia, 1968. Important contribution to theology of worship; Lutheran.

Carroll, Jackson, and Wade Clark Roof. *Bridging Divided Worlds: Generational Cultures in Congregations.* San Francisco: Jossey-Bass, 2002. Case studies of generational differences in churches; in the epilogue the authors argue for "blended," multigenerational churches.

*Chan, Simon. *Liturgical Theology: The Church as Worshiping Community.* Downers Grove, Ill.: InterVarsity Press, 2006. Call for renewal of worship in evangelical churches by a Chinese Pentecostal theologian.

Davies, Horton. *The Worship of the American Puritans, 1629-1730.* New York: Peter Lang, 1990. See pp. 23-25, "The Exclusive Authority of Scripture in Worship"; chapter 5, "Sermons"; pp. 168-71, "Theology of the Lord's Supper." Davies is also the author of *The Worship of the English Puritans.* London: Dacre Press, 1948. See also his *Christian Worship: Its History and Meaning* (New York: Abingdon, 1957) for succinct descriptions of worship traditions ranging from Orthodox to Quaker.

Davies, J. G., ed. *A New Dictionary of Liturgy and Worship.* London: SCM Press, 1986. A standard reference work with a broad range of articles (e.g., "Baptism," "Eucharist," "Architectural Setting," "Liturgies," etc.), with bibliographies.

*Dawn, Marva J. *How Shall We Worship?* Wheaton, Ill.: Tyndale House, 2003. See chapter 1, "What Kinds of Music Should We Use?"; chapter 2, "Who Is Being Worshiped?"

———. *Reaching Out Without Dumbing Down: A Theology of Worship for the Turn-of-the-Century Culture.* Grand Rapids: Eerdmans, 1995.

———. *A Royal "Waste" of Time.* Grand Rapids: Eerdmans, 1999.

*Dix, Gregory. *The Shape of the Liturgy.* London: Dacre Press, 1949. See chapter 2, "Saying and Doing"; chapter 6, "Pre-Nicene Background of the Liturgy." Dix is considered a pioneer in the modern study of history of liturgy.

Farhadian, Charles E., ed. *Christian Worship Worldwide.* Grand Rapids: Eerdmans, 2007. Good resource on a variety of worship styles in churches outside of North America.

Howard, Thomas. *The Liturgy Explained.* Harrisburg, Penn.: Morehouse Publishing, 1981. A very helpful booklet which provides simple explanations of the liturgy for newcomers in an Anglican or Episcopalian context.

Hurtado, Larry. *At the Origins of Christian Worship.* Grand Rapids: Eerdmans, 1999. See chapter 2, "Features of Early Christian Worship."

Johnson, Luke Timothy. *Religious Experience in Earliest Christianity.* Minneapolis: Fortress, 1998. Note pp. 163-79 on the NT awareness of the presence of the risen Christ at the Eucharist and at the fellowship meals.

Johnson, Todd E. "Disconnected Rituals: The Origins of the Seeker Service Movement." In *The Conviction of Things Not Seen: Worship and Ministry in the 21st Century,* edited by Todd E. Johnson, pp. 53-66. Grand Rapids: Brazos Press, 2002. Origins of the Willow Creek "seeker service" in Young Life style youth ministry.

*Jones, Cheslyn, Edward Yarnold, SJ, Geoffrey Wainwright and Paul Bradshaw, eds. *The Study of Liturgy.* Rev. ed. London: SPCK, 1992. A standard reference on the subject, with extensive bibliographies.

Klauser, Theodor. *A Short History of the Western Liturgy.* London: Oxford University Press, 1969. A fine study by a noted Roman Catholic historian of liturgy; see also appendix 2, "Guiding Principles for Designing and Building a Church," on church architecture.

Martin, Ralph P. *Worship in the Early Church.* London: Marshall, Morgan & Scott, 1964. Concise and helpful.

Nichols, James Hastings. *Corporate Worship in the Reformed Tradition.* Philadelphia: Westminster Press, 1968. Valuable history.

Oesterley, W. O. E. *The Jewish Background of the Christian Liturgy.* Oxford: Clarendon, 1925. Important study of the roots of early Christian liturgy ("liturgy of the Word") in the early practices of the synagogue and temple: reading of Old Testament lessons, psalms, prayer, the "Shema" as a creedal confession. (For a brief survey, see Paul P. Levertoff, "Synagogue Worship in the First Century," in *Liturgy and Worship,* ed. W. K. L. Clarke [London: SPCK, 1932], pp. 60-77.)

*Old, Hughes Oliphant. *Worship That Is Reformed According to Scripture.* Atlanta: John Knox Press, 1984. Highly recommended; Old has been influential in liturgical renewal in Presbyterian circles; studied history of liturgy under J. J. von Allmen (see above).

Peterson, Erik. *The Angels and the Liturgy.* New York: Herder & Herder, 1964. A brief but theologically rich discussion by a Catholic scholar of the presence of the angels in Christian worship, based on a reading of biblical texts and early Christian liturgies.

Plantinga, Cornelius, Jr., and Sue A. Rozeboom. *Discerning the Spirits: A Guide to Thinking about Christian Worship Today.* Grand Rapids: Eerdmans, 2003. See chapter 2, "The Rise of Contemporary Worship."

Rayburn, Robert G. *O Come, Let Us Worship.* Grand Rapids: Baker, 1980. Rayburn taught systematic theology at Covenant Seminary.

Ryken, Philip Graham, Derek W. H. Thomas and J. Ligon Duncan III, eds. *Give Praise to God: A Vision for Reforming Worship*. Phillipsburg, N.J.: Presbyterian & Reformed, 2003. Helpful essays by Presbyterian and Reformed scholars.

Sample, Tex. *The Spectacle of Worship in a Wired World: Electronic Culture and the Gathered People of God*. Nashville: Abingdon, 1998. The impact of media on generations born since 1945.

Schmemann, Alexander. *For the Life of the World: Sacraments and Orthodoxy*. Crestwood, N.Y.: St. Vladimir's Seminary Press, 1973. Russian Orthodox perspective on worship and sacraments. Note especially the essays "Worship in a Secular Age" and "Sacrament and Symbol": secularism is seen as a "heresy" of Christianity; in true worship and "sacramentality" the things of creation are seen to have a natural purpose of pointing to and revealing the heavenly world; in the liturgy creation is being returned to God.

*Senn, Frank C. *Christian Liturgy: Catholic and Evangelical*. Minneapolis: Fortress, 1997. Major study of history and theology of liturgy; Lutheran perspective. See also Senn's earlier study, *Christian Worship and Its Cultural Setting* (Philadelphia: Fortress, 1983), where he argues that Protestant appreciation of ritual can be informed by modern studies in comparative religion and anthropology.

Simon, Ulrich. *Heaven in the Christian Tradition*. New York: Harper & Bros., 1958. Note especially chapter 8, "Heaven in Christian Worship," for important biblical insights on the participation of the church's worship on earth with the worship now taking place in heaven.

Thielen, Martin. *Ancient-Modern Worship*. Nashville: Abingdon, 2000. A practical guide to blended worship.

Torevell, David. *Losing the Sacred: Ritual, Modernity and Liturgical Reform*. Edinburgh: T & T Clark, 2000. Argues that the reforms of Vatican II had the unintended consequence of reducing the sense of transcendence and mystery in Roman Catholic worship; argues for renewed appreciation of ritual, especially in its bodily dimensions.

*Torrance, James B. *Worship, Community, and the Triune God of Grace*. Downers Grove, Ill.: InterVarsity Press, 1997. Important insights on the *trinitarian* nature of worship in the NT: "to the Father, through the Son, in the Spirit." Argues that most worship services today are functionally "deistic" (God is absent), "Pelagian" (worship is thought to be possible by *human* activity alone) and "unitarian" (focused on Jesus, forgetting the Father and the Spirit).

Wakefield, Gordon. *An Outline of Christian Worship*. Edinburgh: T & T Clark, 1998. A convenient historical survey, updating W. D. Maxwell, *An Outline of Christian Worship* (1936).

Webber, Robert. *Ancient-Future Faith*. Grand Rapids: Baker, 1999.

———. *The Biblical Foundations of Christian Worship.* Nashville: Star Song, 1993.

*———. "The Crisis of Evangelical Worship." Chapter 6 (pp. 86-101) in *Worship at the Next Level: Insight from Contemporary Voices.* Edited by Tim Dearborn and Scott Coil. Grand Rapids: Baker, 2004.

———. *Planning Blended Worship.* Nashville: Abingdon, 1998.

*———. *Worship Is a Verb.* Waco, Tex.: Word, 1985. See chapter 1, "Winds of Change" ("four things that were disturbing me . . . five new insights"; Webber's pilgrimage).

———, ed. *The Complete Library of Christian Worship.* 7 vols. Nashville: Star Song, 1994.

Wegman, Herman. *Christian Worship in East and West: A Study Guide to Liturgical History.* New York: Pueblo Publishing, 1985. A valuable outline of liturgical history from the NT period to modern times by a Dutch Roman Catholic scholar; note pp. 229-33 for helpful descriptions of how the Mass was perceived at the lay level in late medieval Catholicism.

*White, James F. *A Brief History of Christian Worship.* Nashville: Abingdon, 1993. Best brief introduction to the subject.

———. *Introduction to Christian Worship.* Nashville: Abingdon, 1990. White is United Methodist and a leading American liturgical scholar.

———. *Protestant Worship: Traditions in Transition.* Louisville: Westminster John Knox, 1989. Best introduction to the entire historical range of Protestant worship traditions.

White, Susan J. *Christian Worship and Technological Change.* Nashville: Abingdon, 1994. More questions than answers.

Witvliet, John D. *Worship Seeking Understanding.* Grand Rapids: Baker, 2003. Note especially chapter 8, "Theological Issues in the Frontier Worship Tradition in 19th Century America" (the impact of Charles Finney).

York, Terry W. *America's Worship Wars.* Peabody, Mass.: Hendrickson, 2003. Examines issues raised by the introduction of contemporary worship styles since the 1960s.

Church Music

Brooks, David. "The Segmented Society." *New York Times,* November 20, 2007 <www.nytimes.com/2007/11/20/opinion/20brooks>. On increasing segmentation in popular music and culture and the need for a "musical canon" for greater cultural cohesion.

Dawn, Marva. *How Shall We Worship?* Wheaton, Ill.: Tyndale House, 2003. See chapter 1, "What Kinds of Music Shall We Use?"

Day, Thomas. *Why Catholics Can't Sing: The Culture of Catholicism and the Triumph of Bad Taste.* New York: Crossroad, 1992. Trenchant observations by a Catholic musicologist on contemporary music in the American Catholic churches; how reforms of Vatican II were a "mixed bag."

Dean, Talmage W. *A Survey of Twentieth Century Protestant Church Music in America.* Nashville: Broadman Press, 1988. See chapter 22, "Evaluations and Philosophies."

Gelineau, Joseph. *Voices and Instruments in Christian Worship.* London: Burns & Oates, 1964. See pp. 148-58, "Musical Instruments."

Hamilton, Michael. "The Triumph of the Praise Songs: How Guitars Beat Out the Organ in the Worship Wars." Chapter 5 (pp. 74-85) in *Worship at the Next Level: Insight from Contemporary Voices.* Edited by Tim Dearborn and Scott Coil. Grand Rapids: Baker, 2004.

Hayburn, Robert F. *Papal Legislation on Sacred Music 95 A.D. to 1977 A.D.* Collegeville, Minn.: Liturgical Press, 1979. See chapter 1, "Early Popes"; chapter 12, "Conclusions"; p. 400: musical instruments should not "partake of a worldly style" and should aid and enhance worship.

Howard, Jay R., and John Streck. *Apostles of Rock: The Splintered World of Contemporary Christian Music.* Lexington: University Press of Kentucky, 1999. See pp. 205-20, "Historical Roots to Contemporary Music."

Hustad, Donald P. *Jubilate! Church Music in the Evangelical Tradition.* Carol Stream, Ill.: Hope Publishing, 1981. See pp. 96-105, "Early Church"; pp. 287-91, "Instruments in the Church."

———. *Jubilate II: Church Music in Worship and Renewal.* Carol Stream, Ill.: Hope Publishing, 1993.

Jourdain, Robert. *Music, the Brain, and Ecstasy: How Music Captures Our Imagination.* New York: Avon Books, 1997. Insights from neurobiology, physiology and psychology about our experience of music.

Quasten, Johannes. *Music & Worship in Pagan and Christian Antiquity.* Washington, D.C.: National Association of Pastoral Musicians, 1983. See chapter 4, "Music and Singing in the Christian Liturgy of Antiquity."

Sendrey, Alfred. *Music in the Social and Religious Life of Antiquity.* Madison, N.J.: Farleigh Dickenson University, 1974.

"Snowbird Statement on Catholic Liturgical Music" (1995) <www.canticanova .com/articles/liturgy/art9o4.htm>. See especially parts 3 and 4 on practices; Catholic musicologists on post-Vatican II developments.

Stapert, Calvin R. *A New Song for an Old World: Musical Thought in the Early Church.* Grand Rapids: Eerdmans, 2007.

Storr, Anthony. *Music and the Mind.* New York: Ballantine, 1993. Neurobiology and music; cf. Jourdain above.

Westermeyer, Paul. *Te Deum: The Church and Music*. Minneapolis: Fortress, 1998. See "Postscript," pp. 311-20, on recent trends; extensive bibliography.

White, James F. *Introduction to Christian Worship*. 3rd ed. Nashville: Abingdon, 2000. See pp. 117-29 for a concise overview of the history of music in the churches.

Wilson-Dickson, Andrew. *The Story of Christian Music*. Oxford: Lion Publishing, 1992. An illustrated history from Gregorian chant to Black Gospel; p. 76: first indisputable evidence for the use of organs in liturgy (12th cent.).

Wren, Brian. *Praying Twice: The Music and Words of Congregational Song*. Louisville: Westminster John Knox, 2000. Note especially chapter 4, "Contemporary Worship Music" (argues for "critical acceptance"); see also recommended resources on pp. vi-viii.

Art and Visual Media

Butler, Tanja. "A Transfigured Vision: Art and Worship in Community." *Stillpoint*, Fall 2007, pp. 4-5. "Authenticity," "appropriateness" and "accessibility" as criteria for liturgical art.

Crowley, Eileen. *A Moving Word: Media Art in Worship*. Minneapolis: Fortress, 2006.

Dillenberger, John. *The Visual Arts and Christianity in America*. Chico, Calif.: Scholar's Press, 1984. From the colonial period to the nineteenth century; influence of English Protestantism in impoverishing art in the church; chapter 1, "English Christianity and the Visual Arts of the Colonies"; pp. 157-61, "Epilogue" for summary and overview.

Hipps, Shane. *The Hidden Power of Electronic Culture: How Media Shapes Faith, the Gospel, and the Church*. Grand Rapids: Zondervan, 2005. Applies media theories of McLuhan and Ong to church ministry; contrasts print and visual cultures; how media and electronic technologies are not value-neutral.

Jensen, Robin M. *The Substance of Things Seen: Art, Faith, and the Christian Community*. Grand Rapids: Eerdmans, 2004.

Miles, Margaret. *Image as Insight: Visual Understanding in Western Christianity and Secular Culture*. Boston: Beacon Press, 1985. Note chapter 5, "Vision and the 16th c. Protestant and Roman Catholic Reforms"; chapter 6, "Image and Language in Contemporary Culture"; pp. 146-50, "Training in Image Use."

Wilson, Kent. *For the Sake of the Gospel: A Media Ministry Primer*. Minneapolis: Fortress, 2006.

Wilson, Len, and Jason Moore. *Digital Storytellers: The Art of Communicating the Gospel in Worship*. Nashville: Abingdon, 2002. Some helpful observations on digital media from a pro-media, somewhat postmodern theological perspective; for a more critical view, see Marva Dawn above.

Church Architecture

Kilde, Jeanne H. *When Church Became Theatre: The Transformation of Evangelical Architecture and Worship in Nineteenth-Century America.* New York: Oxford University Press, 2002. Influence of Finney and revivalism on auditorium/ theatre styles of church architecture.

Loveland, Anne C., and Otis B. Wheeler. *From Meetinghouse to Megachurch: A Material and Cultural History.* Columbia: University of Missouri Press, 2003. Shows continuity of twentieth-century megachurch use of auditorium/theatre style of architecture with nineteenth-century revivalism and move to per-former-focused, "entertainment" worship styles.

Torgerson, Mark A. *An Architecture of Immanence: Architecture for Worship and Ministry Today.* Grand Rapids: Eerdmans, 2007.

Williams, Peter W. *Houses of God: Region, Religion, and Architecture in the United States.* Urbana: University of Illinois Press, 2000. Broad survey of American religious architecture; illustrated.

Periodicals

Call to Worship: Liturgy, Music, Preaching & the Arts (PCUSA perspective; articles and resources for worship)

Reformed Worship (resources for congregational worship; Christian Reformed)

Worship (Roman Catholic/ecumenical perspective; published by the monks of St. John's Abbey in Collegeville, Minn., who have been influential in the modern movement of liturgical renewal)

Worship Arts (United Methodist; articles and liturgical resources)

Websites

HymnSite.com <www.hymnsite.com> (search hymn texts for a word or phrase)

NetHymnal <www.cyberhymnal.org> (words and tunes for over 3,600 hymns)

Reformed Worship: Resources for Planning and Leading Worship <www .reformedworship.org> (see *Reformed Worship* periodical above)

The Text This Week: Lectionary, Scripture Study and Worship Links and Re-sources <www.textweek.com> (from Dubuque Theological Seminary; texts, commentaries, images, music, graphics)

Worship Map <www.worshipmap.com> (links, music, arts, liturgy, software)

Select Bibliography

Books

Abbott, Walter, ed. *The Documents of Vatican II*. New York: Corpus Books, 1966.

Adams, Doug. *Meeting House to Camp Meeting: Toward a History of American Free Church Worship from 1620 to 1835*. Saratoga, Calif.: Modern Liturgy Resource Publications, 1981.

Allmen, J. J. von. *The Lord's Supper*. London: Lutterworth, 1969.

———. *Worship: Its Theology and Practice*. New York: Oxford University Press, 1965.

Anderson, Walter Truett. *Reality Isn't What It Used to Be*. San Francisco: HarperOne, 1992.

Aquinas, Thomas. *Summa Theologiae*, 3A.73-78 In *The Eucharistic Presence*. Vol 58. Edited by William Barden. New York: McGraw-Hill, 1964.

Bell, Catherine. *Ritual Perspectives and Dimensions*. New York: Oxford University Press, 1997.

———. *Ritual Theory, Ritual Practice*. New York: Oxford University Press, 1992.

Bellah, Robert. *Habits of the Heart: Individualism and Commitment in American Life*. Berkeley: University of California Press, 1985.

Berger, Peter, and Thomas Luckmann. *The Social Construction of Reality*. Garden City, N.J.: Doubleday, 1967.

Borgmann, Albert. *Crossing the Postmodern Divide*. Chicago: University of Chicago Press, 1992.

Bradshaw, Paul. *The Search for the Origins of Christian Worship*. New York: Oxford University Press, 2002.

Bradshaw, Paul, and John Melloh, eds. *Foundations in Ritual Studies*. Grand Rapids: Baker Academic, 2007.

Brilioth, Yngve. *Eucharistic Faith and Practice: Evangelical and Catholic*. London: SPCK, 1930.

Brunner, Peter. *Worship in the Name of Jesus.* St. Louis: Concordia, 1968.

Bulgakov, Sergius. *The Bride of the Lamb.* Edinburgh: T & T Clark, 2002.

Butler, Tanja. *Icon: Visual Images for Every Sunday.* Minneapolis: Fortress, 2000.

Calvin, John. *Institutes of the Christian Religion.* Translated by Ford Lewis Battles. Philadelphia: Westminster Press, 1960.

———. *Theological Treatises.* Edited by J. K. S. Reid. Philadelphia: Westminster Press, 1954.

Carroll, Jackson, and Wade Clark Roof. *Bridging Divided Worlds: Generational Cultures in Congregations.* San Francisco: Jossey-Bass, 2002.

Carson, D. A. *Becoming Conversant with the Emerging Church.* Grand Rapids: Zondervan, 2005.

Cave, Alfred. *The Scriptural Doctrine of Sacrifice.* Edinburgh: T & T Clark, 1877.

Cerfaux, Lucien. *The Church in the Theology of St. Paul.* New York: Herder & Herder, 1959.

Chan, Simon. *Liturgical Theology: The Church as Worshiping Community.* Downers Grove, Ill.: InterVarsity Press, 2006.

Chenderlin, Fritz. *Do This as My Memorial: The Semantic and Conceptual Background and Value of Anamnesis in I Corinthians 11:24-25.* Rome: Biblical Institute Press, 1982.

Clark, Francis. *Eucharistic Sacrifice and the Reformation.* London: Basil Blackwell, 1960.

Cooke, Bernard J. *The Distancing of God: The Ambiguity of Symbol in History and Theology.* Minneapolis: Fortress, 1990.

Cooke, Bernard J., and Gary Macy. *Christian Symbol and Ritual: An Introduction.* New York: Oxford University Press, 2005.

Cullmann, Oscar. *Early Christian Worship.* Chicago: Henry Regnery, 1953.

Cullmann, Oscar, and F. J. Leenhardt. *Essays on the Lord's Supper.* Richmond: John Knox Press, 1958.

Davies, Horton. *The Worship of the English Puritans.* Westminster: Dacre Press, 1948.

Dawn, Marva. *How Shall We Worship?* Wheaton, Ill.: Tyndale House, 2003.

———. *Reaching Out Without Dumbing Down.* Grand Rapids: Eerdmans, 1995.

de Zengotita, Thomas. *Mediated: How the Media Shapes Your World and the Way You Live in It.* New York: Bloomsbury, 2005.

Dearborn, Tim, and Scott Coil, eds. *Worship at the Next Level.* Grand Rapids: Baker, 2004.

Dijksterhuis, E. J. *The Mechanization of the World Picture.* New York: Oxford University Press, 1969.

Dillenberger, John. *The Visual Arts and Christianity in America: The Colonial Pe-

riod Through the Nineteenth Century. Chico, Calif.: Scholars Press, 1984.

Dix, Dom Gregory. *The Shape of the Liturgy*. London: Continuum, 1945; 2005.

Duffy, Eamon. *The Stripping of the Altars: Traditional Religion in England, c. 1400-1580*. New Haven: Yale University Press, 1992; 2005.

Dunkle, William F., Jr., and Joseph D. Quillian. *Companion to the Book of Worship*. Nashville, Abingdon, 1970.

Eliade, Mircea. *The Sacred and the Profane: The Nature of Religion*. New York: Harper & Row, 1957.

Farrow, Douglas. *Ascension and Ecclesia: On the Significance of the Doctrine of the Ascension for Ecclesiology and Christian Cosmology*. Grand Rapids: Eerdmans, 1999.

Finney, Charles. *Lectures on Revivals of Religion*. Edited by W. G. McLoughlin. Cambridge: Harvard University Press, 1960.

Geertz, Clifford. *The Interpretation of Cultures*. New York: Basic Books, 1973.

Gelineau, Joseph. *Voices and Instruments in Christian Worship*. London: Burns & Oates, 1964.

Gergen, Kenneth. *The Saturated Self*. New York: Basic Books, 1991.

Gerrish, Brian A. *Grace and Gratitude: The Eucharistic Theology of John Calvin*. Minneapolis: Fortress, 1993.

Gibbs, Eddie, and Ryan Bolger. *Emerging Churches: Creating Christian Community in Postmodern Cultures*. Grand Rapids: Baker Academic, 2005.

Giles, Kevin. *What On Earth Is the Church?* Downers Grove, Ill.: InterVarsity Press, 1995.

Gill, Jerry H. *The Possibility of Religious Knowledge*. Grand Rapids: Eerdmans, 1971.

Gross, Martin L. *The Psychological Society*. New York: Random House, 1979.

Gunton, Colin. *The Promise of Trinitarian Theology*. Edinburgh: T & T Clark, 1991.

Guzie, Tad W. *Jesus and the Eucharist*. New York: Paulist Press, 1974.

Hageman, Howard G. *Pulpit and Table: Some Chapters in the History of Worship in the Reformed Churches*. Richmond: John Knox Press, 1962.

Hart, Daryl G. *John Williamson Nevin: High Church Calvinist*. Phillipsburg, N.J.: Presbyterian & Reformed, 2005.

Hauerwas, Stanley, and William Willimon. *Resident Aliens: Life in the Christian Colony*. Nashville: Abingdon, 1989.

Heelas, Paul, and Linda Woodhead. *The Spiritual Revolution: Why Religion Is Giving Way to Spirituality*. Malden, Mass.: Blackwell, 2005.

Hipps, Shane. *The Hidden Power of Electronic Culture: How Media Shapes Faith, the Gospel, and the Church*. Grand Rapids: Zondervan, 2005.

Hoon, Paul. *The Integrity of Worship: Ecumenical and Pastoral Studies in Liturgical Theology.* Nashville: Abingdon, 1971.

Horrocks, Christopher. *Marshall McLuhan and Virtuality.* Duxford, U.K.: Icon Books, 2000.

Huizinga, Johan. *Homo Ludens.* London: Routledge, 1998.

Hurtado, Larry W. *At the Origins of Christian Worship.* Grand Rapids: Eerdmans, 2000.

Jeremias, Joachim. *The Eucharistic Words of Jesus.* New York: Charles Scribner's Sons, 1966.

Johnson, Luke Timothy. *Religious Experience in Earliest Christianity.* Minneapolis: Fortress, 1998.

Jourdain, Robert. *Music, the Brain, and Ecstasy: How Music Captures Our Imagination.* New York: William Morrow, 1997.

Jungmann, Joseph. *The Mass of the Roman Rite.* New York: Benziger Bros., 1951.
———. *Pastoral Liturgy.* New York: Herder & Herder, 1962.

Kasemann, Ernst. *Essays on New Testament Themes.* London: SCM Press, 1964.

Kimball, Dan. *The Emerging Church: Vintage Christianity for New Generations.* Grand Rapids: Zondervan, 2003.

Klauser, Theodor. *A Short History of the Western Liturgy.* London: Oxford University Press, 1969.

Kodell, Jerome. *The Eucharist in the New Testament.* Wilmington, Del.: Michael Glazier, 1988.

Kraft, Charles H. *Christianity with Power: Your Worldview and Your Experience of the Supernatural.* Ann Arbor, Mich.: Servant Publications, 1989.

Lakoff, George, and Mark Johnson. *Metaphors We Live By.* Chicago: University of Chicago Press, 1980.

Langer, Susanne K. *Philosophy in a New Key: A Study in the Symbolism of Reason, Rite, and Art.* New York: Mentor, 1948.

Leath, Paul Brooks. "The 'In Christ' Phrase of Paul: A Genetic and Interpretive Study of the Interrelationship of the Pauline Mysticism and Concept of Salvation." Th.D. thesis. New Orleans: New Orleans Baptist Theological Seminary, 1946.

Lehmann, Helmut T. *Meaning and Practice of the Lord's Supper.* Philadelphia: Muhlenberg Press, 1961.

Lovejoy, Arthur O. *The Great Chain of Being.* New York: Harper & Row, 1936.

Luther, Martin. *Word and Sacrament.* Edited by Robert Fischer. Vol. 37, *Luther's Works,* edited by Helmut T. Lehmann. Philadelphia: Muhlenberg Press, 1961.

Marshall, I. Howard. *Last Supper and Lord's Supper.* Grand Rapids: Eerdmans, 1980.

Martin, Ralph P. *Worship in the Early Church*. London: Marshall, Morgan & Scott, 1964.

Mascall, E. L. *Christ, the Christian and the Church*. London: Longmans, Green, 1946.

Mathison, Keith. *Given for You: Reclaiming Calvin's Doctrine of the Lord's Supper*. Phillipsburg, N.J.: Presbyterian & Reformed, 2002.

May, Gerhard. *Creatio Ex Nihilo: The Doctrine of "Creation out of Nothing" in Early Christian Thought*. Edinburgh: T & T Clark, 1994.

McCracken, George E., ed. *Early Medieval Theology*. Library of Christian Classics 9. Philadelphia: Westminster Press, 1957.

McCracken, Grant. *Transformations: Identity Construction in Contemporary Culture*. Bloomington: Indiana University Press, 2008.

McDonnell, Kilian. *John Calvin, the Church, and the Eucharist*. Princeton: Princeton University Press, 1967.

Meyrowitz, Joshua. *No Sense of Place: The Impact of Electronic Media on Social Behavior*. New York: Oxford University Press, 1985.

Miles, Margaret. *Image as Insight: Visual Understanding in Western Christianity and Secular Culture*. Boston: Beacon Press, 1985.

Minear, Paul. *Images of the Church in the New Testament*. Philadelphia: Westminster Press, 1960.

Nevin, John W. *The Mystical Presence, and Other Writings on the Eucharist*. Edited by Bard Thompson and George H. Bricker. Philadelphia: United Church Press, 1966.

Nichols, James Hastings. *Corporate Worship in the Reformed Tradition*. Philadelphia: Westminster Press, 1968.

Niehaus, Jeffrey J. *God at Sinai: Covenant and Theophany in the Bible and Ancient Near East*. Grand Rapids: Zondervan, 1995.

Nouwen, Henri. *Here and Now: Living in the Spirit*. New York: Crossroad, 1994.

Old, Hughes Oliphant. *The Patristic Roots of Reformed Worship*. Zurich: Theologischer Verlag, 1975.

———. *Worship That Is Reformed According to Scripture*. Atlanta: John Knox Press, 1984.

Otto, Rudolf. *The Idea of the Holy*. New York: Oxford University Press, 1931.

Ouspensky, Leonid, and Vladimir Lossky. *The Meaning of Icons*. Crestwood, N.Y.: St. Vladimir's Seminary Press, 1982.

Panikulam, George. *Koinonia in the New Testament: A Dynamic Expression of Christian Life*. Rome: Biblical Institute Press, 1979.

Pannenberg, Wolfhart. *Systematic Theology*. Vol. 3. Grand Rapids: Eerdmans, 1998.

Pelikan, Jaroslav. *The Vindication of Tradition.* New Haven, Conn.: Yale University Press, 1984.

Perrin, Norman. *Rediscovering the Teaching of Jesus.* New York: Harper & Row, 1967.

Plass, Ewald. *What Luther Says.* St. Louis: Concordia, 1959.

Polanyi, Michael. *Personal Knowledge: Towards a Post-Critical Philosophy.* New York: Harper Torchbooks, 1984.

Powers, Joseph M. *Eucharistic Theology.* New York: Herder & Herder, 1967.

Raphael, Melissa. *Rudolf Otto and the Concept of Holiness.* Oxford: Clarendon, 1997.

Reid, J. K. S. *Our Life in Christ.* Philadelphia: Westminster Press, 1963.

Reumann, John. *The Supper of the Lord: The New Testament, Ecumenical Dialogues, and Faith and Order on Eucharist.* Philadelphia: Fortress, 1985.

Ridderbos, Herman. *Paul: An Outline of His Theology.* Grand Rapids: Eerdmans, 1975.

Rieff, Philip. *The Triumph of the Therapeutic.* Chicago: University of Chicago Press, 1987.

Ringgren, H. *Sacrifice in the Bible.* London: Lutterworth, 1962.

Ritschl, Dietrich. *Memory and Hope: An Inquiry Concerning the Presence of Christ.* New York: Macmillan, 1967.

Robinson, John A. T. *The Body.* Philadelphia: Westminster Press, 1952.

Ryken, Philip Graham, Derek W. H. Thomas and J. Ligon Duncan III, eds. *Give Praise to God: A Vision for Reforming Worship.* Philipsburg, N.J.: Presbyterian & Reformed, 2003.

Sample, Tex. *The Spectacle of Worship in a Wired World.* Nashville: Abingdon, 1998.

Sasse, Hermann. *This Is My Body: Luther's Contention for the Real Presence in the Sacrament of the Altar.* Minneapolis: Augsburg, 1959.

Schillebeeckx, Eduard. *The Eucharist.* New York: Sheed & Ward, 1968.

Schmemann, Alexander. *The Eucharist.* Crestwood, N.Y.: St. Vladimir's Seminary Press, 1987.

Schmidt, Leigh Eric. *Holy Fairs: Scotland and the Making of American Revivalism.* 2nd ed. Grand Rapids: Eerdmans, 2001.

Searle, John. *The Construction of Social Reality.* New York: Free Press, 1995.

Sendrey, Alfred. *Music in the Social and Religious Life of Antiquity.* Madison, N.J.: Farleigh Dickenson University, 1974.

Senn, Frank. *Christian Liturgy: Catholic and Evangelical.* Minneapolis: Augsburg, 1997.

Stephens, W. P. *The Theology of Huldrych Zwingli.* Oxford: Clarendon, 1986.

Stone, Darwell. *A History of the Doctrine of the Holy Eucharist.* London: Long-mans, Green, 1909.

Taft, Robert F. *Beyond East and West: Problems in Liturgical Understanding.* Rome: Pontifical Oriental Institute, 1997.

Thielen, Martin. *Ancient-Modern Worship.* Nashville: Abingdon, 2000.

Thompson, Bard. *Liturgies of the Western Church.* Philadelphia: Fortress, 1961.

Torevell, David. *Losing the Sacred: Ritual, Modernity and Liturgical Reform.* Edin-burgh: T & T Clark, 2000.

Torrance, James. *Worship, Community and the Triune God of Grace.* Downers Grove, Ill.: InterVarsity Press, 1997.

Torrance, Thomas F. *Space, Time and Resurrection.* Edinburgh: T & T Clark, 1976.

Tozer, A. W. *The Knowledge of the Holy: The Attributes of God: Their Meaning for the Christian Life.* Harrisburg, Penn.: Christian Publications, 1961.

Ugolnik, Anthony. *The Illuminating Icon.* Grand Rapids: Eerdmans, 1989.

Underhill, Evelyn. *Worship.* New York: Harper & Bros., 1937.

Wagner, Peter. *Discover Your Spiritual Gifts.* Ventura, Calif.: Regal Books, 2002.

Webber, Robert E. *Ancient-Future Faith.* Grand Rapids: Baker, 1999.

———. *Planning Blended Worship.* Nashville: Abingdon, 1998.

———. *Worship Is a Verb.* Waco, Tex.: Word, 1985.

Wegman, Herman. *Christian Worship in East and West.* New York: Pueblo Pub-lishing, 1985.

Wells, David. *The Courage to Be Protestant: Truth-Lovers, Marketers, and Emer-gents in the Postmodern World.* Grand Rapids: Eerdmans, 2008.

———. *God in the Wasteland: The Reality of Truth in a World of Fading Dreams.* Grand Rapids: Eerdmans, 1994.

———. *No Place for Truth.* Grand Rapids: Eerdmans, 1993.

Wentz, Richard E. *John Williamson Nevin: American Theologian.* New York: Ox-ford University Press, 1997.

White, James F. *A Brief History of Christian Worship.* Nashville: Abingdon, 1993.

———, ed. *Documents of Christian Worship.* Louisville: John Knox Press, 1992.

———. *Protestant Worship: Traditions in Transition.* Louisville: Westminster John Knox, 1989.

Wilson, Len, and Jason Moore. *Digital Storytellers: The Art of Communicating the Gospel in Worship.* Nashville: Abingdon, 2002.

Wilson-Hartgrove, Jonathan. *New Monasticism: What It Has to Say to Today's Church.* Grand Rapids: Brazos Press, 2008.

Witvliet, John D. *Worship Seeking Understanding.* Grand Rapids: Baker Academic, 2003.

Wren, Brian. *Praying Twice: The Music and Words of Congregational Song.* Louisville: Westminster John Knox, 2000.

Wright, N. T. *The Resurrection of the Son of God.* Minneapolis: Fortress, 2003.

Zizioulas, John. *Being as Communion: Studies in Personhood and the Church.* Crestwood, N.Y.: St. Vladimir's Seminary Press, 1993.

———. *Communion and Otherness.* New York: Continuum, 2006.

———. *Remembering the Future: An Eschatological Ontology.* Edinburgh: T & T Clark, 2008.

Zwingli, Ulrich. *Commentary on True and False Religion.* Edited by Samuel McCauley Jackson and Clarence Nevin Heller. Durham, N.C.: Labyrinth, 1981.

Articles

Allen, Thomas G. "Exaltation and Solidarity with Christ: Ephesians 1:20 and 2:6." *Journal for the Study of the New Testament* 28 (October 1986): 103-20.

Bauckham, Richard. "Creation's Praise of God in the Book of Revelation." *Biblical Theology Bulletin* 38, no. 2 (Summer 2008): 55-63.

Blair, Edward P. "An Appeal to Remembrance: The Memory Motif in Deuteronomy." *Interpretation* 15 (1961): 41-47.

Brooks, David. "The Segmented Society." *New York Times,* November 20, 2007 <www.nytimes.com/2007/11/20/opinion/20brooks/>.

Butler, Tanja. "A Transfigured Vision: Art and Worship in Community." *Still Point,* Fall 2007, pp. 4-5.

Carr, Nicholas. "Is Google Making Us Stupid? What the Internet Is Doing to Our Brains." *Atlantic,* July/August 2008, pp. 56-63.

Ciferni, Andrew. "The Rituals of Dinner." *Assembly* 18, no. 3 (May 1992) <http://liturgy.nd.edu/assembly18-3 aciferni.shtml/>.

Cranfield, C. E. B. "Divine and Human Action: The Biblical Concept of Worship." *Interpretation* 12 (1958): 385-98.

Culpepper, R. Alan. "Realized Eschatology in the Experience of the Johannine Community." In *The Resurrection of Jesus in the Gospel of John,* edited by Craig R. Koester and Reimund Bierenger, pp. 253-76. Tübingen: Mohr Siebeck, 2008.

Gaffin, Richard B. "Union with Christ: Some Biblical and Theological Reflections." In *Always Reforming: Explorations in Systematic Theology,* edited by A. T. McGowan, pp. 271-88. Downers Grove, Ill.: InterVarsity Press, 2006.

Gerrish, B. A. "The Lord's Supper in the Reformed Confessions." *Theology Today* 23, no. 2 (1966): 224-43.

Gordon, T. David. "Why Weekly Communion?" <www.opc.org/os.html?article_id=104?>.

Gozzi, Raymond, Jr. "Mass Media Effects in High and Low Context Cultures." In *Mass Media Effects Across Cultures,* edited by Felipe Korzenny and Stella Ting-Toomey, pp. 55-66. London: Sage Publications, 1992.

Jones, R. Tudor. "Union with Christ: The Existential Nerve of Puritan Piety." *Tyndale Bulletin* 41, no. 2 (1990): 186-208.

Kaiser, Christopher B. "Climbing Jacob's Ladder: John Calvin and the Early Church on Our Eucharistic Ascent to Heaven." *Scottish Journal of Theology* 56, no. 3 (2003): 247-67.

Klauck, Hans-Josef. "Lord's Supper." In *Anchor Bible Dictionary,* edited by David Noel Freedman, 4:362-72. New York: Doubleday, 1992.

Koenig, Sarah. "This Is My Daily Bread: Toward a Sacramental Theology of Evangelical Praise and Worship." *Worship* 82, no. 2 (March 2008): 141-61.

Lathrop, Gordon W. "New Pentecost or Joseph's Britches? Reflections on the History and Meaning of the Worship Ordo in the Megachurches." *Worship* 72 (1998): 521-38.

Laughlin, Charles D. "Ritual and Symbolic Function: A Summary of Biogenetic Structural Theory." *Journal of Ritual Studies* 4 (1990): 15-40.

McCue, James F. "The Doctrine of Transubstantiation from Berengar Through Trent: The Point at Issue." *Harvard Theological Review* 61 (1968): 385-430.

Miller, Herb, and Lyle Schaller. "Transitioning Through Worship Transitions." *The Parish Paper: A Resource for Congregational Leaders* 12, no. 1 (July 2004): 1-2.

Ramstedt, Martin. "Metaphor or Invocation: The Convergence Between Modern Paganism and Fantasy Fiction." *Journal of Ritual Studies* 21, no. 1 (2007): 1-15.

Rapaport, William J. and David R. Koepsell. "The Ontology of Cyberspace: Questions and Comments." SUNY Buffalo Department of Computer Science Technical Report 95-25 and SUNY Buffalo Center for Cognitive Science Technical Report 95-09. Two papers originally presented at the Tri-State Philosophical Association Meeting, St. Bonaventure University, April 22, 1995. <http://citeseer.ist.psu.edu/31641.html>.

Rapoport, Amos. "Spatial Organization and Built Environment." In *Companion Encyclopedia of Anthropology,* pp. 450-52. London: Routledge, 1994.

Schattenmann, J. "Fellowship." In *New International Dictionary of New Testament Theology,* edited by Colin Brown, 1:639-44. Grand Rapids: Eerdmans, 1975.

Sibley, Laurence C. "The Church as Eucharistic Community: Observations on John Calvin's Early Eucharistic Theology." *Worship* 81, no. 3 (2007): 249-67.

Sommerlath, Ernst. "Lord's Supper." In *Encyclopedia of the Lutheran Church,* edited by Julius Bodensick, 2:1337-39. Minneapolis: Augsburg, 1965.

Steeves, H. Peter. "A Phenomenologist in the Magic Kingdom: Experience, Meaning, and Being at Disneyland." In *The Things Themselves: Phenomenology and the Return to the Everyday,* pp. 147-79. Albany: SUNY Press, 2006.

Steinmetz, David C. "Scripture and the Lord's Supper in Luther's Theology." *Interpretation* 37 (1983): 253-65.

Stendahl, Krister. "The Apostle Paul and the Introspective Conscience of the West." *Harvard Theological Review* 56 (1963): 199-215.

Wilken, Robert Louis. "The Link Interview." *Christian History* 57 (1998): 44.

Zeilinger, Anton. "A Foundational Principle for Quantum Mechanics." *Foundations of Physics* 29 (1999): 631-43.

Acknowledgments

I would like to express my sincere appreciation to the following people who have contributed in various ways to the development of this book.

To the trustees of Gordon-Conwell Theological Seminary, for their continuing support of the sabbatical program that facilitates such writing and research projects.

To my faculty colleagues—David Wells, Richard Lints, Adonis Vidu, Peter Anders, Patrick Smith, Peter Kuzmic, Moonjang Lee, Tim Tennent, Garth Rosell, Gwenfair Adams, Gordon Isaac, David Horn, Todd Johnson, Frank James, Soo-Chang Steven Kang, Gary Parrett, Jeff Arthurs, Ed Keazirian, Catherine Kroeger, Robert Mayer, Eldin Villafane and Sam Schutz—for their encouragement and helpful suggestions.

To the students at Gordon-Conwell who have interacted with this material in my theology classes.

To friends at Christ Church of Hamilton and Wenham, whose beautiful, liturgical life exemplifies many of the principles discussed in this book.

To Jurgen Liias, whose observations on the sense of the "real absence" of Christ in many Protestant worship services stimulated fresh theological reflection.

To Gary Deddo and the staff at IVP Academic, for the valuable editorial and stylistic improvements they have provided.

And especially to my wife, Robin, for her partnership in the early development of this project and for constant encouragement. It is with pleasure and appreciation that I dedicate this book to her.

I had already completed the research and writing of this book, and had independently arrived at a notion of a local church that is "deep, thick and different" (chap. five) before encountering Jim Belcher's fine book, *Deep Church* (IVP Books). I believe that *Worship and the Reality of God* can help provide a theological and philosophical basis for a renewal of worship and life in the local church that is indeed "deep."

Name and Subject Index

Allen, Thomas C., 94n. 35

Allmen, J. J. von, 86n. 23, 101, 115, 149

anamnesis, 138

ancient-modern worship, 193

Anderson, Walter Truett, 39n. 5, 47

Apostles' Creed, 153

Aquinas, Thomas, 121, 122, 168

Augustine, St., 119

Barth, Karl, 13n. 5

Bauckham, Richard, 88n. 26

Baudrillard, Jean, 46nn. 22, 24

Bell, Rob, 29

Bellah, Robert, 68

Berengar of Tours, 122

Berger, Peter, 44n. 19

body of Christ, 149

Boice, James Montgomery, 11, 100n. 45

Book of Common Prayer, 136, 186

Borgmann, Albert, 46n. 24

Bradshaw, Paul, 118n. 11

bride of Christ, 151

Brilioth, Yngve, 145

Brunner, Peter, 86n. 23

Bulgakov, Sergius, 63n. 62

Bunyan, John, 48n. 28

Butler, Tanja, 191

Calvin, John, 77, 98, 117n. 5, 124, 128, 129, 139, 151, 160, 165

Campolo, Tony, 27

Carr, Nicholas, 15n. 7

Carson, D. A., 29n. 27

Carter, Stephen, 83n. 18

Cerfaux, Lucien, 64n. 64

Chalmers, Thomas, 17n. 11

Chan, Simon, 61n. 56, 186

Coleridge, Samuel Taylor, 105n. 56

Cooke, Bernard, 80n. 12

Covenant Theological Seminary, 30

Cranfield, C. E. B., 62n. 61, 100

Cullmann, Oscar, 117, 145

Cyprian, 61

Da Vinci Code, 42

Darby, John Nelson, 27

Darwin, Charles, 21

Davis, Nathaniel, 69n. 72

Davis, Philip, 41n. 12

Dawkins, Richard, 41

Dawn, Marva, 80n. 10, 97n. 41

Dennett, Daniel, 41

Denver Seminary, 10

Descartes, 67, 153

Diksterhuis, E. J., 81n. 13

Dillenberger, John, 80n. 8

Dix, Dom Gregory, 97n. 41, 121, 123, 166

Duncan, J. Ligon, 11n. 3

Dunham, John, 51

Eck, Diana, 14n. 6, 40n. 8

Edwards, Jonathan, 55n. 42, 135

Eliade, Mircea, 95

Eller, Cynthia, 41n. 12

Emerging Church, 29n. 27

Finney, Charles, 13n. 5, 85, 134

Formula of Concord, 125

Fourth Lateran Council, 121

Freud, Sigmund, 21

Gay, Peter, 80n. 12

Geertz, Clifford, 89n. 27

Gergen, Kenneth, 69

Gerrish, Brian, 77n. 2, 129n. 47

Gibbs, Eddie, 29n. 27

Giles, Kevin, 61n. 58

Giltinan, Martha, 74n. 83

Gordon, A. J., 28n. 24

Gordon-Conwell, 10, 28n. 24

Graham, Billy, 26, 85
Grenz, Stanley, 185
Gross, Martin, 68
Grudem, Wayne, 31
Gruder, Darrell, 61
Gunton, Colin, 59n. 50
Guth, Alan, 52n. 36
Guzie, Tad, 121
Hafemann, Scott, 31n. 31
Hansen, Collin, 31n. 31
Harris, Sam, 41
Hart, David Bentley, 59n. 49
Hawking, Stephen, 53
Hawkins, Greg, 29n. 26
Heidegger, Martin, 53n. 37
Heinecken, Martin, 116
Henry, Carl F. H., 26
Hippolytus of Rome, 118
Hipps, Shane, 185, 192
Hitchens, Christopher, 41
Hodge, Charles, 77n. 3, 132
Hoehner, Harold, 72
Hologram, 159, 164
Hoon, Paul, 93n. 33
Horrocks, Christopher, 46n. 23
Huizinga, Johan, 104, 105n. 54, 108
Hurtado, Larry, 101, 109n. 63, 141
Hybels, Bill, 13n. 5, 85
incarnation of Christ, 155
Isaac, Gordon, 27n. 23
Jaekle, Charles, 88n. 25
Johnson, Mark, 158
Jones, Gregory, 70

Jungmann, Joseph, 121n. 18
Kaiser, Christopher B., 128n. 45
Kang, Steve, 100n. 44
Kant, Immanuel, 67, 68, 81, 133
Kasemann, Ernst, 140
Kimball, Dan, 29n. 27, 40, 61
King, Patricia, 28n. 25
Klauck, Hans Josef, 117
Klauser, Theodor, 120n. 16
Koenig, Sarah, 99n. 42
Kraft, Charles, 44, 182
Lakoff, George, 158
Langer, Susanne, 157
Lathrop, Gordon, 85
Lee, Moonjang, 26n. 21
Locke, John, 67, 68
Lossky, Vladimir, 80n. 9
Loughlin, Gerard, 110n. 64
Lovejoy, Arthur O., 82n. 15
Luther, Martin, 98, 124, 126, 127-28, 151, 160, 162, 190
Marburg Colloquy, 127
Martin, Ralph P., 101, 109n. 63
Marsden, George, 83n. 18
Marshall, I. Howard, 142
Marx, Karl, 21
Mascall, Eric, 72
Mason, Lowell, 202
The Matrix, 16
May, Gerhard, 51n. 33
Maynard, Beth, 185n. 5

McCracken, George, 121n. 21
McCracken, Grant, 17n. 10
McCue, James, 121n. 20
McDonnell, Kilian, 77n. 2
McGavran, Donald, 180
McLaren, Brian, 29
memorial view, 139
Meyrowitz, Joshua, 56n. 43
Miles, Margaret, 80n. 8
Minear, Paul, 62n. 60, 64n. 65, 175
Miranda, Roberto, 179
Moltmann, Jürgen, 59n. 50
Moore, Russell, 20n. 16
Moule, Bishop Handley, 146
mystical union, 138, 149
Neuhaus, Richard John, 83n. 18
Nevin, John W., 132
Nichols, James Hastings, 79n. 7
Niehaus, Jeffrey, 51n. 31
Nouwen, Henri, 43n. 15
Novak, Michael, 45n. 20
Ockenga, Harold John, 26
Old, Hughes Oliphant, 77n. 2
Old Princeton, 30
Orthodox Presbyterian Church, 30
Otto, Rudolph, 55, 82
Packer, J. I., 11n. 2, 37, 38

Pannenberg, Wolfhart, 62n. 59

Parkinson, Cally, 29n. 26

Parrett, Gary, 100n. 44

Perrin, Norman, 117, 169

Pilgrim's Progress, 48n. 28

Piper, John, 30, 197n. 25

Plato, 96n. 39

Polanyi, Michael, 159

Postmann, Neil, 185

Powers, Joseph, 120n. 16

Presbyterian Church in America, 30

Radbertus, Paschasius, 121, 122

Ramstedt, Martin, 47n. 26, 107n. 59

Ratramnus, 122

Reformed Theological Seminary, 30

Reid, J. K. S., 73

Reiff, Philip, 68

Ridderbos, Herman, 72

Ritschl, Dietrich, 119

Robertson, Pat, 28

Robinson, John A. T., 149

Rosell, Garth, 26n. 20

Ryken, Phillip, 11n. 3

Sample, Tex, 80n. 10

Sanneh, Lamin, 18

Savoy Declaration, 131

Schaff, Philip, 132

Schillebeeckx, Eduard, 156

Schmemann, Alexander, 129n. 46

Scotus, Duns, 156

Searle, John, 105n. 55

Second Vatican Council, 130, 157

Senn, Frank, 187

Sibley, Laurence, 77n. 1

Steeves, H. Peter, 47n. 25

Steinmetz, David, 160

Stendahl, Krister, 119, 132

Stone, Darwell, 122

Symbol, 129

Tappert, Theodore, 124n. 29

Thielen, Martin, 185

Thomas, Derek, 11n. 3

Thompson, Bard, 97n. 41

Torevell, David, 110n. 64

Torrance, James, 63n. 63

Tozer, A. W., 11n. 2, 37, 61

transubstantiation, 35, 121

Trent, Council of, 130

Truman Show, 16

Twitchell, James, 69n. 72

Vidu, Adonis, 59n. 49

Vitz, Paul, 84n. 19

Wagner, Peter, 28

Wallis, Jim, 27

Warfield, B. B., 42n. 14

Webber, Robert, 38, 69

Webber, Timothy, 27n. 23

Wegman, Herman, 118n. 10

Wells, David, 11n. 2, 30n. 28, 49n. 29, 56, 95n. 38

Wesley, John, 45, 55n. 42, 136

Westminster Shorter Catechism, 74

Westminster Theological Seminary, 30

White, James F., 81n. 14, 85n. 20, 116, 168

Wilken, Robert Louis, 166, 167

William of Ockham, 52

Willow Creek Community Church, 9, 28, 29, 40, 85

Wilson-Hartgrove, Jonathan, 32n. 33

World of Warcraft, 35, 108

Wright, N. T., 12n. 4

Zeilenger, Anton, 89n. 28

Zengotita, Thomas, 70, 106n. 58

Zizioulas, John, 49n. 30, 59, 87n. 24, 175, 178

Zwingli, Ulrich, 77, 124, 126, 128, 151, 160, 162

Scripture Index

Genesis
1:2, *102*
1:31, *154*
18:27, *55*
20:11, *56, 82*
28:10-22, *82*

Exodus
3:5, *50*
3:14, *50, 51*
19–24, *174*
19, *97*
19:10-25, *97*
19:16, *54*
19:18, *54*
24, *97, 196*
24:3, *98*
24:8, *98*
24:9-11, *98*
24:18, *98*
34, *196*
35:30-35, *191*
40, *196*

Deuteronomy
5:2-3, *92*
5:2-4, *138*
8:14, *45*
8:18, *45*
12, *140*
12:7, *141*

12:11-12, *141*
12:18, *141*

1 Kings
8, *196*

1 Chronicles
23:5, *201*
25, *201*
25:1, *201*
25:2, *201*
25:7, *201*

Psalms
27:4, *58*
84:1, *191*
96:9, *58*
97:5, *24, 33, 182*
102:26, *49*
104:32, *182*
139:7-10, *154*
148, *94*

Proverbs
8:30-31, *57, 154*

Song of Solomon
2:4, *152*

Isaiah
4:2-6, *197*

4:5-6, *94, 102*
6, *10*
6:1-4, *54*
6:3, *54*
6:5, *54*
6:8-9, *54*
44:3, *144*

Ezekiel
10, *196*

Joel
2:28-32, *144*

Zephaniah
3:17, *57*

Haggai
2:6, *49*
2:7, *196*

Zechariah
8:3, *196*

Matthew
3, *129*
17:5, *196*
18:20, *94, 109,
146, 157, 161,
204*
22:2-14, *150*

24:29, *49*
24:35, *49*
26:28, *151*
28:20, *94, 101,
109, 160, 161,
205*

Mark
2:20, *150*

Luke
9:16-17, *143*
10:21, *57*
15:5, *57*
15:6, *57*
15:9, *57*
15:23, *58*
22:19, *143, 165*
24:13-35, *142,
143, 205*
24:25-27, *142*
24:30, *143*
24:30-31, *142*
24:35, *142*
24:51-52, *104*

John
1:1-3, *57*
1:3, *154*
1:14, *102, 196*
2:1-11, *150*

3:29, *150*
4:23, *174*
4:23-24, *95*
4:24, *63, 94, 95*
6:53-57, *144*
6:63, *127*
14:16, *71, 102, 178, 197*
14:16-17, *195*
14:18, *161*
14:23, *71*
15, *113, 131*
15:1-8, *148*
15:5, *71*
15:11, *57*
16:7, *161*
20:26, *161*

Acts
1:4, *144*
2, *85, 178, 196, 197*
2:38, *195*
2:42, *116, 144*
2:42-47, *205*
2:46-47, *57, 144*
10, *144*
10:41, *144*
13:1-3, *54*
20:7, *144, 145*
20:8, *145*
20:8-12, *144*
20:12, *145*

Romans
4:25, *147*
8:9, *177*

8:21-22, *91, 94*
8:29-30, *65*
10:9, *139*
12:1-2, *175, 184*
12:2, *170*

1 Corinthians
5:4, *66, 90, 94, 96, 161, 170, 195*
6:19, *195*
7:31, *53*
10–11, *121*
10:11, *92*
10:16, *140, 204*
10:16-17, *205*
10:16-20, *139*
10:17, *117, 167, 205*
10:18-19, *140*
10:20, *141*
11, *204, 205*
11:10, *94*
11:17-22, *148*
11:17-34, *142*
11:18, *145*
11:18-22, *168*
11:20, *145*
11:20-22, *137*
11:23-24, *139*
11:23-26, *204*
11:24, *138*
11:26, *139*
12:3, *139*
12:7, *194*
12:9, *194*
12:11, *198*

12:13, *71, 148, 195*
12:27-28, *145*
14:13, *198*
14:23-25, *66, 95*
14:25, *90, 161, 170, 195*
14:26, *64*
14:29, *198*

2 Corinthians
3:18, *94, 111, 196*
4:17, *110*
4:18, *53, 182*
5:17, *34, 71*

Galatians
3:28, *73*

Ephesians
1:4, *63, 65, 71, 93, 154, 177*
1:4-6, *10*
1:4-11, *63*
1:6, *10*
1:12, *10, 74*
1:19, *169*
1:20, *72, 94, 162*
1:22, *162*
1:22-23, *64, 197*
1:23, *110*
2:6, *72, 94, 96, 162, 176, 183*
2:15, *73, 168, 181, 200*
3:19, *60, 177*

4:3, *195, 200*
4:3-6, *73*
4:10, *162*
4:13, *177*
4:16, *195*
5:18, *201*
5:18-20, *178*
5:18-21, *201*
5:19, *201*
5:20, *202*
5:22-33, *150*
5:25, *150*
5:29-30, *150*
5:32, *150*
6:1-3, *181*

Philippians
2:11, *139*
3:20, *74*

Colossians
1:16, *154*
3:1-2, *54, 74*
3:1-4, *183*
3:3, *184*
3:4, *183*

1 Thessalonians
5:19-20, *198*

2 Timothy
3:16, *198*

Hebrews
1:2, *154*
6:5, *92, 93, 96*
10:19, *102, 152*

10:21-22, *152*

10:25, *109*

12:18-29, *174*

12:22, *102, 197,*
 204

12:22-23, *96*

12:22-24, *55, 93,*
 94

12:22-29, *174*

12:28, *55, 204*

12:29, *55*

13:8, *101*

James

4:14, *49*

1 John

4:1, *198*

Revelation

1:10, *93*

3:20, *143, 161,*
 170, 206

4–5, *93*

4, *88, 93*

4:8, *54*

19, *93*

19:6-7, *58*

19:7, *206*

19:9, *206*

20:11, *49, 87, 97,*
 111

21–22, *59, 65,*
 91, 155

21:16, *65, 110*

22:17, *170*